DAYS OF SPLENDOR, HOURS LIKE DREAMS

Four Years at a Small College in the Still North (1963–1967)

Charles A. (Chuck) Hobbie

iUniverse books may be ordered through booksellers or by contacting:

iUniverse
1663 Liberty Drive
Bloomington, IN 47403
www.iuniverse.com
1-800-Authors (1-800-288-4677)

Because of the dynamic nature of the Internet, any web addresses or links contained in this book may have changed since publication and may no longer be valid. The views expressed in this work are solely those of the author and do not necessarily reflect the views of the publisher, and the publisher hereby disclaims any responsibility for them.

Any people depicted in stock imagery provided by Thinkstock are models, and such images are being used for illustrative purposes only. Certain stock imagery © Thinkstock.

ISBN: 978-1-5320-1865-7 (sc)
ISBN: 978-1-5320-1866-4 (e)

Library of Congress Control Number: 2017903199

Print information available on the last page.

iUniverse rev. date: 04/26/2017

Other Books by Chuck Hobbie
Buffalo Wings (A Childhood Memoir)
The Time of the Monkey, Rooster, and Dog—A Peace Corps Volunteer's Years in Korea

Dartmouth College seal on door of Nichols High School Library, Buffalo, New York; photo courtesy of Blake Walsh and Nichols School

Baker Library tower at twilight, June 1966

Dartmouth Row, Dartmouth College, March 1964

To my beloved best friend and wife, Young, and to my great children, Jason and Amy, who have tolerated my college stories and love of Dartmouth for many decades. To my brother, John, '57; sister, Cecilia; sister-in-law, Olivann Hobbie; and brother-in-law, John Pehle—who supported me with their letters, encouragement, and love throughout my college years. To the class of 1967— particularly my roommate for three years, Peter Thomas, '67—who prompted and shared such incredible memories; Dartmouth graduates throughout the world—especially my amazingly fun Dutch roommate 1966–67, Willem deHaas, '69—whose friendships have warmed my heart; and current and future Dartmouth students, faculty, and staff, who keep the granite, still north, and hill winds of New Hampshire in trust.

* * *

In grateful memory and honor of my mother, Alix Bray Hobbie, and my father, John Hayes Hobbie, who sacrificed so much to enable me to attend an incredible college; the outstanding Dartmouth faculty—especially Chauncey Allen, Richard Eberhart, Collette Gaudin, Alan Gaylord, Werner Kleinhardt, Richard Regosin, and Paul Zeller—whose friendships and teaching greatly enhanced my life; and my departed college friends—classmates and others—whose voices and laughter are still fondly remembered.

* * *

In appreciation of Tri-Kap brother and Dartmouth alumnus Homer Bezaleel Hulbert (1863–1949), class of 1884, who understood 130 years ago that the world's problems are our problems and was one of the first Americans to address those problems in my wife's homeland, the future Republic of Korea.

It is, Sir, as I have said, a small college.
And yet there are those who love it!

Peroration, Dartmouth College Case, Daniel Webster, March 10, 1818[1]

The still north remembers them,
The hill winds know their name,
And the granite of New Hampshire
Keeps a record of their fame.[2]

---

[1]   Daniel Webster, as quoted by Francis Lane Childs, "A Dartmouth History Lesson for Freshmen," *Dartmouth Alumni* magazine, December 1957.

[2]   Richard Hovey and Harry R. Wellman, "Men Of Dartmouth," in *Dartmouth Song Book*, ed. Paul R. Zeller (Hanover, NH: Dartmouth Publications, 1950), 2–3.

Dartmouth Night bonfire, October 1963

Connecticut River near Middle Wigwam Dormitory, Dartmouth College,
September 1964

Dartmouth College Green, September 1964

Dartmouth College Christmas trees on Green, December 1963

Dartmouth College Glee Club in front of the Hopkins Center, October 1966;
photo courtesy of Dartmouth College

Dartmouth Row from Baker Library tower looking southeast, January 1966

Baker Library tower and weathervane, May 1967

CONTENTS

Foreword 13

Introduction 17

Prologue 21

Chapter 1—Vox Clamantis 25

Chapter 2—"Pea Green Freshmen" 34

Chapter 3—"Five Hundred Gallons of New England Rum" 47

Chapter 4—"Dartmouth's in Town Again—Team, Team, Team!" 58

Chapter 5—"Et Tu Quoque, Mi Fili!" 68

Chapter 6—"Ho a Song by the Fire" 79

Chapter 7—Long White Afternoons 95

Chapter 8—Road-Tripping 108

Chapter 9 —"Gay Young Sophomores" 126

Chapter 10—"Tri-Kap Marching" 146

Chapter 11—"Drunken Juniors" 161

Chapter 12—"Grand Old Seniors" 182

Chapter 13—Dartmouth Undying 203

Epilogue 207

Freshmen versus upperclassmen tug-of-war (latter won), November 1963

Canoeing on the Connecticut River, Dartmouth College, July 1966

FOREWORD

My friend and classmate Charles (Chuck) Hobbie arrived in Hanover, New Hampshire, already in love with "the College on the Hill" by virtue of having an older brother in the class of 1957, having attended Dartmouth's summer camp for young boys at the Moosilauke Ravine Lodge, and having spent high school summers working and hiking in the White Mountains. Along with some academic, athletic, and musical skills, Chuck brought with him to Hanover a family heritage of record keeping, photography, and letter writing. He already understood that history is made by, and mirrored in, every individual's life, as his letters home and to friends reflect.

Readers of this detailed, well-written, and unpretentious memoir will enjoy its hilarious student life anecdotes, admiring profiles of favorite professors, and poetic visions of North Country trails and slopes. But I think the book's underlying sustenance lies in the positive personal relationships, values, and growing self-confidence described (and demonstrated) by the author along the way.

In keeping with the Robert Frost poem, young Chuck gazed down many roads in Dartmouth's academic woods during freshman year. Then, about the time he hit the organic chemistry bump on the path to medical school, he became a bit infatuated with a charming female French instructor and decided to major in French. Perhaps responding to President Dickey's urging that Dartmouth men prepare for dealing with "the world and its troubles," Chuck pursued a foreign study term in France, as well as summers of "research" in Sweden.

Back in Hanover, our man eventually decided to change majors from French to English (no female instructors are mentioned). He thereby belatedly launched a rewarding foray into Chaucer, Shakespeare, the American novel, and American poetry, accompanied by Sanborn House teas, breakfasts at Lou's Restaurant with faculty luminaries such as poet Richard Eberhart, and Tri-Kap lectures and social events with professors Bond, Gaylord, and others.

Throughout his demanding academic schedule, Chuck enjoyed the "Dartmouth Dining Association" (what a great name for work-study pot-scrubbing!); a busy calendar of Glee Club performances and concert tours; numerous skiing, "road," and hiking trips; a venture into crew; and even a few fraternity parties. He recalls places familiar to an older generation of alumni, such as his many visits to Bartlett Tower, near the "Old Pine" stump up the hill behind the observatory, in order to enjoy stirring views of the campus and surrounding hills. And, like generations of Dartmouth men, he also valued the top of the tower as a wonderful spot to take a date. If you read this book closely, you will gain new insight into part of the tower's history—and you will smile.

This book will be appreciated by all members of the Dartmouth family but especially by the Dartmouth class of 1967. Chuck's detailed recollections of our time at Dartmouth will rekindle your own memories, as they did mine. None can forget the busloads of anxious young ladies huddling in Alumni Gym for the freshman mixer, the mandatory physical fitness test, spooky Doc Benton stories at Moosilauke, our freshman beanies worn everywhere and then burned after losing the traditional tug-of-war, and the shock and sadness of President Kennedy's assassination. We danced to "Shout" with the Isley Brothers themselves in Alumni Hall and sang "We Shall Overcome" with our dates after the Peter, Paul, and Mary concert. We enjoyed Green Key chariot races, golf course sleep outs, and "Hums" on the steps of Dartmouth Hall.

Chuck documents at least one of the campus social troubles we all experienced fifty years ago that is still an issue today. Drinking, of course, was an almost mandatory rite of passage. Now, as then, the drinking problem is tethered to the challenge of establishing meaningful relationships with the opposite gender when you are young. But we persevered in our pursuit of such relationships, despite the all-male environment in the 1960s. Chuck deserves perhaps a special commendation for his tenacity in this difficult area—a persistence that is well documented in this book.

In retrospect, as Chuck's memories suggest, our years at Dartmouth also saw the stirrings of political activism on campus prompted by our growing awareness of issues of civil rights and the propriety of the Vietnam War. Antiwar "vigils" on the Green and lectures from Archibald MacLeish, William O. Douglas, Allen Ginsberg, Malcolm X, George C. Wallace, and others sowed some seeds of discontent on the granite fields of the Hanover plain. And we ended every day listening to the Glee Club's haunting rendition of "Dartmouth Undying" when WDCR (Dartmouth College Radio) signed off.

It wasn't *Animal House* exactly,[3] but most of us had a pretty good time at Dartmouth, despite its rigorous academics and noninflated grading. This book recalls a generally content and "simpler" time—before the arrival of perhaps an even happier time of coeducation and cultural diversity.

Bob Davidson, '67
Former senior executive, US Department of Education
Former president, Dartmouth Club of Washington, DC
Former Dartmouth alumni councilor

---

[3] *Animal House* is a 1978 American film comedy based in part on experiences of a screenwriter at the Alpha Delta Phi fraternity house at Dartmouth College.

Winter Carnival statue "Snow Business" on Dartmouth Green
in front of Baker Library, February 1965

The granite mountains of New Hampshire's Presidential Range
north of Dartmouth College, November 1963

Dartmouth College Green and Baker Library, February 1964

INTRODUCTION

_____

On Saturday, September 14, 1963, a windy night, I boarded a midnight bus in Buffalo, New York, for Albany, New York, where I changed to a bus bound for White River Junction, Vermont. By noon the next day, I had arrived at Dartmouth College to begin a new life.

In each of the fifty states, in Puerto Rico, and in nineteen foreign countries, young men were similarly boarding buses, trains, and planes, or driving, to New Hampshire to begin an adventure together as members of the class of 1967.

The adventure occurred in the last decade of the two centuries of all-male culture at Dartmouth. While that in itself made our college years somewhat unique, looking back through the lens of fifty years of change in the world, I realize now what I did not understand then—that the time of our adventure together in the sixties set the stage for some of the great cultural and historic events of American society: the revolution in civil rights, the Vietnam War, space exploration, and the digital age.

The year in which most of us turned eighteen had already been an eventful year, presaging the following tumultuous decade. In Buffalo I often listened to Lake Erie's winds for guidance as to coming weather. If the winds whispering off of the lake that September night could have conveyed the most significant occurrences of the past eight months to the New Hampshire hill winds awaiting me, they would have murmured of the following forecasting events.

In January, George Wallace became governor of Alabama, defiantly proclaiming in his inaugural speech, "Segregation now, segregation tomorrow, and segregation forever!" The same month, African American student Harvey Gantt entered Clemson University in South Carolina, which was the last state to hold out against racial integration. Several weeks later, the publication of _The Feminine Mystique_ by Betty Friedan launched the reawakening of the women's movement in the United States as women's rights organizations spread.

Gideon v. Wainwright, issued on March 8 by the Supreme Court, revolutionized the rights of defendants by requiring state courts to provide counsel in criminal cases for defendants who could not afford to pay their own attorneys. Another group of much younger men revolutionized popular music in the same month, bursting on the pop culture scene in England with their debut LP album, *Please Please Me*.

Early the next month, volunteers from the Southern Christian Leadership Conference commenced a campaign in Birmingham, Alabama, against segregation with a sit-in at a segregated restaurant. A week later, Martin Luther King Jr., Ralph Abernathy, Fred Shuttlesworth, and others were arrested in a Birmingham protest for "parading without a permit." King's *Letter from Birmingham Jail* issued on April 16. Shortly afterward, thousands of African Americans, many of them children, were arrested while protesting segregation in Birmingham, Alabama. Public Safety Commissioner Eugene "Bull" Connor later unleashed fire hoses and police dogs on the demonstrators.

Above the Earth on May 15, astronaut Gordon Cooper orbited in *Mercury 9*, which was the last Mercury mission of the National Aeronautic and Space Agency, known as NASA. As the American space program advanced toward a moon landing six years later, the army of the Republic of Vietnam poured chemicals on the heads of Buddhist protestors. The United States, in response, threatened to cut off aid to Ngo Dinh Diem's regime.

The first week in June, the initial group of Peace Corps volunteers to serve in Guinea began their training at Dartmouth. On June 11, Alabama Governor George Wallace stood in the door of the University of Alabama to protest against integration before stepping aside and allowing African Americans James Hood and Vivian Malone to enroll. On the same day, President John F. Kennedy delivered a historic civil rights address in which he promised a civil rights bill and asked for "the kind of equality of treatment that we would want for ourselves."

The next day, Medgar Evers, a black civil rights activist from Mississippi, was assassinated in Jackson, Mississippi. In another famous speech at the end of June in besieged West Berlin, Germany, President Kennedy declared, "Ich bin ein Berliner."

NASA launched Syncom, the world's first geostationary (synchronous) satellite, in July. About the same time, a mathematician in New Hampshire applied for a National Science Foundation grant to bring a GE-225 computer to his college and to build the first fully functional general-purpose time-sharing system.

On August 5, the United States, United Kingdom, and Soviet Union signed a nuclear test ban treaty. James Meredith became the first black person to graduate from the University of Mississippi on August 18.

Later that month in the wake of what became known as the Xá Lợi Pagoda raids of the South Vietnamese army, the Kennedy administration ordered the United States embassy in Saigon to explore alternative leadership in South Vietnam, preparing the ground for a coup against South Vietnamese President Diem and deepening American entanglement in Vietnam.

On August 28, Martin Luther King Jr. delivered his "I Have a Dream" speech on the steps of the Lincoln Memorial to an audience of 250,000 participants in the March on Washington for Jobs and Freedom.

My first day as a freshman on campus, a bomb exploded 1,200 miles away in the Sixteenth Street Baptist Church in Birmingham, Alabama, killing four young African American girls and injuring twenty-two church members.

We started our college adventure together against this background of recent occurrences. Each of us viewed these events differently, just as each of us had a subsequent college experience unique to our own vision of ourselves and of the world. The only sure thing about the following pages is that my reminiscences of those years differ considerably from recollections of my classmates. My fondest memories are often remembrances not shared by many others, perhaps due to the halcyon haze infusing my view from the mountain summit of half a century of joyful trails, or more probably because different trails then and in our subsequent lives have variously shaped our perceptions of what occurred during our college odyssey.

Nevertheless, I write of my memories for two reasons. First, on the occasion of the class of 1967's fiftieth reunion in June 2017, on the eve of both the 250th anniversary in 2019 of the founding of Dartmouth in 1769 and the 200th anniversary of the historic Supreme Court argument by Daniel Webster in 1818, and on the 175th anniversary of the 1842 founding of Kappa Kappa Kappa, I hope that my words will bring as many smiles and as much pleasure to my male and female friends—who were such good companions so long ago—as writing these words has brought me in the past year.

Second, I write in the hope that this memoir will in small measure at least express my profound gratitude to my family and to the faculty, college staff, alumni, fellow students, and others—including the women from other schools and countries with whom I corresponded or whom I dated and the people I met in Sweden and France—who extended so much kindness, support, and friendship to me during my college years.

View east from Bartlett Tower of Baker Library, White Church steeple,
Connecticut River, and Vermont's Green Mountains, June 1964

Dartmouth football, October 1963

PROLOGUE

Robert Frost wrote of his two roads. He sighed at the recollection.[4] Two trails often have diverged in the woods for me, and I took the one all travel by. It was not hard to choose. My feet just followed my socks and my shoes.

All trails have a beginning and an end. Most begin with hope—the anticipation of the summit wind in your face, endless views in your eyes, and rest for muscles. Some trails end in elation, some in emancipating pain, some in cloudy shrouds. Some trace wispy threads across the sky. Others plunge through cool glades or etch lines across sheer cliffs. One climbs granite peaks in fourteen states.

A trail—like time—is not a place but a dimension. What you see and where you are on a trail depend on the trailhead, what songs you hear from the birds and the breeze, the sensation of rocks or moss under your feet, the straining of your body, the warmth of the sun, the cairns you follow, and your memory of past turns and encounters.

Trailheads are known; few know the source of watery trails. The rivulet from the mountain spring joins a millenary of unknown others before sweeping to the ocean. The river voyager knows that trails and rivers are both predestined; both follow well-trodden tracks; both carry those who pursue them toward a known end. Both are multidimensional.

Sometimes trails and rivers cross. One such crossing lies just north of the junction of Vermont's White River with the longest river in New England. The trail stretches approximately 2,100 miles from Mount Oglethorpe, Georgia, to Baxter Peak on Mount Katahdin in central Maine, undulating through the Appalachian Mountain range that straddles the eastern United States from north to south. It is aptly known as the Appalachian Trail, or AT. The river—New England's mighty Connecticut—arises from a small pond that sits about three hundred yards south of the United States' border with Quebec, Canada, in northern New Hampshire and runs south 410 miles to the Atlantic Ocean. The trail and the river cross in the foothills of the White Mountains at a special place: a small college town called Hanover, New Hampshire.

Throughout my life, I have hiked many sections of the AT in half a dozen states and glided on many

---

[4]   "… I shall be telling this with a sigh, Somewhere ages and ages hence: Two roads diverged in a wood, and I—I took the one less traveled by, And that has made all the difference." Robert Frost, "The Road Not Taken," in *The Oxford Book of American Verse*, ed. F. O. Matthiessen (New York: Oxford University Press, 1962), 556–557.

stretches of the Connecticut. My passages along that trail and on that river were always exhilarating and soul stretching, filled with the vistas, encounters, ecstasies, aches, and music that have altered and illuminated my life. At the end of each journey I have wondered if the purpose of the passage—the business of life—is merely the acquisition and communicating of memories, and whether at the end this is all that there is—through our DNA or otherwise. There is no sigh in that reality.

Four years of my life's course on that trail and river are especially significant in my memory because that was a time—like so many people's college years—when I awakened to the world outside of my beloved home town of Buffalo, New York. It was a time when, to paraphrase a great twentieth-century college president, Ernest Martin Hopkins, I learned not how to make a living but rather how to live. I also learned from my own great college president, John Sloan Dickey, that the world's troubles are my troubles. The awakening was an intense and sometimes difficult interlude in the rush of my life at that place where the AT and Connecticut intersect. It was also a joyful and fulfilling crossing.

So these are my recollections of the "splendor … of … her days" and the "hours that passed like dreams"[5] during my years at Dartmouth College in which I hiked many trails and glided along many waterways in the more than thirty-two thousand New Hampshire acres belonging to Dartmouth and elsewhere. My letters home and to many friends during 1963–67, returned to me over the years, as well as carefully preserved letters I received then have revived the memories of those years that fill these pages.

In four short years, I came to love the legends of several great men, the stump of a lone pine on a hill, the wisdom of many amazing teaching minds, the smell of drifting smoke wraiths from bonfires on the green, the rustle of the hill winds, the swoosh of skis on snow, green eggs and ham, the straining of synchronized oars, the fire goblins flickering in faculty hearths, the library bells, the flaming autumn foliage, the aches of granite trails, the songs floating on the campus, "sharp and crispy mornings," and the "gleaming, dreaming walls … miraculously builded" in the hearts of all who know Dartmouth.[6]

---

5   Franklin McDuffee, "Dartmouth Undying," *Dartmouth Song Book*, 8–9.

6   Ibid.

Students, dates, and faculty on summit of Mount Moosilauke (4,810'),
New Hampshire, June 1966

Students on Dartmouth College Green, November 1964

"Nine Freshmen" performing, January 1964 (I am third from right)

Lounge and fireplace of "the Hop" (Hopkins Center for the Arts),
Dartmouth College, October 1963

Chapter 1—Vox Clamantis

The scream was unearthly. The sound split the late autumn air and echoed from the buildings on either side of the street. It seemed to come from the sky, the ground, and all sides. At first I thought it was a wounded animal. I scanned the area around me in alarm. The street was deserted. The noise stopped before I could get a fix. Then it came again. This time it sounded like a wail of anguish from a mother who had lost a child. It came from inside a small building just ahead of me on the right side of the street.

It was an Indian summerlike day with temperatures around sixty degrees. The sun was warm on my face. Winter was about one month away officially. I was on my way to pick up my shirts at the local laundry. My routine my freshman year was that every Friday afternoon I took my shirts and other laundry to a small building located about one block behind the magnificent new Hopkins Center for the Arts that had opened the previous year.

The laundress was a small, older, friendly woman with an Irish brogue. In the first two months of college, Mrs. Gilbert had become a friend—someone who always asked about how I was adjusting to college life and was sympathetic when I told her how much I missed my girlfriend at home. Her laundry was cheaper than the College Cleaners or Gordon's Linen Service, both of which charged you for pickup and delivery. As I flung open the front door to the laundry, the wail cut the November calm like that of a banshee, and then I heard sobbing.

I looked around the seemingly empty store. The television in the corner of the room was on. I recognized the soap opera *As the World Turns*, which was one of my mother's favorites. Over the counter in the front of the store, I could see the clock in its usual place on the back wall. It was around two thirty. The Dartmouth Winter Carnival posters from the past, which I admired every time I visited the laundry, were on the wall to the right, and opposite them, in its usual place, was an oversize portrait of an Irish American president. All seemed in order.

Except for a hurried breakfast and an even more abrupt lunch at Thayer Dining Hall that day, I had spent all morning and the first part of the afternoon at Baker Library, high in the stacks, where I loved to study. It was my special alcove. Around two o'clock, I had picked up my small laundry bag of shirts in Topliff Hall after leaving my armful of books in my room. The weather was so pleasant for late November that I had decided to walk around the campus, circle Occom Pond, and run errands in Hanover's two-block downtown.

Occom Pond was one of my favorite places at Dartmouth. It was a small body of water located just north of most of the campus, adjacent to the golf course and below Occom Ridge. As I walked around the pond, admiring its reflection of the birches, pines, blue sky, and puffy clouds on that calm day, I thought of the pond's namesake of whom most of us had learned for the first time in the orientation lectures in September.

Samson Occom was among the great men integral to Dartmouth's history. He was an eighteenth-century Presbyterian cleric without whose assistance Dartmouth College would never have existed. This remarkable Native American of the Mohegan Nation raised the funds in England and Scotland—exactly two hundred years before the period of this memoir—which Eleazar Wheelock used to found Dartmouth College in 1769. Among many other noteworthy accomplishments, Reverend Occom was the first Native American to publish his sermons and writings in English. By means of his lectures and his sermons, he raised overseas about 11,000 English pounds—an enormous sum—which was an amount greater than that raised in the British Isles by any other American educational institution before the revolution.[7]

Thanks in large part to Occom, I was happily in my first term at Dartmouth College, enjoying that peaceful November day while I ran several errands. As I entered the laundry, I dropped the bag. Behind the counter, I could see my Irish friend lying on the floor, convulsed in sobs. I knelt next to her silently, not knowing what to say. Her weeping confused and disturbed me. News bulletins were interrupting *As the World Turns*. What the hell was going on?

"They shot him," she sobbed. It was all I could understand. I glanced around in concern but saw no one else in the front room or in the back room where she often worked. Had someone tried to rob her laundry and hurt her husband? I asked her if I should call for help. After several minutes, she managed to whisper to me, through her moans, "They killed the president."

I first thought that someone had killed Dartmouth's beloved president, John Sloan Dickey. He had just greeted me and the other freshmen in the Tower Room at Baker Library at our matriculation two months ago, shaking each of our hands and personally welcoming us to Dartmouth. Then I heard Walter Cronkite on on *CBS News* say that President Kennedy had been pronounced dead in Dallas. It was about two thirty on November 22.

That day, hour, and minute were the rarest of moments in my life, when I remember precisely where I was and what I was doing, although it was more than half a century ago. I recall the shocked faces around me; the seeming indifference of the wind, trees, and birds on the college green; the cancellation of classes and of the annual tug-of-war between freshmen and upperclassmen and of the football game against arch rival Princeton; the two-inch headline in the *Boston Globe*; the special

---

[7] Ralph Nading Hill, ed., *The College on the Hill—A Dartmouth Chronicle* (Hanover, NH: Dartmouth Publications, 1964), 28.

two-page edition of the *Dartmouth*; and the buildings draped in black bunting for weeks. It was the lowest point of my Hanover years and one of the few moments of my college years that I recall with a sigh.

Something within me also died that afternoon. It was as though a trail or river I was familiar with had somehow vanished. Perhaps the end of youthful vigor and vision in the White House signaled the end of my own youth.

I heard a white-throated sparrow singing in the November chill outside the laundry. Its familiar call—"Sam Pea-bo-dy"—had changed to "Jack Ken-ne-dy." I thought of the brown bird, warbling from a bleeding throat, in Whitman's lament of another president's death almost a century ago in *When Lilacs Last in the Dooryard Bloom'd*:

> Come lovely and soothing death,
> Undulate round the world, serenely arriving, arriving,
> In the day, in the night, to all, to each,
> Sooner or later delicate death.[8]

Eight months before my shock that day of sighs, I was anxiously awaiting a letter from Dartmouth in response to my application for admission. It arrived in March. Like so many of my high school classmates, I was fortunate to have been accepted at some of the best colleges and universities in the country to attend after graduation from high school: Dartmouth, Yale, Harvard, Cornell, Princeton, and Colgate. This was not due to my abilities, which were average at best, but rather to the wonderful preparation I received from my parents and other family and friends and from my teachers at Public School No. 56 and at Nichols High School in Buffalo, New York. My parents could have saved the cost of five of my six applications for college admittance in 1963. The school for Native Americans had been my choice for college as early as the second grade. Several influences accounted for my youthful infatuation.

At Christmas in 1953, my brother John, '57, brought back from his freshman year at Dartmouth College a compelling record of Dartmouth songs performed by the Glee Club in which he sang. He gave it to my parents as a gift. It was the first long-playing (LP) record we had. Our family had recently purchased a turntable, which played the relatively new LP records that were appearing on the market to replace the scratchy old 78 rpm records. Even at the age of eight years old, I appreciated the great improvement in sound quality represented by that first 33 1/3 rpm record called *A Program of Dartmouth Music*.

There were ten Dartmouth songs on the record performed by the Glee Club. Paul R. Zeller was identified as the director. (I did not know at that time that Paul Zeller would later become a favorite

---

[8]   Walter Whitman, "When Lilacs Last in the Dooryard Bloom'd," in *The Oxford Book of American Verse*, ed. F. O. Matthiessen (New York: Oxford University Press, 1962), 388.

professor and close friend.) Most of the songs had been composed or set to music fifty years or more before. The lyrics were printed on the back of the album "sold by James Campion, Hanover, N.H."

Within a month, I had memorized all of the songs and could sing them lustily. My two favorites were "Eleazar Wheelock" and the "Hanover Winter Song." The former alluded to Dartmouth's beginning as a school for Native Americans. I had no idea what was meant by the *Gradus ad Parnassum*," which accompanied Reverend Wheelock when he founded Dartmouth in 1769 together with the "sachem" of the tribe and was concerned that, according to the song, not only did the sachem have ten wives but also the "big chief matriculated."[9] Was he supposed to be doing that?

I also liked the phrase "wine-witch glitters in the glass" from the "Hanover Winter Song." Who was that wine-witch and where did she come from? The words sounded ominous, as did the song's reference to the "wolf wind" and "ice gnomes marching."[10]

Another favorite song was "Pea Green Freshmen." I thought a lot about "Pollard's Smut Class," which was mentioned in the song, wondering what that meant.[11] Even at the age of eight, I was curious about smut.

Brother John embellished the songs with his stories of skiing, his Dartmouth Outing Club and Cabin and Trail Club exploits, his roommates and classmates, including Chick Igaya (the talented Japanese skier who competed for Japan in the 1952, 1956, and 1960 Olympic Games, winning a silver medal in the slalom in 1956, and who won a record six NCAA titles and five national titles while competing for the college) and conductor Erich Kunzel Jr. (the famous conductor of the Cincinnati Pops Orchestra and Cincinnati Philharmonic Orchestra), his fraternity life at Phi Kappa Psi, and the faculty and visiting lecturers whose wisdom he absorbed, including the renowned arctic explorer Vilhjalmur Stefansson and the poet Robert Frost.

Despite not knowing the meaning of some of the songs, I thought that the recording was the best record I had ever listened to, and I blessed James Campion—whoever he was—for selling it to my brother.

Three years later, I attended a camp for young boys. It was located at the foot of Mount Moosilauke—a 4,810-foot-high mountain in the southwestern part of the White Mountains in New Hampshire. As the tenth highest and most southwestern of the 4,000-foot summits in the White Mountains, it juts impressively up from their foothills about fifty miles from Hanover. The AT passes over the summit of the mountain, emerging above tree line for the first time in the trail's northward passage since its beginnings in Georgia. According to legend, the mountain's name is derived from a contraction of the Native American words *moosi* ("bald") and *auke* ("place"). My head could now be called the same thing.

---

[9]   Hovey, "Eleazar Wheelock," *Dartmouth Song Book*, 6.

[10]   Hovey, "Hanover Winter Song," *Dartmouth Song Book*, 36.

[11]   Anonymous, "Pea Green Freshmen," *Dartmouth Song Book*, 84.

On the east side of the mountain, there is a steep ravine at the headwaters of the Baker River called Jobildunc Ravine. The camp—named after the ravine—was run by Dartmouth College at Moosilauke Ravine Lodge at the foot of Mount Moosilauke. Dartmouth owns the mountain and built the lodge. The camp counselors were all Dartmouth students. Dartmouth students also served as the crew at the lodge, working for the college.

My brother was a crewmember and cook at the Ravine Lodge during the summer of 1956, between his junior and senior years at Dartmouth. Thanks to John, I spent two weeks during each of the summers of 1956 and 1957 at Camp Jobildunc, hiking, canoeing, and camping in the White Mountains, which had already claimed my soul on earlier visits with my family.

About half of the time, the twenty or so Jobildunc campers ate meals at the lodge and slept in the Nate Emerson bunkhouse, a little ways from the lodge. The rest of the time, we were hiking around northern New Hampshire and Maine, or camping on Mount Moosilauke's heavily wooded slopes amidst crystal streams, century-old trails, and soft winds, which kept the mosquitoes away and blew pine fragrances through our tents.

One summer, after days of paddling practice on the Connecticut, the Jobildunc campers went camping and canoeing in Maine on the Rangeley Lakes. My arms ached from the paddling for the entire week, but otherwise I loved canoeing on those incredibly peaceful and lovely lakes.

Like my beloved Lake Erie, however, these lakes could be moody. Our canoes were swamped during a sudden storm one blustery afternoon. We all survived, but wet sleeping bags and clothes made us appreciate the morning sun and drying breezes on an island in Mooselookmeguntic Lake.

On another trip, the camp visited the Second Dartmouth College Grant in northeastern New Hampshire, which is a twenty-seven-thousand-acre wilderness area near the Diamond Peaks just south of the Canadian border. I panned for gold in the Swift Diamond River and found a few flakes. We stayed in several of Dartmouth College's shelters and cabins on the Grant, visited timbering operations, and ate with rough lumberjacks at a logging camp kitchen, with tasty food in tremendous quantities. The apple and cherry pies were the best I ever ate!

At the College Grant, we were taught how to build a firebreak in the path of a forest fire. We labored for days with picks, scythes, axes, and shovels to clear an area about three hundred yards by thirty yards to protect a cabin from the likely route of a fire. The work was backbreaking and hot. I imagined how horrible it must be to construct a firebreak with an actual fire bearing down on you.

When we stayed near the Moosilauke Ravine Lodge, a fire blazed in the lodge's huge fireplace in the evenings after dinner when the temperature dropped. Just after dark, the campers gathered before the hearth in comfortable chairs and listened to the story of old Doc Benton.

Doc Benton was a vampire-like village doctor from the early nineteenth century, who lived in the town of Benton on the north side of the mountain, had discovered the secret of everlasting life while studying in Germany, and still roamed the Mount Moosilauke area, preying on animals and people alike. The tale (which I repeat in part below) lasted over an hour and was punctuated throughout, at appropriate moments, by sound effects from the crew, such as muffled moans, clanking chains, and horrific screams, calculated to scare the pants off any listeners. I was terrified but loved that story, which I probably heard at least three dozen times.

The heads of the camp during my two summers there were Dartmouth student outdoorsmen: Brad Leonard, '56, the first summer, and then Dick Sanders, '57. With the students who ran the camp—such as Danny Monahan (son of Dartmouth's College Forester, Bob Monahan) and Fred Turner, '59 (one of my brother's best friends from Buffalo)—they taught us how to chop wood, build fires without matches, construct shelters in the woods, cook simple meals, and otherwise survive on our own. We learned first aid and orienteering with a compass and contour maps. Our counselors taught us that hiking above the tree line in a storm is extremely dangerous. "Lightning, wind, and hypothermia are the enemies," they drilled into our heads. "Get down into the woods for cover during storms." Before the end of the camp, each of us had to stay by ourselves in the woods and survive for two days with nothing more than a sleeping bag, ax, two sandwiches, and a candy bar. I learned a lot.

The Dartmouth counselors made Mount Moosilauke come alive for us. Through them, we came to know its trails intimately: the Beaver Brook Trail, Benton Trail, Gorge Brook Trail, Ridge Trail, Asquamchumauke Trail, and the Carriage Road—several of which were also part of the AT. We learned to track Mount Moosilauke's animals and recognize its birds. And we came to understand its moods—sultry on a hot, clear, summer day; exuberant on a clear, cold night with thousands of stars above; mysterious in the morning with clouds cloaking the summit and high shoulders; and chillingly dangerous below storm clouds and rising wind.

Twelve years after my Jobildunc experience, I discovered a plaque on the windswept summit of the mountain. Its inscription—echoing a verse of Dartmouth's alma mater—memorialized the father of our camp director and was one any devout outdoorsman would covet: "The still North remembers him; the hill winds know his name; and the granite of New Hampshire keeps a record of his fame." After two years of camp there, I understood and deeply appreciated the references to "the still North," "the hill winds," and "the granite of New Hampshire." Each was a companion that accompanied me throughout my college years and is still with me. It was hardly surprising that several of the eleven- and twelve-year-old boys who were my compatriots during the camp sessions in 1956 and 1957, such as Mike Gonnerman, '65, and Terry Ruggles, '66, were fellow students at Dartmouth seven years later.

The third Dartmouth influence in my early life was a subtler one. I began Nichols High School in Buffalo in 1959. It was a country day school for young men in grades four through high school. Virtually every day during my high school years, I entered the library at Nichols through stained-glass doors on which the seal of Dartmouth was etched in colorful glass. One day I finally noticed it and stopped before it, transfixed. The seal depicted several Native Americans, a colonial building with a cross-topped steeple, pine trees, deciduous trees, and the words *Vox Clamantis In Deserto*. The Nichols librarian, Mrs. Stewart, told me that this Latin phrase translated to "A Voice Crying in the Wilderness" and was biblical in origin.[12]

I liked the figures and the trees on the seal. I have always loved stories of Native American cultures and history and admired their historical leaders, such as the Mohawk chieftain Joseph Brant (whom I later learned was an early graduate of Eleazar Wheelock's school for Native Americans in Connecticut—Dartmouth's precursor). My Mohawk classmate in elementary school—Kathy Henry—with her long braided hair was my first Native American friend.

Trees were also important to my childhood, and I appreciated their presence in the seal—several pines and what looked like elms or maples. But what I really loved about the seal were the words. What a wonderful motto for a college, particularly one situated in the foothills of the White Mountains, which were still "wilderness" for a young boy from the city! Whatever it meant—a voice crying for help, a voice of dissonance, or one spreading truth or wisdom—it inspired me. I resolved to add my voice to the one crying in the wilderness and have always been thankful that I realized that early goal.

---

[12] The "Voice of one crying out in the wilderness" in *The Bible: Containing the Old and New Testaments*, Revised Standard Version (New York: 1946), Matthew 3:3; Mark 1:3; Luke 3:4; and John 1:23.

Wim deHaas, '69, Tracy Johnson, '68, Phil Davey, '67,
Paul Fitzgerald, '68, Hampton Rich, '69, and dates, Mount
Moosilauke, New Hampshire, September 1966

Rollins Chapel, Dartmouth College, June 1964

Moosilauke Ravine Lodge, Dartmouth College, September 1964

Chapter 2—"Pea Green Freshmen"[13]

My brother had several pieces of advice for me as I prepared for my first year at Dartmouth: prepare in advance for the physical fitness test given at the beginning of the freshman year—especially the rope climb; don't get drunk; and don't worry too much about women. I followed his first piece of advice.

My sister, Ceci, who is seven years older than me, also wished me to be kind to my dates, if I ever had any. I wondered what she meant by that, but I hope that I fulfilled her wish.

The week that followed my arrival in White River Junction by bus from Albany was full of orientation activities. After the shuttle bus to Hanover dropped me off on the Green, I was assigned a room—114 Topliff Hall—and a roommate—Peter Albert Thomas, from Moorestown, New Jersey.

Pete was about my height (six feet), a little heavier and stockier than me, and looked like a good athlete, which he was. He had short brown hair and had been on his high school's varsity football, swimming, and tennis teams. I soon discovered that he was also a musician, having played trombone in his high school band and orchestra. Like me, he had sung in his school's glee club. We were similar in many ways in our interests, and I guessed from his manner that our economic backgrounds were also similar—solidly middle class. His broad grin and outgoing demeanor told me from the beginning that he would be a fine roommate!

We were both given a class of 1967 green-and-white beanie and told that we had to wear it at all times. I also picked up a 1967 beer stein from the Dartmouth Co-op on Main Street, initiating a lifelong relationship with both the co-op and beer.

The beanie marked you as the lowest of the low on campus and obligated you to help all upperclassmen upon request as they moved into their dorms and fraternities. What a difference three months can make! In June, I had graduated as a proud senior from my high school. Seniors at any school carry the rank like a crown. In September, I was suddenly one of many beanie-crowned servants of all upperclassmen. I soon learned to avoid walking past all dormitories and fraternity houses in those first weeks on campus, skulking instead behind buildings and in back alleys as I made my way to classes or to the Hopkins Center, so as to avoid being conscripted to carry trunks, scrub floors, move furniture, or worse for demanding sophomores.

---

[13] "Where, O where are the pea green Freshmen?" Anonymous, "Pea Green Freshmen," *Dartmouth Song Book*, 6.

Upperclassmen, looking for freshmen slaves, often lurked outside the main entrance to Topliff Hall on Wheelock Street. Topliff was a huge old brick dormitory, filled to the brim with freshmen. From our first-floor room, which overlooked Crosby Street and the tennis courts then located on the west lawn of Alumni Gymnasium, Pete and I made sure that no upperclassmen could be seen on the back side of the building before we slunk out.

The day after my arrival, I went across the street to the gym to check out the physical fitness test scheduled in several days. All freshmen had to take this test, which required you to run a certain distance within a prescribed time and to swim fifty yards within one minute, among other physical tasks, as well as to climb a twenty-foot-high rope. The latter requirement was my only concern. If I didn't pass the test and thereby failed to demonstrate sufficient physical proficiency to opt out of physical education, I would be required to take physical education for six terms—during my entire freshman and sophomore years.

I had been thinking about that rope climb ever since my brother first mentioned it. Because I had earned varsity letters in track as a quarter miler and half miler in high school, the running was no problem. I had swum competitively in elementary school in Buffalo and captained the city championship swimming team only four years before, so the swimming test would be easy. But that rope climb was an unknown skill. I was worried to death. With uncharacteristic foresight, I acted to avoid a potential problem.

The first person I bumped into at the office of the Athletic Department was an engaging man who introduced himself as "Whitey." I asked him where I could view the rope that was part of the physical fitness test.

"Why do you want to see the rope?" he asked with a broad smile. "Don't you know how to climb one? It is pretty easy. If you have a minute, I'll show you how," he offered, chuckling to himself. He led me into a corner of the gym, and there it was—one and one half inches thick and seemingly several hundred feet long, stretching up to the ceiling and beyond.

Noting my concern, Whitey (who turned out to be the coach of the varsity lacrosse and soccer teams—Whitey Burnam) again offered to teach me how to climb the rope, which he promptly did. Under his direction, I quickly learned how to wrap a foot around the rope for support as I "inchwormed" up and to ease myself slowly down without getting rope burns. Coach Burnam shook my hand and wished me luck as I thanked him and left.

When I reported my experience to roommate Pete, he was unimpressed. Pete, who as I have already mentioned was an excellent high school athlete, later easily passed all of the physical fitness test requirements except the rope climb and ended up having to take physical education for two years. Despite having passed the physical fitness test and thereby being able to eschew any further physical exertions at Dartmouth, the next week I decided to try out for frosh crew, which turned out to be about as physically demanding as any sport could possibly be!

Later that afternoon, I passed a group of about twenty fellow freshmen on West Wheelock Street, who asked me to join them in "borrowing" a cannon from the village green of a nearby town. The plan, I was told, was to wheel the cannon from the town onto the Dartmouth Green in broad daylight. The escapade was to be the first of many that would establish our class's reputation as an audacious, unconventional, and unique assemblage of young men. I walked about a quarter of a mile with my classmates and then left the group with an excuse, unsure as to how audacious, unconventional, and unique I wanted to be perceived in my first days of college.

In addition to the physical fitness test, freshmen were also required to take a battery of tests for purposes of placing them at the proper academic level, permitting them to demonstrate sufficient proficiency in a subject or degree requirement so as to be qualified to opt out of it, or providing guidance with respect to a student's vocational aptitude (the so-called Strong Vocational Interest Test). These tests took place during freshman week.

To be awarded the bachelor of arts degree, a Dartmouth student had to complete thirty-six term-courses (three per trimester or nine per year), including English 1 (a so-called freshman seminar designed to enhance writing ability), three terms of a foreign language, and at least four courses chosen from the course offerings of each of the academic divisions—the humanities, the sciences, and the social studies. He was also required to spend one summer on campus and to experience, as deeply as possible, soft September sunsets, long cool shadows floating on the campus, and the drifting beauty where the twilight streams.[14]

I wanted to do well on the language and English tests in particular, because I had decided to follow the premed curriculum and hoped to do well enough in the English and foreign language tests to satisfy those requirements initially so as to allow me to focus entirely on math and science courses. (This early focus in college was clearly a product of a delusional mind—just beginning to manifest itself in my eighteenth year—which had too quickly forgotten my struggles with chemistry and physics in high school.)

Because of four years of French in high school with Nichols teachers Al Sutter, Jim Herlan, and David Hershey—all excellent teachers—I received high enough grades on the French test to be able to place out of the first two terms of French. I would have to take only one term of a foreign language. What a relief! I decided to complete my language requirement immediately, which I did in my first term. I then had a one-year (ill-advised) hiatus from French literature and language study, which fortunately only lasted until the talented and sultry French instructor Colette Gaudin—she of the model-like face and body and husky, seductive voice—came to my attention in my sophomore year.

The English composition test was the other major challenge I worried about. We were all given

---

[14]   "Who can forget her soft September sunsets? Who can forget those hours that passed like dreams? The long cool shadows floating on the campus, The drifting beauty where the twilight streams?" McDuffee, "Dartmouth Undying," *Dartmouth Song Book*, 8–9.

several pieces of English literature—poems and short stories—and told to write two or three pages critiquing two of them (whichever we chose). These essays were to be written outside of class but without the aid of any textbooks or other sources. Dartmouth had an honor system, like the one at my high school in Buffalo, so we were trusted to write the compositions on our own and to turn them in by the end of the week.

The person administering the composition test to the twenty freshmen in my group was a likeable, first-year assistant professor named Carnicelli. On the day the results were announced, I received a note from him, asking me to come to his office. I had no idea what he wanted.

Professor Carnicelli was holding my composition test when I walked into his office. He asked me to sit down in a chair next to his desk.

"Mr. Hobbie, are you aware of Dartmouth's honor system?" he asked in a stern voice. When I replied affirmatively, he continued:

"It seems to me that you have either copied someone else's work in your essays or taken these critiques from a literary source. Plagiarism is a serious offense at Dartmouth, and I am recommending your suspension, and possibly expulsion, for cheating."

I was dumbfounded. I denied the accusation vehemently and asked what I could do to prove my innocence.

After pausing for a minute, Professor Carnicelli said that I could write a critique of a poem in his office to demonstrate my ability. He suggested that I choose one of Robert Frost's poems and gave me one hour to compose my essay. I chose "Stopping by Woods on a Snowy Evening," which has always been a favorite poem and one of the first that I ever memorized in elementary school.

After about an hour, I handed my paper to him. He read it and then said that he had been wrong and apologized for doubting my honesty. I was tremendously relieved! I never had a course with Professor Carnicelli, but when we met occasionally on campus during the next four years, he always treated me as a friend and asked how I was doing. Most importantly, he gave me a high enough grade on the composition test that I did not have to take any English writing course.

There was a special "Freshman Issue" of the *Dartmouth*—America's oldest college newspaper—which I picked up soon after my arrival. It was published daily by the student newspaper staff and cost seven cents. On the front page was a "Freshman Week Schedule" that included, besides the language testing and English composition testing that I have already described, a Green Key reception for freshmen and their families and the first meeting of the class of 1967 on Monday, September 16; conferences with faculty advisers and a lecture on "Dartmouth's Past" by Professor Francis Childs on Tuesday; matriculation on Thursday; physical ability tests and a football demonstration by Coach Bob Blackmun on Friday; and picnics with student advisers and a freshman mixer on Saturday. Of these events, besides the physical ability tests, English composition, and French language tests mentioned above, three stand out in my mind among the hectic activities of freshman week.

Meeting with my faculty adviser—Dr. Norman Arnold of the Biology Department—forced me to focus on what course of academic study I wished to pursue, beyond indicating that I intended to go to medical school after college (like about 40 percent of my classmates). I had already selected my three courses for the fall term: Chemistry 1, Greek and Roman Studies, and third-year French. Professor Arnold, who was a fine mentor for my first two college years, mentioned that another Biology Department professor, Dr. Gene Likens—who was a friend of my brother—was waiting to see me to welcome me.[15] With this warm introduction to the Biology Department, I was confident that biology would be my choice when we selected our majors at the beginning of the sophomore year.

On Thursday, the class of 1967 gathered at Baker Library. Baker Library was an overwhelmingly handsome building with great nooks and crannies in which to study, comfortable chairs from which to gaze out over the Green and distant purple mountains through the huge windows, and appealing study areas—one of which was decorated by the renowned and extraordinary room-length mural of Jose Clemente Orozco entitled *The Epic of American Civilization*.[16] Earlier in the week, we had all enjoyed a grand tour of the library and orientation to its collections and card catalogue system. The nine floors of open stacks housing over one million books—the largest undergraduate library in the country—amazed and delighted me. Any student had direct access to any book at virtually any hour of the day. Except for books in the rare book collection, a student could check out as many books as he wished. Even then I felt that this incomparable resource was the perfect building for the center of the campus—as the repository of the record of human learning up to that moment and as the symbol of the height and breadth of the intellectual achievement to which we had access at Dartmouth. Not the least of the charm of Baker were its chimes, audible everywhere on campus and evincing a constant musical celebration, every quarter hour, of the joy of learning.

This morning we were to visit a part of the library I had not yet seen. In a long line stretching onto the Green, we climbed the steps to the library's striking Tower Room to meet personally the president of Dartmouth, John Sloan Dickey. I was tremendously impressed at matriculation when I first entered the Tower Room, which was located in the center of the third floor of the library above the card catalogue hall. It later became one of my favorite study areas with its formidable collection of books of all kinds, quiet atmosphere, cozy armchairs, and lovely views of the Green. I especially appreciated in this room the ornate fireplace at one end, the forty-inch cast bronze statue of a western Native American on horseback, with his palms uplifted in supplication, in the center of the room, and the portrait on one wall of William Legge, second earl of Dartmouth, after whom the college was named. The statue was called *Appeal to the Great Spirit* and reflected aptly my own feelings on several subsequent occasions when I was confronted with a deadline for a paper or a challenging exam.

---

[15]   In 2002, President Bush awarded Dr. Likens the 2001 National Medal of Science—the nation's highest science award—for his contributions to the field of ecology.

[16]   Designated in 2013 as a National Historic Treasure.

As I approached him, President Dickey greeted me warmly from the desk at which he was seated, shook my hand, and signed the paper officially enrolling me.

"Welcome to Dartmouth College," he said. "I hope that you will enjoy your years here!"

"Thank you, sir," I mumbled, not knowing what to say. "I'm glad to be here!"

After having repeated this formality over eight hundred times that day, President Dickey must have been exhausted! None of my high school classmates experienced this personal touch from the presidents of the other universities they were attending.

The third memorable event that week was on Saturday night of freshman week. A so-called mixer for freshmen in the Alumni Gymnasium featured a dance with women from half a dozen or so New England colleges. The freshmen in our corridor in Topliff Hall were excited about the mixer and talked about it for days beforehand. Few of us had experienced a mixer before. Our upperclassman adviser, Hans Krichels, a genial sophomore who lived in Topliff, generally described to us what we could expect and suggested that we should be prepared in case a young woman—whom we would hopefully meet at the dance—wished to engage in sexual activity. The question was where could we buy condoms without attracting undue attention or ridicule?

Topliff Hall's facility manager, an older man named Larry, suggested that either Eastman's Drugstore or a small store called Edith's—both on South Main Street—sold condoms. With a great deal of uneasiness, I went to scout out the feasibility of such a salacious purchase in broad daylight, carrying enough collected money to secure condoms for several of my classmates.

After determining that I was not being followed by the campus sex police and was not otherwise under surveillance, I slunk by Eastman's and Edith's and decided that Edith's was the better source (two young women, from whom I was not anxious to purchase my objective, were handling sales at the counter in Eastman's). I managed to slide into Edith's unobserved and to purchase from Edith—a short older woman with frizzy red hair—as quickly and stealthily as I could, several boxes of premoistened Fourex XXXX condoms (three to each box). They were expensive, but Edith assured me that they were the best! My Topliff classmates were impressed with my purchase and thanked me profusely.

On the night of the mixer, Pete and I arrived in front of Alumni Gymnasium just as a dozen or so buses started to pull up at the curb and disgorge smartly dressed young women. The women walked in a long line from the bus at curbside up the lengthy walk to the front door and disappeared inside but not before my classmates and some upperclassmen had lined up along both sides of the front walk to check them out, forming a sort of gauntlet. I was surprised and somewhat shocked at this arrangement. The comments from the hundreds of guys as the women walked by were not exactly designed to place the women at ease or to put them in a friendly, receptive frame of mind when the dancing began. I thought of my sister and of how I would feel if she were the subject of such rude treatment.

During the mixer, I recall meeting and dancing with several nice girls, but I had a girlfriend whom I had seen only the previous weekend before I left Buffalo and was not interested in a new relationship. I left after an hour, rather unimpressed with the social dynamics of a mixer held in the cavernous gymnasium. I also noticed that the girls seemed to favor the upperclassmen, who were adept at beguiling the most attractive women on the dance floor. The box of condoms sat forlornly unopened in my desk drawer in my room until the following summer.

Convocation took place on the first Monday after Freshman Week— September 23. The exercises in Alumni Gymnasium opened the 195th year of the college. We sang "America the Beautiful" and "Men of Dartmouth" and listened to speeches by Tucker Foundation Dean Richard Unsworth, the president of the Undergraduate Council (William Slade Backer, '64), and President Dickey. Dickey's speech was inspiring, as all of his speeches were during my college years.

The next day, not far from Topliff Hall and only several hundred yards from the white trail markers on East Wheelock Street tracking the AT past the gymnasium, I discovered the highest point on the Dartmouth campus—Observatory Hill—where there is an impressive stone tower built by successive classes at Dartmouth during the period 1885–95 (according to the plaque on the tower). The tower is named after Dartmouth's eighth president, Samuel Colcord Bartlett, who suggested the construction of the tower to replace the college's nearby "Old Pine" after its demise. From the top of the tower, I had an unobstructed view west across the campus to the Connecticut River and the Green Mountains just beyond, north toward the town of Lyme and the White Mountains beyond, and south toward the towns of Etna, Lebanon, and West Lebanon (the latter being the location of the liquor store that was the font of liquid pleasure for residents of the dry town of Hanover). Mount Ascutney (3,130') was visible on the southwestern horizon on the opposite side of the Connecticut River about twenty-four miles from Hanover.

Bartlett Tower became a favorite place. It was like a secret scenic overlook on a mountain trail—the kind of place you discover if you are lucky, which is close enough to the trail to be easily accessible, where your mind marvels at the sweep of the view and your soul is uplifted sufficiently to continue climbing the trail. The tramp up its seventy-one dark steps to the top was illuminated about one-third of the way up and again at the two-thirds mark by two open windows in the stone wall, each with its own view of the surrounding woods and providing just enough light to draw you upward. At the top, you emerged onto a small room, open on all sides, with vistas in every direction of purple mountains, green forests of pine and fir, the campus of colonial brick buildings, the blue river, and puffy white clouds.

On that first visit, as my gaze took in the town of Hanover and the campus, I wondered if previous Dartmouth students—such as Nelson Rockefeller, Theodor Geisel (a.k.a. Dr. Seuss), or Robert Frost (all heroes of mine)—had been as thrilled at this tower as I was. It was a metaphor for the Dartmouth experience: a struggle up dark, steep circular stairs in which an occasional burst of light through narrow windows illuminates the climb but at the top of which the amazing view—and the sense of belonging to the wonderful academic community and town spread below—together soon erase any memory of the darker twists of the passage. (Unlike the tower's view, which over the passage of time has been obscured by the surrounding trees—like so many special places and memories—the sense of the Dartmouth community has thankfully continued to thrive.)

My next thought was that this was a great place to bring a date. My high school girlfriend—Lindsey Jewel—would be the first girl I brought up to the top of Bartlett Tower, I vowed. At sunset it would be extremely romantic, and with any luck, the dark climb up the narrow stairs might offer opportunities to clutch her hand or even better. I could already hear my dear Lindsey laughingly commenting on the phallic symbolism of the tower.

After that first visit to Bartlett Tower, I visited it at least once every season for four years (except when I was studying abroad), usually with my camera and binoculars. From it I watched the amazing crimson glory of the Dartmouth campus and nearby mountains in the autumn, the driving snow that cloaked the surrounding pines and bent the white birches on Observatory Hill each winter, the arousing of the forests with their puffy, light green haze creeping into the canopy each May, and the wheeling of the red-tailed hawks riding the summer wind currents above the Connecticut. Virtually every one of the several dozen women who visited me at Dartmouth over the next four years climbed the tower with me. Lindsey never joined me there.

My father also enjoyed Bartlett Tower. Dad was a pharmacist, a graduate of Cornell, and a fine tenor, besides being a warmhearted, gregarious man of gentle humor. When he arrived for Fathers' Weekend in mid-February 1964, the hills around Hanover were veiled in a foot of snow. The bare outlines of the maples and elms on campus traced filigree patterns of limbs and twigs against leaden skies. No remnants remained of the glory that for a brief week or two had emblazoned Dartmouth with the gorgeous reds, oranges, and yellows that only a New England autumn can claim. The view from the tower was still awe-inspiring.

Pete Thomas's father also visited for the weekend. Pete's father was a high school teacher, coach, and otherwise like my father in many ways. Fathers stayed in the dorms with their freshman sons.

Our dorm room was a corner room with windows on two sides. Each room in Topliff Hall had bunk beds, two desks, two desk chairs, two comfortable chairs, and two chests of drawers. Pete and I had purchased a cheap purple rug for the floor and separated the bunk beds into two beds, placed on opposite walls of the room. It was a small room and quite cramped, but the two windows gave us more light than most of our dorm mates enjoyed. Pete had a Dartmouth banner on his wall. I had a green-and-white banner inherited from my brother, which archly proclaimed, "When better women are made, Dartmouth men will make them."

A picture of his high school sweetheart "Sue" adorned Pete's desk. I had a picture of Lindsey on mine. A picture of a high school sweetheart seemed obligatory on the desks of most of my friends in the first months of that first year. By the start of the second term in January, most of these pictures had disappeared, regretfully including Lindsey's.

We had also purchased curtains at an auction in nearby West Lebanon. In a somewhat accidental purchase, we had bid on what we thought were two pairs of curtains at two dollars per pair, not understanding at first that we were actually bidding on nine sets. So we ended up with enough curtains for most of the rooms on our corridor and with a bill of eighteen dollars, which for us was a small fortune. I have never bid on anything at an auction again, but at least we provided amusement for the local patrons, who seemed to enjoy the confusion of a couple of smart-alecky boys from the college!

The auction was the first of many adventures that Pete and I had together. He was always a gracious friend. We seemed to share a very similar outlook on life, which was generally optimistic, looking for positive experiences, and full of humor. Pete was exceptionally caring toward others and me. I do not remember having a quarrel with him even once in the course of four years, unless it was over who was the most attractive Playmate of the Month in a given year (Pete's subscription to *Playboy* was a Godsend). His parents had raised him well.

We both wore our beanies faithfully during the fall term and joined in the traditional tug-of-war on the college green between the freshmen and the upperclassmen. If the freshmen won the tug-of-war, our beanies could be burned in the bonfire for the next home football game. A fire hose gushed water at the midpoint of the rope, dousing students unlucky enough to be pulled through it. Pete and I were toward the back of the rope, but we still got wet when the upperclassmen ended up winning the tug-of-war for the first time in years (I suspected that they cheated by tying their end of the rope to the elms on the east side of the college green). Disgruntled classmates then stormed Thayer Dining Hall, formally known as the Dartmouth Dining Association or DDA, and created a mess there for student workers at the dining hall to deal with. Most beanies were burned or otherwise discarded anyway thereafter. I still have mine.

During Fathers' Weekend, our fathers slept in our beds in Topliff Hall. Pete and I tried to sleep in our sleeping bags on the floor between the two beds. It was like sleeping between two chainsaws, each with a slightly different pitch and cutting speed. The two nights were pure torture! Al Thomas bested my father with his snores, but Dad held his own. Despite two nights with virtually no sleep, Pete and I both enjoyed showing our fathers around the campus and taking them to classes.

I know that my dad wanted me to go to his alma mater—Cornell University—and was disappointed that I followed my brother to Dartmouth instead. But he never said anything about this to me and seemed to have a good time that weekend. It was so good to see him! Dad left Hanover on Sunday, just missing a major snowstorm in the afternoon, which caught Pete's father and forced him to return to Hanover for a third night of cutting wood in our room.

Dad was always interested in directories of names. When we took trips, he would scan the telephone directories in motel rooms to see if there were any Hobbie families in the area or other names of interest. He picked up my copy of the *Green Book '67* from my desk soon after he arrived and started to peruse it.

The *Green Book '67* was a college publication of freshmen photos and biographical information provided to entering freshmen at the start of the winter term. It was probably the college book I referred to most often when I was a student and in subsequent years, annotating my classmates' news and deaths next to their pictures. On the inside of the front cover and first page was a map of the campus highlighted with an image of the Dartmouth shield, which I have already described.

On the inside of the back cover was the Dartmouth College Telephone Directory of numbers for emergencies, dormitories, fraternities, and college organizations and offices. The first fifteen pages documented in pictures my class's adventures during the fall semester, ranging from meetings with the dean of freshmen, Al Dickerson, and President Dickey, to departures by bus on the freshmen trips, building our first bonfire in the middle of the Green, the postponed tug-of-war against upperclassmen, the awesome Big Green football machine (1963 Ivy League Champions with a 7–2 record), and orientation to the most important building on campus—the fine-looking Baker Library.

All 824 members of the class of 1967 were then individually pictured with a short statement of each student's high school achievement and current college address. Seven hundred and forty of us, or about 90 percent, would graduate four years later.[17]

My father was most interested in the geographic directory of my classmates, quickly advising me that I was the only member of my class from Buffalo, New York, and that there were ten classmates from the surrounding Niagara Frontier area. Over time, as we traded rides back and forth to Dartmouth in the ensuing four years, I became good friends with most of these boys: Ted Preg (Clarence Center, NY); Dwight Campbell, Rix Jennings, and Andy Mack (East Aurora, NY); Chris Light (Hamburg, NY); David Brooks (Niagara Falls, NY); and Mike Gfroerer, Dave Watt, and Don Wehrung (Tonawanda, NY). Chuck Slade (Orchard Park, NY) was the only one of the Western New Yorkers whom I never got to know well. Andy Mack had been a classmate at Nichols High School, commuting to Buffalo from East Aurora.

Dad was especially pleased that there were three classmates from Tonawanda, which was his birthplace. My father also reported that there were 110 presidents of their high school classes and sixty-four football captains among my classmates. There were also three African Americans and eight Asian Americans. Of course, there were no female classmates. (The lack of racial and gender diversity at

---

[17]   "740 Seniors Graduate Tomorrow" in the *Dartmouth* (June 10, 1967), 1.

college was the only significant manner in which my college years were deficient relative to the rich diversity of my later life in the Washington, DC, area.) As I suspected was true for every incoming freshman class, the 1967s also had the highest average Scholastic Aptitude Test scores of any new class in Dartmouth's history.

At the back of the *Green Book* was a helpful directory of mostly New England women's colleges with directions, distances from Hanover, key telephone numbers (main switchboard and dormitory numbers), and a cryptic description of the typical date (even then, I cringed when I first read these). Bennington, Bradford, Colby Junior, Green Mountain, Mount Holyoke, Pine Manor, Skidmore, Smith, Vassar, Wellesley, and Wheaton were listed.

It was intriguing to know that "Bennington is a small school, but there are those who like long, straight hair[;]"[18] "Skidmore girls are reputed to have a pleasant level of intelligence [and] … there is a good chance that your date has taken a bath [Saratoga Springs][;]"[19] "What's Smith like? Ask any conservative guy on your floor—he'll tell you. If you still want to call after asking, the number is JU4–2700[;]"[20] or "At Wellesley College Dartmouth has a rather formidable image, and the girls are sometimes reluctant to date the beasts from the hills."[21] I wondered if my grandmother, who played on Wellesley's basketball team in 1898, would have considered me a "beast."

A Mount Holyoke date told me later that year that the Holyoke girls also consulted the *Green Book* with its pictures and biographies of Dartmouth's freshman class. But they called it something else, similar to the children's book by Maurice Sendak, which also was published in 1963: *Where the Wild Things Are.*

---

[18]   *Green Book of 1967*, vol. LIII (Hanover, NH: Dartmouth Publications, 1963), 134.

[19]   Ibid., 137.

[20]   Ibid.

[21]   Ibid., 139.

Dartmouth students waiting for buses of dates to arrive in front of the
Hanover Inn, May 1964

Moosilauke Ravine Lodge, dam, and swimming pool on
Baker River, June 1957

Sandra Amy Ingalls, June 1963

Peter Albert Thomas, '67, April 1966

Albert Thomas with Pete
Thomas, '67, February 1964

Chuck Hobbie, June 1965

Chapter 3—"Five Hundred Gallons of New England Rum"[22]

The girl in my arms was silent and still. Her breathing was barely audible, causing tiny puffs of vapor in the icy night air. The blue eyes I so admired were closed. I had been carrying her for what seemed like hours. My arms and my heart ached. My mind was racing as I crossed the college green beneath a thousand suddenly censorious stars and the despairing bare limbs of the silent elms.

Throughout elementary school, I had experienced a progression of crushes on various girls who were classmates. Every year, it seemed, there was someone new. One year it was brown eyes and brown hair that delighted me, then red hair and green eyes, and then blonde hair and blue eyes. I thought then that I was in love with each.

I was lucky that I dated some wonderful young women during high school, who tolerated my relative inexperience in matters of the heart and sex. Indeed, several I obsessed about day and night for months, and one I worshiped as though she were a goddess.

As I became familiar with the great romances of literature, however, I began to worry that I would never find the girl who must exist out there with whom I could feel true kinship and the sort of all-consuming love that was on what I imagined to be the highest level of human feeling—a girl like Fitzgerald's Daisy Buchanan, Austen's Emma Woodhouse or Elizabeth Bennett, Shakespeare's Juliet Capulet, or Tolstoy's Anna Karenina. Literature also taught me of the dangers of such a love, suggesting that it often had a horrific price. Nevertheless, I wanted to experience it and for the first three years of high school longed for it, hoping to find it in the girls I knew and with whom I was infatuated.

On the AT in New Hampshire in 1962, on the summit of Mount Madison in the Presidential Range, a fifteen-year-old named Sandi suddenly appeared with her parents. I was working that summer as a hutman for the Appalachian Mountain Club (AMC) at the Madison Spring Huts, located at an elevation of 4,805 feet on the shoulder of the most northern of the peaks of the Presidential Range. Six young men staffed this site that summer, cooking meals for hikers, maintaining the hut and its sixty-two bunks for overnight guests, packing food and other supplies and equipment daily up

---

[22] "Eleazar was the faculty, and the whole curriculum was five hundred gallons of New England rum." Hovey, "Eleazar Wheelock," *Dartmouth Song Book*, 6.

almost four miles and 3,600 feet in elevation from Randolph, New Hampshire, and serving as guides, environmental stewards, and emergency rescue personnel as needed.

Sandi Ingalls was the beautiful, demure sister of a crewmate. She had blonde hair, blue eyes, and an alluring voice and manner. I was immediately smitten by her, but it was quite by accident that we ended up together and by ourselves on the summit of Mount Madison the evening that we first met, as the reds, yellows, and oranges of the sunset elegantly yielded to the greens, blues, and purples of a night sky ablaze with stars and a full moon. It was as though the gods had recognized my ignorance in matters of intimacy and sent Sandi to the mountaintop to teach me.

After hours of snuggling together to keep warm, in the moonlight we stumbled down the AT to the huts to discover that the hut crew had locked us out, forcing us to sleep together in the small accessory hut used for storage and overflow guests. That night was the first of many together. Sandi stayed for almost a week. I was a physical wreck. But my heart and mind were full of her smell, her touch, her warmth, and her murmurings. She was my first love. I found in her insights and experiences, her love of life, and her affinity with intimacy—not to mention her soft skin and creamy neck—the nature and cause of the passion of the literature, poetry, music, and other great art, which I had come to appreciate in the first seventeen years of my life.

Fifteen months later, I walked on the AT down East Wheelock Street in Hanover—sixty-five miles south of Mount Madison—with Sandi almost unconscious in my arms. It was dark and very cold, and the hill winds were gusting that Columbus Day eve. No snow had yet fallen in Hanover, but the weather was wintry already. Sandi seemed lifeless. What had started out as a poignant evening of revisiting past romance had quickly turned into a very chilling situation.

She was sixteen by then and had arrived from New York City earlier that day by train to visit me for the weekend. Dartmouth was to play Brown in football the next day, having beaten Bucknell University and the University of Pennsylvania on the two previous weekends. It was to have been a glorious football weekend. I had looked forward to her arrival for weeks. Although she had a boyfriend at home in Dobbs Ferry, New York, a large part of my heart still belonged to her, despite my overwhelming feelings for Lindsey—my girlfriend of the past six months. My heart was in pain for the girl in my arms. It was one of the saddest and scariest moments of my life.

After meeting at the train station in White River Junction late that afternoon, we had taken the shuttle bus back to Hanover and walked over to the house on Valley Road where Sandi would be staying on Friday and Saturday nights. Residents of Hanover opened up their homes to house visitors on football weekends because there were virtually no commercial lodgings in Hanover or in the nearby area, except for the prohibitively expensive Hanover Inn. Weeks before any weekend when a student needed to arrange for housing for a guest, the list of available beds for rent in private homes was posted in College Hall. For a small fee—about two dollars per night—students assured that female guests would have a place to sleep other than dormitory or fraternity rooms, which supposedly were strictly off limits at night to women.

With other classmates and their dates, Sandi and I had an early dinner together at Thayer Dining Hall and then went to Topliff Hall. Although the town of Hanover was a dry town in which alcoholic beverages could not be purchased, some of the five hundred gallons of New England rum with which Dartmouth's founder—Eleazar Wheelock—had devised the 1769 first curriculum (according to the song "Eleazar Wheelock"[23]) lingered on campus almost two centuries later, courtesy of the West Lebanon liquor store. I had illicitly procured a bottle of this beverage, which was probably the most popular alcoholic drink for freshmen—rum mixed with equal amounts of Coke. I introduced Sandi to roommate Pete Thomas and to our neighboring dorm mates in Topliff—Jeff Childs, Bill Kirkpatrick, Stan Brown, Jim Schlough, Pete Lysaght, Gene Tabor, and Jay Boekelheide,[24] most of whom also had dates and were imbibing the same rum and Coke drinks. We were having a very good time.

Suddenly, after two drinks, Sandi became extremely ill—first vomiting repeatedly and then retching uncontrollably. I had no idea what to do. By this time, it was after ten o'clock (the agreement with the landlords of the beds we rented for our dates specified that the girls had to be back at the houses by eleven). She was in no shape to walk, so I decided to carry her. I was frantic with worry since I had never encountered this level of apparent intoxication. It was about half a mile to Valley Road. When I rang the doorbell, the lady of the house refused to admit Sandi in her condition. What to do?

My first thought was that I would ask the Monahan family, who lived nearby on Conant Road, for help. Bob Monahan was the Dartmouth College forester, whose sons I knew from the AMC and from Camp Jobildunc. The Monahan's house was familiar to me because I had had dinner with the Monahans several times.

I finally decided that I had to take Sandi immediately to Dick's House—Dartmouth's infirmary—located on the opposite side of the campus from Valley Road. I carried her across the campus, and she was admitted about midnight. After I had waited until about two o'clock in the morning, a young intern advised me that Sandi was okay now. I told the intern that I didn't understand how Sandi could have become so drunk after only two drinks over a four-hour period. He replied that the alcoholic content of her blood had been just above the legal level of intoxication, indicating in view of the severity of her physical symptoms—which could not be accounted for by the relatively low level of alcohol in her system—that she was probably allergic to rum.

The next morning, we left the infirmary, and Sandi rested at her lodging until noon, still feeling quite sick. She insisted on going to the Brown football game with me. A friend from Brown with whom I had worked at the Madison Spring Huts—Tony MacMillan—went to the game with us.

---

23   Ibid.

24   After graduation, as far as I know, Jay was the only of the 1967s to win an Academy Award.

Tony had a flask of rum, which he tried to share with us, but the very smell of rum made both Sandi and me feel nauseous. To this day, I cannot drink or even smell rum. Dartmouth, at least, beat Brown 14–7.

Sandi gamely tried to enjoy the weekend despite her physical condition. We went to the Occom Inn on North Main Street for dinner on Saturday night, although she could eat hardly anything, and then walked around the campus in the evening. On Sunday morning, we climbed Bartlett Tower and kissed as we listened to the awakening town and campus, before I sang in Rollins Chapel at the college's Columbus Day service and then took her to the train station in White River Junction early on Sunday afternoon.

She never accepted my entreaties to come back to Dartmouth—I certainly understood why—but I visited her several times at her home in Dobbs Ferry, New York, afterward, and Sandi wrote often during her college years at Bucknell University. We relit the spark between us almost ten years later in Washington, DC, before she moved to England, and have remained good friends for over fifty years.

On the following Monday morning, I received invitations to visit the dean of freshmen, Albert Dickerson, and the dean of the college, Thaddeus "Thad" Seymour. Both were friendly, caring men whom I had met repeatedly at functions in the first months on campus, but I was more than a little concerned that the weekend's visit to Dick's House had been reported to Dartmouth's administrative officers and that I might be in a great deal of trouble. My concern was justified.

I met Dean Dickerson first and then Dean Seymour at their offices in Parkhurst Hall, explaining to each the events of the past few days. Both said that I had done the right thing in getting Sandi to the infirmary, expressed concern that Sandi was only sixteen, and advised me that I had used up one of my three strikes at Dartmouth (three strikes and you are out!). Dean Dickerson reminded me that serving alcoholic beverages to a person under the age of twenty-one was a violation of New Hampshire law. I assured both deans that I would not repeat this mistake, and they sent me on my way. (The next, and last, time that I conversed at length with Dean Seymour was under much happier circumstances, when he congratulated me in 1967 on the citation for outstanding writing [a weird play I wrote in the style of Dylan Thomas] awarded me by then United States poet laureate—Dartmouth professor Richard Eberhart.) I never had another drink of rum at Dartmouth.

But I thought about rum a lot. Every time I went to Thayer Dining Hall and viewed the attractive Hovey Grill mural there, one panel of which depicted Eleazar with a bowl of rum, dispensing drinks to Native Americans, I thought of Sandi.

To decorate the Richard Hovey Grill in the new Thayer Dining Hall, which opened in September 1937, Walter Beach Humphrey, '14, did a series of large oil paintings illustrating the song "Eleazar Wheelock." Colorful and painted with evident affection, they included many clever touches, but when they were completed and put on public display in the spring of 1939, they apparently shocked the prudish with their bevy of bare-breasted Native American maidens. Then Dartmouth president

Ernest Martin Hopkins reportedly didn't see how a mural with a subject as seemingly safe as "Eleazar Wheelock" could be controversial. "How would you as president of Dartmouth College like to be shown years from now surrounded by a lot of naked Indian girls?" one upset alumnus asked him. President Hopkins reportedly replied that he wouldn't mind at all, that he would in fact be quite pleased.[25]

The mural provoked a lot of discussions among my classmates a quarter of a century after its unveiling. The Hovey Grill, which the mural embellished, was located on the lower floor of Thayer Dining Hall and was a place where you could take a date and relax over a snack or coffee in a more intimate setting than the brightly illuminated and noisy dining hall in general provided. The mural's depiction flowed from the song by Richard Hovey that I loved: "Eleazar Wheelock," which mocked Dartmouth's founder as a "very pious man" utilizing alcohol—in the form of rum—to leverage the founding of the college. Most of my classmates and I loved the Hovey mural for its irreverent depiction of Eleazar Wheelock and its caricature of the circumstances surrounding the founding of Dartmouth. It delighted me that the college tolerated, and in fact had apparently commissioned, a painting that mocked religion, sobriety, and any idea that the college had been founded for noble purposes. No other college or university that I knew of would have allowed such satire. Most would have covered the mural or otherwise hidden it. It was a noteworthy and jocular testament to freedom of expression in academia.

Over the next four years, several of my dates pointed out that the mural's depiction of half-dressed women in a variety of poses could be considered somewhat lewd and demeaning to women. I thought about that, but neither my sister nor my mother found the mural offensive when I asked for their opinion. Naked women were the subjects of many acclaimed works of art, some of which were displayed in Dartmouth's own Hood Museum.

Until another classmate—Melvin Boozer—once pointed out to me that a Native American might find the mural offensive in depicting Indians as ignorant and inebriated, this thought had never occurred to me. Mel was an African American and one of the very few racial minorities in our class. I got to know him quite well while working with him at Thayer Dining Hall, considered him a good friend, and often discussed race relations and politics with him. He was much more intellectually mature than most of my classmates. I respected his opinion. He later was elected vice president of our class.[26] If the mural had depicted African Americans in such a manner, Mel suggested, he would have been very angry. That was food for thought.

After the Columbus Day weekend with Sandi, I tried to focus on the primary reason I was at Dartmouth (well, at least one of the primary reasons). Of my three courses during the fall term of that

---

[25]   Charles E. Widmayer, *Hopkins of Dartmouth: the Story of Ernest Martin Hopkins and His Presidency of Dartmouth College* (Hanover, NH: University Press of New England, 1977), 184.

[26]   After Mel's service in the Peace Corps in Brazil, the Socialist Party nominated him in 1980 for the office of vice president of the United States. Delegates to the convention of the Democratic Party that year also nominated him by petition at the convention. He was the first openly gay person ever nominated for the office and the only classmate so honored.

first year, I liked the Greek and Roman Studies course best. It met on Mondays, Wednesdays, and Fridays for sixty-five minutes each morning from nine fifteen until ten twenty. Essentially, the course was an introduction to Greek literature in translation from Homer to Plotinus. In high school, I had read and enjoyed Homer's *Odyssey*, but this course opened my eyes to the writings and historical and cultural background of so many other Greek literary giants. I was enthralled and thought seriously about changing my future major to the classics.

The class of about forty students met in a lecture room in Dartmouth Hall, where, through lectures and discussions, we explored the writings of Homer (*The Iliad*), Aeschylus, Sophocles, Euripides, Aristophanes, Herodotus, Thucydides, Plato, Aristotle, and Plotinus. We used excellent translations of these works by a famous Dartmouth classicist, Richmond Lattimore, '26. I remember in particular that the chairman of the Classics Department, Professor Wiencke, who presented many of the lectures, was an enthralling teacher, as was an associate professor named Doenges, who told us of his experiences in excavations of many Greek sites.

The head of the Chemistry Department taught Chemistry 1. I had struggled with chemistry in high school, but Professor Walter Stockmayer was such a compelling, enthusiastic teacher that I actually enjoyed his classes. I did not enjoy the chemistry laboratories, however. The chemistry course met four times each week from eight o'clock until five after nine, plus a one-hour laboratory in the afternoon—all in Steele Hall. I got a B in the course.

My third course in the autumn was French 3, conducted entirely in French, which I found easy and enjoyable, because of four years of high school French. There were about a dozen students in the class, many of whom were upperclassmen. The class met in Thornton Hall on Tuesdays, Thursdays, and Saturdays in the morning from eight o'clock until five after nine, with one-hour language laboratories on Wednesday and Friday afternoons. A fine, young assistant professor by the name of Richard Regosin was the primary lecturer. We focused most of the nine-week course on developing a mastery of spoken and written French in undertaking linguistic and thematic analyses of selected texts. Stendhal's *Le Rouge et le Noir* and *Terre des Hommes* by Antoine de Saint-Exupéry were the major works we addressed.

The fall term seemed to fly by! In high school, I worked very hard but had tended to take it easy at the beginning of each term, sharpening my focus in time for midterm exams and final exams. Regrettably, I had developed a parallel tendency to procrastinate until the very last minute, especially if a paper or other project was involved. At Dartmouth, I realized after several weeks that the shortness of the just-over-two-months term demanded that I buckle down to work immediately.

I also became aware of how fortunate I was to be taught by excellent teachers—always professors / assistant professors and often the head of a department—in relatively small classes (except for the introductory science courses, which tried to accommodate huge numbers of premed students taking the required chemistry, biology, mathematics, and physics courses). In all but one of the thirty-eight courses that I took at Dartmouth, including three courses taught by professors overseas and two summer courses, I thought that the teachers were extremely competent and empathetic. The single exception occurred in my sophomore year when an unfortunate faculty member, who was obviously emotionally compromised in his life and in the classroom, ultimately took his own life one dark winter evening. I remember him with great sadness.

The fall term was also the start of a roller-coaster ride as far as my grades were concerned. I ended the term with a 3.7 average (out of 5), or just under a B average. I should have worked much harder. In ensuing terms, overall my grade point average dipped as low as 2.3 (C minus) twice, despite my efforts to study harder, to be tutored in organic chemistry, and to reduce my extracurricular activities.

Perhaps my most difficult terms were the winter term of my freshman year, when I got a C minus in Biology and a D in Chemistry, and the winter term of my second year, when I got a D in Organic Chemistry and a C minus in Religion. My worst grades seemed to come during the winter terms in my first two college years. Perhaps my great love of skiing had something to do with that.

I recall being quite stressed and upset about grades as the spring term was beginning. Just before my birthday in April 1964, I received an unexpected letter from my brother John, who then was spending a year in Sweden with his family doing research at the Institute of Limnology, Uppsala University. John's letter was just the birthday present I needed in the form of encouragement. He wrote in part:

> Too bad about the chemistry. Chemists are always like that—the chem majors just sit there and nod their heads as if to say how logical it all is and how obvious. The rest of us wrote like mad and got C's or worse. [Another '57] stayed an extra year at Dartmouth because of a late reporting date for the Air Force. He took only organic chemistry, spent at least five or more hours a day on it, was married, relaxed, etc. and still got a D in it. I plugged along with track, DOC [Dartmouth Outing Club], etc. and only made decent grades in my senior year after I gave up track … Oh well, if I could get into graduate school [University of California at Berkeley] with a few D's, I guess you can …

Getting that letter helped a lot. My sister also wrote to encourage me with references to her problems with courses in her first two years at Mount Holyoke. I felt much better knowing that I was not the only member of our family who experienced some low grades at times in college.

Halfway through my college years, I looked at my overall grade point average of 3.3 (C plus) and decided—along with two-thirds of my fellow premed students (40 percent of my classmates)—that science and premedicine courses were not my strong suits. While I was struggling to decide what major course of study to switch to (from biology), I took solace in as much skiing as I could possibly squeeze into my afternoons. One day at the Dartmouth Skiway, I experienced a sign, or perhaps a vision, suggesting what I should do.

I first saw Madam Gaudin at the Skiway during winter term of my sophomore year. When I asked someone who the stunning, exquisitely graceful skier was whom I had admired on several occasions as she pirouetted down the trails, I was shocked to learn that she was a Dartmouth French teacher. I decided on the spot that I would take her course and several days later mustered the courage to speak to Colette Gaudin in French about my decision. She was gracious, enthusiastic, and welcoming— besides being gorgeous and having a husky, seductive voice like the actress Lauren Bacall—and immediately suggested that I consider studying in France during part of my junior year. As a result of my bewitchment that afternoon, I switched my major to comparative literature with a focus on French literature for my junior year. My world changed. The stress disappeared!

The faculty of the Romance Language Department was simply extraordinary—all were skillful, committed teachers, including several young teachers: Richard Regosin, John Rassias,[27] and Colette Gaudin, among others. I enjoyed French language and comparative literature tremendously!

And I took two great classes with Madam Gaudin, who was one of those riveting teachers who constantly moves around a classroom, speaking directly to individual students, punctuating comments with hand movements, and capturing the attention of all. She was one of the very few females on the faculty at Dartmouth, and I will admit that this novelty had something to do with my enjoyment of her classes. It did not hurt my concentration in her classroom that she often wore a black, loosely knitted sweater—the type that the wearer can see through if it is pulled over the head—and seemed to slowly remove it, stretching it over her head, at least once in each class. Of the approximately ten or so students in the class, most seemed to froth at the mouth (or engage in some other antic in appreciation of what lay beneath the sweater) as soon as the sweater was over her eyes. I was always respectful, suspecting that she could see right through that sweater. My quiet reticence before her provocative sweater removal may have been a reflection of both my great respect for Madam Gaudin and my secret daydream that a faculty member might wish to have an affair with a reverential man a dozen years younger.

I will be grateful forever to Madam Gaudin for her excellent French instruction. As described more fully below, studying comparative literature led to the opportunity to live and to study in France for a term, which was one of the high points of my college years.

Then, lest I fall into the trap described by Ralph Waldo Emerson—"A foolish consistency is the hobgoblin of little minds …" (*Self-Reliance*)—for my senior year I switched majors again to English, although in so doing I committed to taking eight straight English literature courses (plus German 3) my fourth year at Dartmouth, as well as the English comprehensive exam, which had the reputation of being the hardest of the few comprehensive examinations still being required at Dartmouth. For my last six terms, I worked extremely hard, as I mention later in this memoir, and was rewarded

---

[27]   Professor Rassias later taught at Dartmouth for fifty years and in the 1960s developed the "Rassias Method" of teaching languages, which was adopted by the Peace Corps and other well-known language-teaching organizations and is still utilized today.

with an incomparable learning experience as well as (incidentally) with a grade point average of 4.2 (B plus). My last year was a blissful year!

South Wigwam Dormitory and Pete Thomas's Austin Healy, June 1965

Yale-Dartmouth freshmen hockey game, February 1964

Freshmen cheering the Big Green Ivy League
football champions, October 1963

View from summit of Mount Moosilauke (4,810'), May 1964

Moosilauke Ravine Lodge, Dartmouth College, April 1965

CHAPTER 4—"DARTMOUTH'S IN TOWN AGAIN—TEAM, TEAM, TEAM!"[28]

I felt so very *alive* at Dartmouth! I had previously spent four months in Alaska's Brooks Range during the summer of 1961 and worked as a hutman for the AMC for the past two summers in the White Mountains of northern New Hampshire, as I mentioned earlier. In college, I was truly on my own. For the first time in my life, I had the ability to shape my destiny by myself, at least for the next four years.

When I arrived at Dartmouth, I was determined to live every moment of my college experience to the fullest. My Alaskan and White Mountain summers had been joyous but too evanescent. A summer had seemed like a week. I knew, as a result, that my college years would pass with a speed that defies comprehension. I strove to "live at a pitch that is near madness"[29] in the too brief time of my college experience. I only partially succeeded.

Incoming students at Dartmouth have a once-in-a-lifetime opportunity to acquaint themselves with New Hampshire's stately mountains, vast forests, and pristine lakes and rivers and to get to know each other at the same time by participating in a so-called freshman trip. The invitation I received at the end of the summer to join the trip was tempting. I could spend a week before the college term officially began hiking and camping in the White Mountains with my new classmates and spending nights at one of the college's many Dartmouth Outing Club cabins scattered among the nearby mountains or at the Moosilauke Ravine Lodge, where I had spent several happy years as a camper.

Unfortunately, the previous February I had broken my left ankle in high school. During the summer, I had twisted the same ankle on one of the packing trips up Mount Madison while carrying an eighty-pound load up to Madison Spring Huts, reinjuring my broken bone. One month later, my ankle still bothered me enough that I knew a lengthy hiking trip was not advisable. I decided reluctantly to forego the freshman trip, as a result.

In September of my sophomore year, I had a second opportunity to experience the freshman trip and happily accepted the chance to lead one of the freshman trips based upon my activities in the Dartmouth Outing Club, my familiarity with the Mount Moosilauke area trails, and my overall

---

[28] Anonymous, "Football Medley," *Dartmouth Song Book,* 68.

[29] Richard Eberhart, "If I could only live at a pitch that is near madness," in *Richard Eberhart: Selected Poems 1930–1965* (New York: New Directions Publishing Company, 1965), 18.

outdoor survival skills. It gave me great pleasure and a wonderful occasion to get to know the class of 1968 as they entered Dartmouth.

After I arrived in Hanover and heard my new classmates' reports of the fantastic hiking trip that most had experienced, I resolved not only to pursue my love of hiking as much as I could but also to join a team. Nothing promotes friendships like participating in a team sport.

In the 1960s, Dartmouth was a football powerhouse. Led by quarterback Bill King, '63, and center-linebacker Don McKinnon, '63, in 1962 Dartmouth had shut out five foes, beaten Princeton in the finale, 38–27, and gained its first undefeated-untied season (9–0–0) since 1925. The campus was buzzing with excitement over the football team when we arrived at Dartmouth in September 1963.

Coach Bob Blackmun and his team did not disappoint the newest class on campus. After a 17–13 loss at Harvard ended our fifteen-game winning streak, the Green rebounded, won a comeback victory 22–21 at Princeton, and ended a glorious season tied with the Tigers for the Ivy League crown. Football prowess was synonymous with Dartmouth.

Our dominance continued throughout my Dartmouth years. Princeton managed to beat us in 1964 and took the Ivy League Championship, but in 1965 revenge was sweet. Princeton had won seventeen straight games since the loss to Dartmouth in 1963. We were 8–0. At Palmer Stadium at Princeton, classmate Mickey Beard's seventy-nine-yard pass to another '67, Bill Calhoun, clinched Dartmouth's win, 28–14. It was our second undefeated season in four years, and we won the Lambert Trophy as the East's best team. Of course, under the strict application of Murphy's Law to the events of my life, I was in France during the entire spectacular season, spending part of my junior year in Dartmouth's foreign study program at the University of Montpellier. So I missed what was probably one of Dartmouth's greatest football seasons.

Our last fall in Hanover, we were undefeated in eleven straight previous games but failed to make a rain-drenched two-point conversion and bowed to Holy Cross, 7–6. The Green still gained a three-way tie, with Harvard and Princeton (all 6–1), for its fourth Ivy title in five years. I participated in this football glory only as an avid spectator who never missed a home game when I was in town. After all, a book of four home-game tickets cost only $12.50.

Despite my love of football, because of my ankle injury, I knew as a freshman that I could not even think of pursuing a fall sport at Dartmouth that involved a lot of hard running, much less severe physical contact. I had played three years of varsity football and run the half-mile, quarter-mile, and relay events on the varsity track team in high school. I weighed about two hundred pounds, was six feet tall, and was in tremendous condition, as a consequence of lugging sixty- to eighty-pound packs of supplies four miles and 3,600 feet up the Valley Way Trail to Madison Spring Huts on Mount Madison almost every day for the past two summers. But football and track were now out of the question, even if I was good enough in perfect health to make either the freshman football team or the track team at Dartmouth, which I probably was not.

Early in September, as the fiery autumn colors had just begun to creep from the mountain summits toward the valleys, I saw a notice on the huge bulletin board on the first floor of the Hopkins Center near the mailboxes. It solicited interested freshmen to try out for the rowing club. Rowing was not yet a varsity sport at Dartmouth at that time but was considered a club sport. I stopped by the athletic office in the gymnasium to talk with a young man named Andy Geiger, who was the freshman crew coach.

Coach Geiger was enthusiastic about rowing and urged me to try out. He told me that students first began rowing at Dartmouth in 1833, and although it was still a club sport, it was quickly growing in popularity. He expected about fifty freshmen to try out.

The young coach also mentioned that Dartmouth's first professional coach was the legendary professional oarsman, John Biglin, who was also the subject of many Thomas Eakins's paintings from that era. I knew from an art course in high school that one of Eakins's most famous paintings featured two brothers rowing. Remembering that painting, portraying Biglin, I took Coach Geiger's reference as a sign that I should try rowing. Also, my best friend in high school had just written me that he was trying out for Yale's freshman rowing team. It would be great to row against Bob Ramage someday, I thought!

The rowing club trained out of the Dartmouth Rowing Club Boathouse, located on the Connecticut River, which runs along the western edge of the campus, as I have mentioned. The river provides more than forty miles of flat, rowable water, with virtually no powerboats or other traffic. Checking out where the rowing team practiced, I looked north from the Ledyard Bridge, over which the AT crosses the river. I could see the boathouse on the right bank of the river, surrounded by graceful pines and the shimmering foliage of the birch trees hugging the bank. The foothills of Vermont's Green Mountains on the river's west bank and those of the White Mountains on the east bank, just beginning to flare into the reds and oranges that would soon engulf them, dropped to the water's edge. All in all, it looked like a peaceful and alluring setting for an autumn sport. I was hooked.

I soon learned that official crew races against other schools took place in the spring. Rowing club members formed teams that trained for and raced in long distance "head races" in the fall. The frozen Connecticut River forced winter training indoors, where we could expect a continuation of the grueling, intense training I soon began.

Every afternoon in September and October, we had an hour or more of exercising and running several miles after classes. The running was easy enough that even with my healing ankle I was fine. My favorite run during this fall training was east up the AT on the long hill on East Wheelock Street from the college green to Grasse Road, then north through the woods over to Reservoir Road, then west to the Lyme Road (Route 10), and finally completing the 4.8-mile circle by turning south on the Lyme Road toward the golf course and Vale of Tears at the ski jump back to the college green. If I was feeling lazy or had to get back to the college faster than usual, I took a shortcut from the AT north up Rip Road to Reservoir Road, bypassing the longer route up Grasse Road. The latter route tracked

Camp Brook, which ran along parts of both Grasse Road and Reservoir Road, offering glimpses and the music of the clear stream water, swirling and cascading over the granite rocks.

Those were glorious runs! I could run at a leisurely pace and enjoy the crisp autumn air pushed down from Balch Hill and Moose Mountain—parts of the ridge to the east of Hanover. Until late October, on most days I ran in shorts and a T-shirt. In November, I donned a Dartmouth sweat suit I bought for three dollars at the Dartmouth Co-op on Main Street.

The best part about these runs was the opportunity to reflect on life. My high school in Buffalo had instilled in me a great interest in international current affairs. Dartmouth nurtured this interest in almost every nonscience course I took and in the many informal discussions with professors I was just beginning to experience on campus at social events. The year 1963 provided a lot of food for thought on the international scene, such as the Soviets pulling their missiles out of Cuba, Churchill's retirement, the first woman in space (a Russian), and France's opposition to Britain's joining the European Common Market.

The year held even more thought-provoking events at home: the Freedom March earlier in 1963 in Washington, DC, involving about 250,000 civil rights demonstrators, as I mentioned already; the president's sending of troops to Alabama to quell race riots; the signing of the atomic test ban treaty; and the inauguration of the zip code.

Dartmouth's most illustrious contemporary alumnus also was contributing to my reflections: New York Governor Nelson Rockefeller, class of 1930. I was reading Rockefeller's newly released book— *The Future of Federalism*—and enjoying it tremendously. Rocky and his new wife, Happy, visited Hanover in November for the Holy Cross football game, and I shook their hands at a reception after the game at the Leverone Field House.

Some of my reflections on these runs were darker and sadder, as I tried desperately to figure out why my girlfriend Lindsey had precipitously dropped me within a month of our tearful farewell to each other in Buffalo in September. What signs had I missed of the breakup and what could I have done to avoid it? My heart ached after Lindsey wrote me in early October that she had found a new love in the early weeks of her freshman year at William Smith College: some junior at Hobart College named Doug. As I ran, I relived in my mind every minute of our six brief months together.

Lindsey Jewel was smart, personable, athletic, and sensitive. She was also a long-legged, longhaired, gorgeous, blue-eyed blonde, with full lips and a nice figure. Her name—Jewel—fit her perfectly. She was on the precision swimming team at Kenmore West High School in suburban Buffalo when we met in April. We had connected at a deep level immediately. Her parents were wonderful, and she had a cute dog named Nikki. Meeting her was one of the couple of times in my life when I thought that divine intervention had occurred. We dated heavily for the rest of the spring and when I returned from my hutman's job in the White Mountains. She gave me a fine, brown, mohair sweater that she had knit for me for my birthday. I gave her my Nichols High School letter sweater. We both loved

Leonard Bernstein's music in *West Side Story*. More than fifty years later, I still think of her whenever I hear it.

By the end of the summer, we had started a more intimate relationship, emotionally and physically. She was one of the two girls I had met by the end of high school whom I trusted wholeheartedly and loved with every fiber of my being. When we left Buffalo for our respective colleges in early September, we promised to love each other forever, although we agreed that we both should date other students, given the 350 miles separating us. My very first purchase in Hanover after arriving to begin college was a gold Dartmouth pendant and chain that I bought at Ward Amidon Jewelers on South Main Street and sent to Lindsey immediately.

At one level, I understood how a lovely and bewitching girl like Lindsey probably would not remain my girlfriend for long after she left home. In my heart, I feared from the moment of our last kiss that she would meet a new lover and our relationship would end, as it did. I was shocked to my core, however, at the speed with which she dropped me! I learned for the first time in those hours, running in the nostalgia of September and October, the irony that emotional pain could be appealingly transformational, as I strangely found in the depths of despair almost the same sort of emotive plateau of intense feeling and pleasurable stimulation to which my deep love had brought me throughout my relationship with Lindsey. So this was what love and loss were about!

Almost as bad as Lindsey's "Dear John" letter was the one I received from her parents, who blamed me in strong words for breaking up with Lindsey! I was very close to her parents—probably too close. That may have been one reason Lindsey broke up with me. (If my parents recommended a particular girl to me, it was a kiss of death.) After struggling with my feelings for weeks after receiving her parents' letter, I finally wrote to them, advising them of who did what to whom. Of course, when I tried to visit Lindsey at Christmastime during winter break, she refused to see me. I never saw her again. Sweet Lindsey …

There were also not-so-pleasant runs up and down the aisles of the west stands of the football stadium. Running the stadium steps reminded me of my two previous summers in New Hampshire's Presidential Range, when I ran up and down mountain trails as part of my work. The effect on my legs was also similar. At first my legs ached unbearably, but after a few weeks, my leg muscles were rock hard and pain-free!

Rowing was entirely new to me. I had previously rowed an old rowboat at our family's summer cabin on the Canadian shore of Lake Erie and paddled many canoes on various lakes and rivers, including the Connecticut. The discipline of competitive rowing was totally foreign. I had so much to learn! Most of the other about forty-five classmates were equally as ignorant. I recall that Bruce Chasan, Erik Joh, Ed Masters, and Bill Sprong were among them with me. Coach Geiger and several of the more experienced rowers, such as classmate Ted Walkley, struggled to teach us. Even such a basic process as carrying a boat from the boathouse to the pier and placing it in the water took several afternoon practices to master.

We quickly learned that the boats are called shells because the hull is thin like a shell. Our boats' hulls were only about 1/8" to 1/4" thick to make them as light as possible. We were to engage in sweep rowing, where each rower handles a single oar (about twelve and a half feet long). The shells were long and as narrow as possible. Sitting in the shell, each of the eight rowers had his back to the direction the boat was moving. Power was generated using a blended sequence of the rowers' legs, backs, and arms. Each boat was steered by a coxswain sitting in the stern, who used the rudder to steer the boat and verbally coordinated the power and rhythm of the rowers.

Rowers sat on a sliding seat that rolled on wheels along a fixed track called the slide. Our feet were tied into shoes, which were bolted onto footplates in the boat. Oars were held in place by riggers, which extended from the top of the shell's sides. Each person in the boat had a position, starting in the bow. The person closest to the bow was called bow seat. Progressive numbers identified every other rower, except the lead rower, who was the stroke. In each boat, the seats were called bow, two, three, four, five, six, seven, and stroke. Although initially we often changed positions in the shell, by the end of fall training, Ted Walkley was the stroke in our boat. I rowed in seat seven just in back of Ted. Bill Sprong was six just in back of me. As the stroke, Ted was responsible for setting the stroke length and cadence (with the coxswain's help).

The steps of the rowing process or cycle were drummed into our heads. Each step had its own plethora of details and techniques to master. Of course, the overall objective was to move the shell through the water as fast and efficiently as possible, minimizing any motion or alteration in the cycle that would slow forward progress.

Very generally, after we learned how to position our hands on the oar or blade, Coach Geiger taught us how to make the squared blade enter the water with a slight upward motion of the hands and arms. This was called the catch. All rowers had to be as nearly as possible in sync at the catch and thereafter with the stroke. The power that moved the boat was applied to the oar first by the legs, then the back, and finally the arms to pull the oar through the water. The legs created the majority of the power. Even the amount of backward lean on a rower's body affected the power in this fluid motion called the drive. The end of the drive, where the last 20 percent of the power comes from the back, arms, and leaning back, was called the finish.

Following the finish came the release, when the blade was removed from the water with a sharp downward and away motion of the hands. The release started the rowing cycle and preceded the recovery, which was the time we could rest while we bent our legs, slid forward on the slide, and returned to the ready position. The recovery time should always be longer than the drive time, even as much as twice as long as the drive time, but the idea was to move the boat on the pull through (or drive) and take a ride (or rest) on the recovery without sacrificing the very speed that we had generated.

Every muscle in your body is called into play in the sequence of actions just described! I thought that I was in really excellent shape when I started rowing. I soon found that nothing in my past life had prepared me for the excruciating fatigue and persistent ache my body endured at first. As the autumn progressed, however, with the pain came moments of amazing bliss, even euphoria.

I found that the most difficult things to learn were turning the oar to a perpendicular (vertical) position, called "squaring," and turning the blade into a position parallel (horizontal) to the water, called "feathering" the blade, which was performed at the release. I knew how to feather a canoe paddle. Feathering a long oar at a completely different angle was quite another thing, particularly when the action took place quickly and repeatedly.

There were so many details to remember. Until my muscle memory finally kicked in, I was guilty of more than my share of so-called air strokes, where I started the drive before the catch was completed, and skying, when I carried my hands too low during the recovery, resulting in the blade being too high off the water's surface. Any such instances had disastrous effects.

I learned to measure the success of my efforts by watching the wake created by the blade. If my blade left behind little dinky ripples, then I was not pulling hard enough. If I left tidal waves after I lifted the blade out of the water, then I was pulling just right. Within weeks, virtually all of the men in our boat were leaving *tsunamis* in the Connecticut.

We raced against each other and against the junior varsity boats. It was pure joy when we beat the other freshman boats most of the time and occasionally slipped past a junior varsity boat. I recall that I became very aware of the river's strong current, especially during these races. Rowing north against the current was very difficult. When we raced southward, it seemed as though we were flying! There is nothing quite so thrilling as silently gliding down a river, cutting like a knife through the reflections of the autumn colors, sunset, and sky in the water, with the only sounds those of the wind, the straining of the oars, and the rhythmic calls of the cox and stroke.

With the change from daylight savings time in October, suddenly our afternoon practices were taking place in the river shadows of the Connecticut's twilight hours. So we switched to early-morning practices for the last weeks of the season. Sometimes we rowed through an eerie fog as the sun rose over the river. The combination of sunrise and fog transformed the Connecticut into a glowing, golden, liquid canvas on which our dipping oars painted exquisite patterns of circular ripples.

In November we had to use oars to break the ice beginning to form on the Connecticut. By Thanksgiving, the darkness and river ice had driven us indoors for practices at Alumni Gymnasium's jury-rigged training tanks, which were poor substitutes for the transcendental experience of rowing on the river.

In the following months, my courses, work to pay for college expenses, skiing, glee club, and a bout with mononucleosis all combined to still my oar. Until the end of February, I continued to exercise and to lift weights regularly at Alumni Gymnasium. But I never rowed on the Connecticut again, to my deep regret. The autumn trail of the river between banks of yellow-leaved birches and sentinel white pines and firs has remained a favorite among my memories.

Crew practice on the Connecticut River at sunset below
our dormitory window, October 1964

Dartmouth College Band, October 1966

Kappa Kappa Kappa fraternity house, 1 Webster Avenue, January 1966

Dartmouth College Green looking south toward Hopkins Center
and Hanover Inn, January 1964

Tuck Mall, Dartmouth College, October 1963

Chapter 5—"Et Tu Quoque, Mi Fili!"[30]

The accident was a total surprise. Missing my head by about one foot, the football-sized piece of the ornamental, twenty-foot-high ceiling crashed on the floor next to my chair, glancing off of the chair arm and table corner. On impact, it had disintegrated into hundreds of pieces and a cloud of dust.

"Are you all right?" the lady asked, quickly standing up and putting a reassuring hand on my shoulder. "Did it hit you?"

"I'm all right," I replied, shaken but unhurt. My dark suit was now white with plaster dust.

"Let me call the librarian and the custodian to help," she offered and immediately found both in an adjoining room.

With clucks of concern, the Supreme Court librarian quickly offered to call a doctor or to pay for having my suit cleaned. Nothing like this had ever happened before, she fretted. The custodian quickly swept up the mess.

At Topliff Hall twenty years earlier, the custodian was a friendly New Englander named Larry Ragan. Beginning in elementary school, I learned that often one of the most important people to get to know at a school or at any institution is the custodian, sometimes known as the facility manager, janitor, or maintenance man. Larry had taken care of Topliff Hall for more than two decades and in significant ways had mentored many of the hundreds of young men during these years who had called Topliff home, at least for part of the year.

If you were looking for a romantic place to take a date, or a local restaurant with home-cooked food, or somewhere to buy ski wax or condoms, Larry was your man. If a light fixture or plumbing needed attention, he was always there to address the problem. On the several occasions when I was locked out of my room, he had the master key.

Larry also had an endless supply of the dimes needed to make a telephone call in one of the hallway telephones on the first (643-9752), second (643-9845), and third floors (643-9700) servicing the denizens of Topliff. Perhaps most importantly, he was also an older person to talk to when things were

---

[30]   Daniel Webster, as quoted by Francis Lane Childs, "A Dartmouth History Lesson for Freshmen," *Dartmouth Alumni* magazine, December 1957.

not quite going well, providing a comfortable, nonjudgmental nod or a laconic word of sympathy, as appropriate.

I recall once being on an important telephone call with a date in March, deeply involved in a romantic exchange. Suddenly, the line went dead. I was distraught. I checked the other telephones in Topliff and then those next door in New Hampshire Hall. No telephones were working. When I complained to Larry, he replied, "Line's down." As usual, he was right. Heavy rains and ice flows in the rampaging White River had destroyed the bridge over the White River at White River Junction, severing telephone communications between Hanover and the outside world for days. We were really isolated!

I thought of Larry as a typical New Hampshire man (although I recall that he was from nearby Thetford, Vermont). I particularly liked his manner of talking, which was short and to the point. He never wasted words and occasionally salted his comments with the local phrases, speech patterns, and practicality of Grafton County—one of the poorest counties then in Appalachia (except for the relatively wealthy town of Hanover).

On one occasion, my hall mates and I were discussing Dartmouth's revered president, John Sloan Dickey, who had been leading Dartmouth since the year most of us were born. It was hard to imagine what Dartmouth had been like before President Dickey arrived or what it would be like after he retired.

"What do you suppose people will do when Dickey dies?" someone mused.

"Likely they'll bury him," was Larry's reply.

Another time, a classmate from New York City commented to Larry: "You folks up here in the mountains certainly are lost."

"Being lost ain't bad; being found is vexin'," he replied.

When the New Yorker complained upon returning to Hanover's snow in January after Christmas vacation at home—"I guess I shouldn't expect too much from an isolated place like this; why I came back to this wilderness I'll never know"—Larry opined: "We ain't missed you much, son."

Larry told us the story of his brother Jim who lived over in the area of the border between New Hampshire and Maine, close to the state line. In 1961, surveyors told his brother that he didn't live in Maine after all; he lived in New Hampshire.

"Well, thank the good God Almighty!" Jim exclaimed. "I couldn't have stood another of them gol dern Maine winters."

He wouldn't tell us much about his family. Loquacious he was not. I once asked him about his family.

"Well, I got the wife and three kids livin'; another kid in Concord," Larry offered. I didn't ask him if his child was buried in Concord.

When he wasn't bemusing me with his quips, Larry often offered hope, in his own way. As he was the local weather expert, I asked him on several stormy days: "Think it'll stop snowing?" He never failed to reply, "It always has."

Not all New Hampshire men were laconic. One became perhaps this country's best orator.

Not long after I arrived at Dartmouth, I met another freshman, Stan Brown, who lived across the hall from Pete and me on the first floor of Topliff Hall with his roommate, Bill Kirkpatrick, '67. Stan was a lanky, friendly classmate whose claim to fame was that his great-great-great-grandfather was Francis Brown, Dartmouth's third president (1815–20).

President Brown, as Stan soon told me, presided over Dartmouth College during the time of the famous dispute between the State of New Hampshire and the college. Stan's mention of his ancestor was one of those things that you first hear absentmindedly but don't think much about. In the following weeks, however, I thought about what he had told me and decided to find out about the dispute.

A librarian at Baker Library was a font of information. She directed me to a December 1957 issue of the *Dartmouth Alumni* magazine that contained an article by former Dartmouth professor Francis Lane Childs entitled "A Dartmouth History Lesson for Freshmen." Professor Childs had provided a lecture on Dartmouth's history during Freshman Week, which I had missed. His article awakened me to the fascinating history of the school I had just joined and initially answered two questions that my first month at Dartmouth had raised.

The first arose when I noticed on several occasions in my classes that professors were quick to correct any student who referred to the college inadvertently as a "university." "Dartmouth is a college, not a university, we were admonished repeatedly." What was this obsession about distinguishing Dartmouth College from a "university"?

The second question concerned Daniel Webster. It took me a little while to figure out who Daniel Webster was. I confused him with Noah Webster of dictionary fame and for several weeks wondered why portraits of a lexicographer hung prominently in Baker Library and in a building named after Webster on the north end of the Green.

My ignorance was quickly dispelled. This Webster, of course, was *the* Webster I had learned about in high school history: probably the most eloquent politician (congressman, senator, and secretary of state under three presidents) and lawyer of nineteenth-century American history, with the possible exception of Abraham Lincoln. He is Dartmouth's favorite son, for without his powerful legal defense of his alma mater, Dartmouth as I knew it would not have existed.

The defense occurred in the case of *Trustees of Dartmouth College v. William H. Woodward* or, as it is more commonly called, the *Dartmouth College Case*. Sooner or later, every Dartmouth graduate finds out about this case, which was an extremely important one for Dartmouth and for the future of the then forty-year-old United States. A mural in Thayer Dining Hall depicts Daniel Webster's argument to the Supreme Court.

Briefly, as recounted in the article, the legal issue concerned the contract clause of the United States Constitution. When King George III granted a charter to Eleazar Wheelock in 1769, giving him the land to support a new college for Native Americans, a "contract" was created between the then sovereign and Wheelock. The New Hampshire legislature amended this charter forty years later. The legislature tried to make Dartmouth a public institution and to change its name to Dartmouth University. Under the leadership of Stan's ancestor, President Brown, the trustees resisted the effort, arguing that such interference by the state with a contract was unlawful. Daniel Webster argued the case for Dartmouth before the US Supreme Court in 1818 after several adverse decisions in the lower courts.

Chief Justice John Marshall wrote the historic decision in favor of Dartmouth College, thereby paving the way for all American private institutions to conduct their affairs in accordance with their charters and without interference from the state. Even more important for Dartmouth lore than the very significant victory and legal precedent, however, was how the ruling was obtained. Daniel Webster, who graduated from Dartmouth in 1801, gave one of the most eloquent, emotional, and compelling arguments in the history of the court, according to a reliable observer's account.

It took me a while to comprehend why this event—apart from the decision—was so significant to Dartmouth. In fact, I wondered during most of my four years at Dartmouth. Then I understood. The emotional tie to the college. Only a Dartmouth graduate can fully appreciate the affection for Dartmouth expressed by Webster in his deeply moving performance before the Supreme Court of the great Chief Justice Marshall.

The sole contemporary narrative of the argument was written by Chauncey A. Goodrich, professor of oratory at Yale University, who reported on the argument to Yale with respect to Webster's concluding peroration, quoting Webster's words:

> *This, Sir, is my case!* It is the case not merely of that humble institution. It is the case of every college in our Land! It is more! It is the case of every eleemosynary institution throughout our country—of all those great charities founded by the piety of our ancestors to alleviate human misery, and scatter blessings along the pathway of life! It is more! It is, in some sense, the case of every man among us who has property of which he may be stripped, for the question is simply this, "Shall our State Legislatures be allowed to take *that which is not their own,* to turn it from its original use, and apply it to such ends and purposes as they in their discretion shall see fit!" Sir, you may destroy

this little institution; it is weak, it is in your hands! I know it is one of the lesser lights in the literary horizon of our country. You may put it out! But if you do so, you must carry through your work! You must extinguish, one after another, all those great lights of science which for more than a century have thrown their radiance over our land! It is, Sir, as I have said, a small college. And yet *there are those who love it.*

Professor Goodrich then described Webster's demeanor and final words:

Here the feelings, which he had thus far succeeded in keeping down, broke forth. His lips quivered; his firm cheek trembled with emotion; his eyes were filled with tears; his voice choked; and he seemed struggling to the utmost, simply to gain that mastery over himself which might save him from an unmanly burst of feeling. I will not attempt to give the few broken words of tenderness in which he went on to speak of his attachment to the college. It seemed to be mingled throughout with the recollections of father, mother, brother, and all the trials and preventions through which he had made his way into life. Every one saw that it was wholly unpremeditated—a pressure on his heart which sought relief in words and tears. Recovering himself, after a few moments, and turning to Judge [John] Marshall, he said, "Sir, I know not how others may feel (glancing at the opponents of the college before him [some of whom were Dartmouth graduates]), but for myself, when I see my *Alma Mater* surrounded, like Caesar in the senate house, by those who are reiterating stab upon stab, I would not for this right hand have her say to me, '*Et tu quoque, mi fili!*'"[31]

"It is, Sir, as I have said, a small college. And yet *there are those who love it,*" Webster emotionally pled. Every Dartmouth graduate knows these two sentences. They appear on the masthead of the *Dartmouth* and are almost a mantra imprinted in the brain of every alumnus and alumna.

Webster was my first thought when I heard, 165 years after his stirring argument, that the Supreme Court had granted review of one of my cases. I read the above account again as I prepared for my first Supreme Court argument. I was looking for language that could persuade a conservative court of the merit of my position in a case I knew that I would lose. Its acceptance for review by the court in the face of four unanimous and favorable (to my union client and me) decisions by three different US courts of appeals, involving fourteen appellate judges, was extremely ominous (i.e., there was no conflict among the opinions of the lower courts who had all agreed with my position—indeed every judge agreed with me—so there was no need for Supreme Court review).

The grant of the petition for a writ of certiorari (request for review) indicated that then chief justice Warren Burger and company wished to overturn the previous sweeping successes of union attorneys on the issue in many courts that had supported the union's position I championed. The court annually grants about one hundred of the approximately ten thousand petitions for review filed. In my case,

---

31   Ibid.

the federal government had asked for court review. I was not feeling lucky that my case was one of the few accepted. For the life of me, I couldn't figure out how to incorporate Webster's stirring appeals or his quote from Shakespeare's *Julius Caesar* into my argument. "*Et tu quoque*, Chief Justice Burger!" On the morning of the argument, I got up early, dressed in my only dark suit, and put on my Dartmouth tie in honor of Webster. As I prepared for my case on the morning of oral argument in the court's majestic library, I sat at one of the dark mahogany tables underneath an imposing brass chandelier, somewhat cowed by the silence and impressiveness of the room.

Suddenly, above me there was a breaking sound and a piece of the ceiling of the historic library fell on me, brushing my shoulder, my chair, and the table edge and disintegrating with a crash on the floor next to me. I was stunned and covered in white plaster dust. The only other person in the library at the time—Ruth Anne E. Galter, assistant attorney general of Nebraska, who was preparing to defend her state's requirement that licenses of drivers have a picture of the bearer against a religion-based challenge—was equally startled. After confirming that I was all right, she confided that she thought that the accident was intended for her and mentioned a curse associated with her case: *Jensen v. Quaring*.

I rushed home to change my clothes and managed to get back to the court for the one o'clock argument. I had previously argued appeals in over two-dozen cases at the court of appeals level. However, arguing before the Supreme Court was quite a different matter. My half-hour allotment of argument time was far too short (Webster's team had four hours), but I managed to make the points I needed to present to the court.

When the *Wall Street Journal* reported the argument and library incident on its front page the next day (Tuesday), it opined that the accident was a bad omen for the success of my case! Five New York attorneys called me that night to ask if they could represent me in my lawsuit against the Supreme Court … I told them that I would think about such a claim and call them back if I was interested. I now regret that I passed up the opportunity to sue the Supreme Court. Res ipsa loquitur! ("The fact speaks for itself" or negligence is inferred from the circumstances of the injury.)

So instead of a successful, unprecedented lawsuit (with an impeccable witness) against an improbable institutional defendant, millions of dollars in compensatory damages for my emotional distress, and an impressive sobriquet such as Webster's "Black Dan," I was thereafter known in legal circles as "Chicken Little" Hobbie. (The sky is falling! The sky is falling!)

I lost the case: *Cornelius v. Nutt*. Justice Thurgood Marshall, however, wrote a stinging dissent, joined by Justice Brennan, which was some consolation. At least Justice Marshall—one of the greatest justices of all time—agreed with me! Larry would have said about the six members of the court who voted against me (Justice Powell did not participate): "City folks don't know nothin'."

The other words of wisdom imparted by Larry concerned my budget. I complained to Larry that I never had enough money to enjoy college life. His sympathetic response was: "Spend less, earn more."

So for my second term, I kept track of my expenses. My expense list looked like this for the approximately nine weeks between January 1, 1964, and the end of the first week in March:

Mrs. Gilbert (laundry)	$9.00	Chemistry lab book	$ .50
Dartmouth Co-op	$8.60	Stamps	$1.25
Jim Schlough (DDA substitute)	$5.00	Simmons College—road trip	$2.00
Skiing lessons	$13.50	Mixer ticket— Simmons Col.	$1.25
2 meals on trip	$2.00	Laundry 1/16	$ .50
Dance on 1/11	$4.50	Books 1/17	$1.90
Ski tow tickets 1/20 Oak Hill	$2.25	Haircut	$1.50
Ride 1/20	$1.75	Film	$2.85
Books 1/23	$ .50	Developing	$1.85
Lowell—road trip 1/25	$6.10	Hockey game	$2.00
Writing paper	$1.00	Laundry	$2.00
Glee Club concert	$4.00	Birthday cards 2/24	$ .50
Hockey game	$2.00	Stamps	$ .36
Winter Carnival		Variety Night (Hop Center)	$2.00
Dances	$4.00	Skiing	$3.00
Sleigh ride	$3.00	Notebook 2/26	$1.00
Food	$11.85	Misc.	$2.25
Ski jump tickets	$2.00	Dinner 2/29	$6.00
Lodging Kaete Honig	$4.00	Postcards & cards	$ .75
Misc.	$2.25	Stamps	$1.50
Stamps	$1.00	Book	$1.25
DDA substitute 2/9	$2.50	Bindings	$7.00
Movie	$1.60	Glee Club trip 3/7	$1.00
Cleaning	$2.00	Date—Jackson College	$1.00
Stamps	$ .70	Patches	$2.00
Books	$2.00	Cards	$ .35
Valentines	$ .75	Ride home	$5.00
Phone call (long dist. Kaete)	$1.20	Laundry	$3.60

Total: $155.21

(If the budget above seems like very little money relative to today's prices, remember that in 1963—according to my mother's notes—a gallon of milk cost about $1.00, a new car about $3,000, a gallon of gas about $0.30, a loaf of bread about $0.20, and a term's tuition about $400.)

During the same time frame, I managed to earn $33.70, as a result of seventeen babysitting jobs during the term. The going rate in the Hanover area was about $0.60 an hour for student babysitters. Faculty and townspeople posted notes that advertised for babysitters on the bulletin board at the

Hopkins Center, adjacent to the student mailboxes, and on the large bulletin board in the lobby at Thayer Dining Hall. Those bulletin boards were excellent means of communication. Notices of items for sale, odd jobs, road-trippers looking for riders to share costs, beds for dates in townspeople's homes, meetings of various clubs and student activities, and similar notices were posted on them.

When I responded to an ad for a babysitter by calling the telephone number listed in the ad, as long as I was a Dartmouth student, apparently, no other reference was needed. The faculty member usually would pick me up in front of Robinson Hall on the west side of the Green, drive me to the babysitting location, and return me to the Green afterward. I often found the children whom I was hired to babysit were already in bed, so I could get a lot of homework done while earning a bit of extra money.

Where there were very young children not yet retired for the night, I enjoyed reading to them, as my parents had read to me when I was a child. Invariably, one of the children's books available in all faculty homes with young children was a charming, witty narrative that had just been published several years before by a famous Dartmouth author who immortalized his college's color: *Green Eggs and Ham* by Dr. Seuss. It was also enjoyable to visit faculty and others' homes and to see the residential areas surrounding Hanover. I made some fine faculty acquaintances by babysitting their children over the next four years!

Only on one occasion did I have a problem. A faculty member of the math department and his wife arranged to have me babysit their two young sons. He picked me up and drove me to his house. As he and his wife were leaving for their evening out, he handed me a key to the boys' bedroom, told me that they were locked inside, and instructed me not to open the door unless it was a matter of life or death. He repeated these directions for emphasis.

Shortly after the parents had left, I heard a tremendous crash upstairs, which sounded as though a large piece of furniture had been overturned in the boys' room. After much deliberation and concern that something terrible had occurred, I quietly unlocked the door and cracked it open, peering in. The boys rushed at the door ferociously, clearly evincing that they were unhurt and primed to attack me. I managed to pull the door quickly shut and lock it before they crashed into it and started to rattle the doorknob.

I babysat for this family only on two more occasions. I liked the faculty parents but finally decided not only that I could not get any studying done with the boys rampaging above but also that the anxiety prompted by the loud noises upstairs throughout the evening was not worth the money.

Wim deHaas, '69, standing by Glee Club bus, January 1967

Dartmouth College Glee Club, October 1964

Dartmouth College Glee Club, March 1966

Dartmouth College Green, January 1964

Glee Club Officers William
Gibson, '66, Robert Bach,
'66 with Dr. Paul Zeller, Glee
Club director, March 1966

Dr. Paul Zeller, Glee
Club director, April
1966

Dartmouth College Freshman Glee Club, March 1964

Chapter 6—"Ho a Song by the Fire"[32]

I liked Professor Paul Zeller from the moment I first met him in the Faulkner Recital Hall of the new Hopkins Center for the Performing Arts. He had a crew cut, wore glasses, was of medium height and weight, and was about fifty years old. When he smiled, the lines around his eyes deepened into crinkles etched by a lifetime of laughter. His jokes were well known. He was the head of the Music Department and director of the College Glee Club. I was there for an audition for the Freshman Glee Club, also known as the Class of 1967 Glee Club. The audition was one of the most significant events that shaped my freshman year—indeed all of my college years.

A notice posted on the bulletin board at the Hopkins Center instructed interested freshmen to come for auditions on a Tuesday evening at eight o'clock. I showed up early because I was nervous and wanted to watch other auditions before I decided to go ahead. I recognized another classmate, Ora McCreary, who seemed to be one of the two piano accompanists helping with the auditions. I later met the other pianist, John Hargraves, '66. My roommate, Pete Thomas, was coming later. There were several dozen classmates waiting to audition.

"Tell me about your musical background, your hometown, and why you want to join the Freshman Glee Club?" Professor Zeller asked each of us.

"Well," I replied when it was my turn, "I played the violin for seven years until high school, sang in my church choir for five years, and sang in my high school glee club for four years. I am from Buffalo."

"So you came to Dartmouth to get more snow!" He smiled. "I remember Buffalo's winters when I first started teaching music in the suburbs at East Aurora High School in the forties. Some days I couldn't get to work there was so much snow! Say, didn't your brother sing with me a long time ago?" he asked.

He handed each of us in turn a Dartmouth song to sing. Mine was the "Hanover Winter Song," which begins "Ho a song by the fire, pass the pipes, pass the bowl." I knew it by heart already from my childhood love of the Glee Club's record that I mentioned earlier.

Director Zeller stopped me almost immediately and said that he was pleased to welcome me. All of the about two-dozen auditioning classmates that evening were similarly welcomed. Pete also made

---

[32]   "Ho, a song by the fire! Pass the pipes, pass the bowl ..." Hovey, "Hanover Winter Song," *Dartmouth Song Book*, 36.

the club, as did Stan Brown and Peter Keating from our Topliff dormitory corridor. As far as I know, no one failed the audition.

The Freshman Glee Club had about forty other members at first, but after several months, only twenty-five of these remained, including with the four from Topliff Hall the following: Fred Behringer, Rob Chambers, Larry Fabian, Chuck Holtz, Wayne Johnson, John Kornet, Wayne Letizia, Andy Longacre, Andy Mack, Allen McCook, Ora McCreary, John McPherson, Bob Morrow, Bruce Munroe, Frank Mwine, Tony Newkirk, Bob Packer, Joel Plavin, John Steinle, Alan Wapnick, and Kurt Wendelyn. Bill Moore and Ora McCreary were the talented accompanists for the Freshman Glee Club. It was the beginning of four years of a lot of hard work, dozens of concerts and receptions throughout the United States, friendly visits with hundreds of alumni (and their pretty daughters), and sheer joy in music!

There were initially about nine members in each of the four voice categories: first tenor, second tenor, baritone, and bass. I sang bass. Pete was a baritone. Practices were on Tuesday and Thursday nights from six thirty until eight o'clock. the regular Glee Club, which had over one hundred members (fifty of whom usually were selected for the touring Glee Club), practiced after the freshmen from eight o'clock until nine thirty on the same evenings. We soon learned not to miss practices and not to be late. Absences and late arrivals were recorded. Paul Zeller was a strict director.

The Dartmouth Glee Club had the reputation of being a fine singing group—among the best in the country, as well as one of the oldest (founded in 1869). The concert programs, in this regard, quoted what critics had said about past concerts in New York City's Radio City Music Hall: "It is a smartly drilled crew … Their voices are brilliantly displayed in a varied vocal program …" (*New York Mirror*); in Buffalo: "The Dartmouth Glee Club, demonstrating an entertainment prowess which might well be the envy of many professional groups, was cordially applauded …" (*Buffalo Evening News*); in Atlantic City: "It was refreshing to hear the youthful voices, under expert direction, blend in an unhackneyed program of fun and frolic, intermingling its seriousness with humor … It should happen in Atlantic City more often …" (*New Jersey Press*); in Los Angeles: "The group of fifty singers is an exceedingly well-trained organization and has in Paul Zeller a director capable of solid and sensitive music making …" (*California Times*); and in Washington, DC: "In their faultless diction, their easy maintenance of fine intonation, and their complete ease in a wide variety of musical styles, these young men stand high on the list of college glee clubs …" (*Washington Times* and *Times Herald*).

I soon realized that I was privileged to be singing under Paul Zeller's conducting. He insisted that every eye be on him at all times and required that the lyrics be carefully phrased, every syllable expressed, and every consonant articulated, especially those at the end of a phrase. He was a stickler for correct intonation. His evocative hands were constant reminders of the volume required—*pianissimo, forte,* and the other dynamic levels—and he signaled the finish of each line by slowly closing his fingers, as though pinching off the sound. He delighted in unexpectedly improvising with pieces that we knew by heart, calling for a soft voice, when the music stated *forte*, or prolonging the finish of a phrase well beyond what we had practiced, just to trip up a wayward eye. If he were successful, he would laugh irrepressibly and perhaps ask the inattentive singer what had happened the night before to cause such daydreaming.

It was evident that he loved music and conducting. It was equally evident that the members were focused on singing. In one of my letters home, I wrote to my parents that during the rehearsals everyone was so focused that you could hear a pin drop in Faulkner Recital Hall between the practice of each song. I thought that the musicality of the group was awesome.

Each of us was responsible for buying our own uniform for concerts from the James Campion store: dark green blazer, white shirt, Dartmouth tie, and gray slacks. We wore this "uniform" for the first time when we sang at a chapel service.

Initially our concerts were limited to Sunday services at Dartmouth's Rollins Chapel and one concert on the Green before the bonfire on Dartmouth Night. The only church services that I ever attended at Dartmouth were at Rollins Chapel because the Glee Club was providing the music for the service. I was not very interested in religion, and churches interested me even less. But there were several spectacular stained-glass windows in Rollins Chapel that drew my interest when we performed there.

According to the information in the plaques on the chapel's walls, Rollins Chapel was completed in 1885, and at the time of dedication of the chapel, three memorial windows were in place in the chancel and one in each transept. The stained-glass windows throughout the chapel were dedicated to honor the past presidents of the college. As we waited to perform at each of the chapel services, my eyes swept back and forth admiringly on these lovely windows.

So it was a shock in the fall of 1964, at another Glee Club concert in the chapel, when I noticed that the windows had disappeared! The most attractive features of the chapel were gone. Apparently, I later learned, renovations to Rollins Chapel earlier that year resulted in concealment of the five stained-glass windows in the chancel area of the chapel. These windows depicted Christian biblical figures. The then dean of the Tucker Foundation, Richard P. Unsworth, had the windows covered in the face of the declining spiritual interest in students, I was told. Unsworth's idea was that by concealing the windows, students would be more attracted to the chapel. For me, the concealment had the opposite effect.

Our first concert as the Class of 1967 Glee Club was in Rollins Chapel on Sunday, October 13, 1963. That morning, I was still shaky from the previous Friday night's adventure with Sandi, recounted earlier, and worrying about what the college administration would do when it found out. The anthem we sang for the Columbus Weekend Dartmouth College Service, as it was called, went very well, to my surprise (we had only practiced it the previous week): "Emitte Spiritum Tuum" ("Send Forth Thy Spirit") by Bach. I especially was impressed by the organ music played by Professor Milton Gill, who was an extremely skilled musician. (Five years later, almost to the day, Professor Gill died on Moose Mountain near Hanover in a plane crash that took thirty-two lives.)

The second time we sang at Rollins Chapel was the Thanksgiving service on November 17, 1963, held one week before the actual holiday, and five days before the world changed on November 22, as I described earlier. Again, the Class of 1963 Glee Club sang the anthem with the extraordinary organ accompaniment of Professor Gill: "Jubilate Deo" by August Wiltberger. I was extremely happy that the music sounded very polished, because my parents, aunt, and twin cousins were visiting for House Parties Weekend.

Dartmouth had beaten Cornell—Dad's alma mater—the day before, and he said that he was feeling better about the game after he heard the Freshman Glee Club sing so well in the chapel. He often reminisced about his own college days as a member of Cornell's Glee Club in the 1920s, and when talking football, he never failed to remind me of the famous forfeit to Dartmouth of a football victory by Cornell in 1940 as an example of the Big Red's sportsmanship and integrity.

According to Dad, Cornell entered the 1940 contest with eighteen straight victories over a two-year period. Dartmouth held off Cornell's offense for nearly the entire low-scoring game and scored first, kicking a field goal for three points in the fourth quarter. Finally, with less than a minute left in the game, Cornell got the ball on Dartmouth's six-yard line. Cornell expected to have four chances to win the game. After three failed attempts to run the ball, on the fourth down Cornell was penalized for delay of game, and the referee spotted the ball just over the five-yard line in order to replay the fourth down. With nine seconds left on the clock, the Cornell quarterback threw an incomplete pass into the end zone.

Normally, the ball would have gone to Dartmouth, which would have run the clock out and won the game, 3–0. But following the fourth down, although the linesman correctly signaled that it was first down and that the ball should go to Dartmouth, the referee did not agree, gave the ball to Cornell, and placed it on the six-yard line on fourth down when in actuality it was "fifth" down. Cornell's quarterback then threw a touchdown pass, and following the extra-point kick, Cornell won the game 7–3.

Officials discovered their error after reviewing the game films. Cornell's players, coaching officials, and president immediately agreed that Cornell should contact Dartmouth offering to forfeit the game. Dartmouth accepted (I suspect to the great surprise of Cornell). According to Dad, the forfeit probably cost Cornell the national championship, but he loved to point out that Cornell had acted in the highest tradition of honorable and magnanimous conduct. While agreeing that Cornell had done the right thing, I liked to chide Dad by pointing out that the Cornell University president had undoubtedly learned his high moral and ethical behavior as a student at Dartmouth, class of 1905.

Such behavior was on someone else's mind that weekend. The sermon presented at the Rollins Chapel service that morning by the Tucker Foundation dean, Richard P. Unsworth, was entitled "Christian Ethics and Sexual Behavior." I remember thinking at the time that the sermon was too little, too late, since Dartmouth Night had already occurred weeks before, and the Saturday night of House Parties Weekend had been last night. Talk about closing the barn door after the horse has escaped!

I also recall that the woman who arranged the flowers in the chapel at both the October and the November services was the wife of Dean Thaddeus Seymour, whom we all had met at a reception for our class in September. Thad and his wife were a wonderful, compassionate couple who befriended many students. Mrs. Seymour greeted my family warmly when I introduced them to her after the service.

The four Rollins Chapel concerts were not my favorite Glee Club events in my freshman year. Nevertheless, I loved particularly the Easter and Christmas services at which we sang each of the four years of my Glee Club experience. Christmas carols, especially, have always been favorite songs of mine, so the prevacation Christmas concerts there were especially enjoyable.

The Freshman Glee Club also sang for Freshman Fathers' Weekend in February. It was our first concert experience in the venue we came to call home: Hopkins Center's wonderful Spaulding Auditorium, which was a magical concert hall of wood walls and excellent acoustics, seating about nine hundred. For that concert, we formed a smaller group of nine members, which we called the Nine Freshmen: John Kornet, John McPherson, Wayne Letizia, Bob Chambers, John Steinle, Bob Morrow, Andy Longacre, Bob Packer, and me. The program of both the full Freshman Glee Club and the Nine Freshmen was comprised of some of the twenty or so familiar Dartmouth songs.

I remember another concert on March 7, 1964, at Radcliffe University in Cambridge, Massachusetts, with the Radcliffe Freshman Choir. I almost was not able to make the trip to Cambridge because of illness. Shortly after Freshman Fathers' Weekend, my roommate, Pete Thomas, was hospitalized in the college infirmary—Dick's House—with a severe case of mononucleosis. When I was visiting Pete at Dick's House, a doctor there suggested that I have a blood test, which I promptly did. The test results indicated that I was in the recovery stage of mono, and since I seemed to be recovering well enough by myself, hospitalization was not required. One week later, however, I came down with the measles, only weeks before the Radcliffe concert. Happily, by early March both Pete and I were declared to be over our illnesses and fit to travel. I was so exhausted by that time, however, that I remember very little about the Cambridge visit.

Singing with the Freshman Glee Club was a great part of my freshman year and provided several opportunities to travel to women's colleges and to meet freshmen of the opposite gender. But nothing compared to the pure joy and fun of the Varsity Glee Club's concerts, beginning in our sophomore year.

The first of these was the concert of Dartmouth songs on Dartmouth Night in October 1964. We stood on the steps of Dartmouth Hall, facing the Green with our eyes reflecting the dancing tongues of fire of the fifty-foot-high bonfire in the center of the Green. You could feel the heat of the fire through the chilly air, although it was about 150 feet away, and see and smell the wraiths of smoke rising above the Upper Valley.

The sight and smells of the bonfire prompted memories of building the several 1963 bonfires with dozens of my classmates the previous autumn and the excitement of the flames leaping upward through the railroad ties, which we had spent an afternoon collecting along an abandoned railway line not far from Hanover. It had been exhausting work, hefting the ties onto the college's flatbed truck, unloading them on the Green, and carefully stacking them to form the bonfire, even though there were dozens of students, college personnel, and even faculty members participating.

The Glee Club's songs followed a football rally with inspirational words from the incomparable head football coach Bob Blackmun. Our voices rang out over the campus above the excited faces of hundreds of students with their dates. Of course, as in all concerts, the songs concluded with "Men of Dartmouth," whose strains seemed particularly uplifting in the light of the flickering flames in the cool darkness under the elms in front of Dartmouth Row.

In November 1964, in Spaulding Auditorium for House Parties Weekend the concert program, which changed every year, of course, tended to include many of the same songs performed in subsequent concerts during that particular academic year. The House Parties concert program, which had a nice balance of Dartmouth songs, show tunes, poems set to music, and classical pieces, was typical:

Eleazar Wheelock	Richard Hovey, '85; Marie Wurm
Twilight Song	Fred L. Pattee, '88; Benjamin B. Gillette, '88
Song of Peace	Vincent Persichetti
Hope for Tomorrow	Martin Luther King; Jean Berger
Song of the Broad Axe	Walt Whitman; Robert Kurka
Duettino Concertante Nach Mozart	arranged by Ferruccio Busoni
John Hargraves, '66 and Ora McCreary, '67	
The Bounty of Our Age	Jean Berger
If All the World Were Paper	
(from "Three Fancies")	Jean Berger
Fall Comes to Cape Cod	Joseph G. Harrison; John C. Worley
Madame Jeannette	From the free French; Alan Murray
The Pasture (from "Frostiana")	Robert Frost, '96; Randall Thompson
Stopping by Woods on	
a Snowy Evening	Robert Frost, '96; Frank Logan, '52
Fire and Ice	Robert Frost, '96; Frank Logan, '52
Intermission	

Songs by the Injunaires
Two Columbia Songs
Sans Souci
Roar Lion Roar
Come, Fellows, Let Us
Raise a Song   Willard B. Segur, '92; Guy
                                                W. Cox, '93

A Son of a Gun   E. H. Crane, '98
Williams True to Purple   Harry R. Wellman, '07
Football Medley
Dartmouth Touchdown Song   Winsor D. Wilkinson, '10;
                                                Moses Ewing, '13
Dear Old Dartmouth   Rollo G. Reynolds, '10;
                                                Walter Golde, '10
As the Backs Go Tearing by   John Thomas Keady, '05;
                                                Charles W. Doty
Glory to Dartmouth   Anonymous
Dartmouth's in Town Again   H. Lyman Armes, '12; Robert
                                                Hopkins, '14
Dartmouth Undying   Franklin McDuffee, '21;
                                                Homer P. Whitford
Men of Dartmouth   Richard Hovey, '85; Harry
                                                Wellman, '07[33]

We were very fortunate to have had extraordinarily talented accompanists playing with the Glee Club. Bill Moore, '67, accompanied the Freshman Glee Club during 1963–64. John Hargraves, '66, and Ora McCreary, '67, were our superb accompanists afterward. Most of the club's concerts in the period 1963–65 featured at least one piano duet by them, such as the *Duettino Concertante Nach Mozart* at the 1964 concert, which was an extremely difficult arrangement of Mozart's Finale of the Concerto no. 19 in F major, K. 459 by Ferruccio Busoni. Later, during 1966–67, the equally talented accompanists were Warren Finke, '69, and J. Gary Cherry, '69.

An important part of most concerts was a mini concert by the "Injunaires." Paul Zeller originally formed this a cappella singing group of about sixteen members of the Glee Club in 1946 as an offshoot of the Glee Club. They performed a variety of popular tunes set to music by members of the group and combined skillful vocalizations with humor. Stalwarts of the Injunaires in the mid-1960s included originally four 1967s (John Kornet, John McPherson, Bob Packer, and John Steinle).

---

[33]   The Dartmouth College Glee Club, 1964 Fall House Parties Concert Program.

My roommate, Pete Thomas, joined the group in 1966 with Alan Lieberman, '67.[34] I auditioned unsuccessfully for the Injunaires in the spring of 1965, and was disappointed not to be selected. (My nonselection ultimately turned out to be for the best, since I would soon be studying in France and unable to participate anyway.)

Besides the fall concerts at Dartmouth, there were a couple of joint winter or spring concerts with glee clubs from New England colleges such as Riviera College, Smith College, and Mount Holyoke College. These helped to break up the dark, cold winter term and muddy early spring, and I found it refreshing to hear the women's voices joined with ours.

At one of the first of these in my freshman year, I met a lovely older student at the concert with Riviera College—a dark-haired Irish beauty. Maureen O'Brien and I wrote each other for several years thereafter. I took her to several dances at Riviera and had several delightful visits with her and her warmhearted parents in Lowell, Massachusetts, during the next two years. But they wouldn't let her come to Dartmouth …

On several occasions, I was moved almost to tears by the beauty of the music we performed, such as Mozart's *Vesperae solennes de confessore*, K. 339. I remember especially the soloist from the Smith College Choir singing the fifth movement (*Laudate Dominum*) with a voice, face, and demeanor so angelic that the entire Glee Club was transfixed in disbelief and wonder.

Another memorable concert was at the Hopkins Center with the Dartmouth Symphony and the Mount Holyoke College Glee Club in April 1967. Among other pieces we sang was the North American premiere of Pierre Mercure's *Cantate Pour Une Joie* and Francis Poulenc's marvelous *Gloria*.

Each year the club embarked upon an ambitious tour as the college's "goodwill ambassadors," visiting a dozen or more cities in different parts of the United States during the two-week spring vacation break. Dartmouth alumni clubs sponsored the concerts, which were usually followed by receptions with an abundance of sumptuous food and alcoholic beverages. Happily, as well, there were many young women at these events who seemed anxious to meet and to welcome us. Often these girls were either local high school or college students from the Dartmouth families who invited us to their homes for dinner and lodging.

Of these young women, I particularly remember with fondness Sybil Waterman, who was the sister of Glee Club member Dana Waterman, '68. "Sis," as I came to call her, was a delight with her short brown hair and disarming smile. Although she was a junior in high school in Davenport, Iowa, when I met her, she acted much older. We never dated, but we had a correspondence relationship in which

---

[34]   Other members of the Injunaires during 1964–1967 additionally included: 1964: James Cornehlsen '64, Wayne Hill '66, Ned McCook '65, John Macindoe '65, David Plavin '64, Charles Reichart '66, Nicholas Rowe '64, and Steven Ward '64; 1965: Thomas Campbell '65, Donald Macaulay '65, and Andrew Rosenthal '66; 1966: Edward Gundy '68, Eric Jones '68, Stuart Ley '68, and David Peck '68; 1967: Paul Stageberg '68, Michael Hermann '69, William Rollings '69, and Joseph Serene '69.

she wrote charming letters that sustained me through several difficult periods in my senior year and in graduate school, earning my deep gratitude.

The warmth and generosity of the alumni were overwhelming! My major problems, I soon discovered, were overindulging at the delicious preconcert dinners to which we were invited to the point that I was too bloated to sing competently and drinking so much at the postconcert receptions that I was in no condition to perform adequately at the next day's concert! Occasionally, our hosts overindulged as well. I recall on at least two occasions having to help our hostess carry her husband to and from their car and up the stairs to their bedroom!

Sometimes these postconcert parties continued until well after midnight. Since we were under strict orders from Paul Zeller to be at the bus pickup point each morning at eight o'clock sharp, we had to recover lost sleep on the buses or planes between concert destinations. It was exhausting until we got into the rhythm of the concert travel.

Our concert tours covered a different region of the United States each year. In 1965, for example, the Glee Club headed south along the East Coast, singing concerts in Yonkers, New York; Teaneck, New Jersey; Huntington, West Virginia; Washington, DC; Atlanta, Georgia; Miami, Florida; Memphis, Tennessee; Philadelphia, Pennsylvania; and Rochester, New York.

On April Fool's Day that year in Philadelphia, several of the 1966s in the Glee Club arranged a surprise for Paul Zeller at the commencement of the concert. After Director Zeller had come on stage to thunderous applause (he was very popular with audiences) and thanked the audience for their support of the Glee Club and Dartmouth, he opened his music to begin the concert and found instead a playmate centerfold picture of a naked Sally Duberson—*Playboy*'s Miss January. I thought that Paul was going to have a heart attack! But he quickly recovered and laughingly held up the centerfold for the audience to see.

The "big trip" took place the next spring, with visits by air to multiple cities on the West Coast and other western states. On March 18, 1966, we sang in Chicago, followed by a concert in a different city for the next ten nights: Omaha, Nebraska; Denver, Colorado; Seattle, Washington; Portland, Oregon; San Francisco, California; Reno, Nevada; San Diego, California; Los Angeles, California; Houston, Texas; and Oklahoma City, Oklahoma.

Our visit in San Francisco was typical. Pete and I stayed with a Dartmouth host family whose high school daughter and her best friend—who seemed like wild California girls to Pete and me—drove us all over downtown San Francisco in an open red convertible after the concert. We ate at Original Joe's in the North Beach area of the city, tried unsuccessfully to enter the Condor Club nearby to see topless dancer Carol Doda (the girls were too young), and managed to get into the Purple Onion— where Richard Pryor, Phyllis Diller, the Kingston Trio, and the Smothers Brothers, among others, all got their start—for a drink in that famous cellar bar.

In Reno, we were all made honorary citizens of the city and presented with keys to the city. We returned to Boston on March 29, having flown to eleven cities in twelve days, and arrived in Hanover by bus about ten thirty in the evening—exhausted but very happy with the fantastic trip.

The last spring tour for the 1967s was in the Midwest. We left Hanover very early in the morning by bus for Rochester, New York, on March 17, 1967, filling two coaches of the White River Coach Lines with the fifty-five members of the concert tour Glee Club. The next day, we visited Niagara Falls and performed in Buffalo, New York (where my family and hometown friends attended, of course). It was fun introducing Pete Thomas—my great roommate for the past three years—and my then current roommate, Wim deHaas (a fabulous foreign student from Eindhoven, Netherlands) to my family and hometown.

The buses dropped us off in Buffalo at my former school, Nichols High School, where our host families picked us up. Pete stayed with his girlfriend's family (his future wife was Pam Austin, a close friend of mine from Buffalo, mentioned later in this memoir), and Wim and I stayed with my parents. The rest of our itinerary included Cleveland, Ohio; Detroit, Michigan; Cincinnati, Ohio; Indianapolis, Indiana; Saint Louis, Missouri; Beloit, Wisconsin; Minneapolis, Minnesota; Rochester, Minnesota; Chicago, Illinois; and Erie, Pennsylvania.

It was in Beloit that I almost missed the bus on the morning of our departure. We sang at Beloit College. After the concert, there was one of the wildest parties in the Glee Club's history. I danced with a pretty and friendly Beloit student named Sara all evening, who then invited me back to her apartment for the night. We hardly slept at all. The next morning, we woke up at eight o'clock—bus departure time—and I scrambled to get to the rendezvous point, running the half mile or so to the buses. Fortunately, other members, as well as Professor Zeller, were also late, so I was not left behind.

In Erie, members of the Glee Club conjured up another surprise for Paul Zeller. We changed one of the lines of the "Hanover Winter Song" from "And the great white cold walks abroad" to "And in the great white cold walks a broad." The audience didn't pick up the one word addition to the line, or the resulting change in meaning, but Paul couldn't control his laughter.

I particularly remember our hosts during the visit to Rochester, New York: Dr. and Mrs. Henry B. Crawford, '25. Doctor Crawford had retired from teaching at the University of Rochester Medical School and from a distinguished career as an orthopedic surgeon. He was career-wise the typical Dartmouth host—usually a teacher, doctor, lawyer, or business executive. After retirement, he had taken up painting.

"Would you like to see some of Hank's paintings?" Mrs. Crawford asked Wim and me.

"The boys aren't interested in such things," Dr. Crawford interjected and tried to steer the conversation back to Dartmouth and our respective majors.

"One thing you should know," Mrs. Crawford said quietly as she led us into the living room and dining room of their large home, "Hank is totally colorblind. I had to tell him what colors to use when he painted the pictures you see here."

She showed us his oil paintings—mostly landscapes with unbelievably lovely cloud formations—which were some of the most enchanting paintings I had ever seen. There were perhaps a dozen large paintings on the walls. The colors and the shadings of different colors were so subtly realistic that I was literally speechless (very unusual for me). They were amazingly lifelike and depicted nature's shades of color perfectly.

When I mentioned that I thought the hues of color of the trees, other landscape features, sky, and clouds were remarkably true to life, his wife laughed and said that she would take some credit for the colors, since her husband could not tell the difference between them. I was astonished and thought to myself that he had been able to use his inability to see color as a strength that enabled him to discern and paint differences in color gradation far beyond what color-perceiving painters could accomplish.

Dr. Crawford expressed repeatedly to us that his love of art and his talent in painting had been initially nurtured by courses at Dartmouth, despite his color blindness.

"I learned how to live at Dartmouth," he reiterated, "although I waited decades, until the end of my professional career, to pursue my great passion!"

Classmates on that 1967 trip included: Carl Bartholomaus, Stan Brown, Jim Gifford, Jon Hanlon, Pete Keating, John Kornet, Wayne Letizia, Andy Longacre, John McPherson, Dave Millane, Frank Mwine, Clem Page, Joel Plavin, Pete Thomas, Alan Wapnick, and Kurt Wendelyn. Seventeen of us remained from the approximately forty who had first sung with the Freshman Glee Club three years earlier.[35]

Several of these had exceptionally fine voices and were soloists in our concerts. I recall John Kornet singing "Mack the Knife" from *The Threepenny Opera*; Frank Mwine singing "If You Want to Be Happy for the Rest of Your Life," and John McPherson performing "Try to Remember" from *The Fantastiks*. (The title of the latter song aptly characterizes the process involved in writing this memoir.)

The best of our soloists during those Glee Club years, however, had a voice that rivaled Frank Sinatra's—a baritone sound that was as smooth as butter. The voice of Tri-Kap fraternity brother

---

[35] The 1967 spring tour also included the following students. Class of 1968: Robert Burr, Frank Couper, Daniel Graves, Sherwood Gurnsey, Edward Gundy, Eric Jones, Jonathan Lohnes, Gregory Marshall, Jonathan Moody, Kevin O'Donnell, David Peck, William Rupp, Paul Stageberg, and Dana Waterman. Class of 1969: Donald Baird, Gary Bartholomaus, Lawrence Carter, Gary Cherry, Willem deHaas (my Dutch roommate), David Dunning, Christopher Elders, Warren Finke, Flanders Fuenzalida, Richard Gerry, Robert Hagen, Michael Hermann, Roy Hitchings, John Husted, Robert Lefkowits, Loren Lortscher, James Miser, Nicholas North, Hampton Rich, William Rollings, Joseph Serene, Thomas Stickney, John Stonesifer, Donald Syracuse, and David Tee.

Tony (Ginteras) Dambrava, '68, was simply amazing and is the one solo voice I remember best, singing "One Girl."

In the spring of 1967, we also traveled to Montreal, Canada, to perform at "Expo '68," which was a type of world fair taking place in Montreal. We sang two concerts in an open-air pavilion. In addition to singing, I was called upon to announce the pieces that we sang in both English and French. Considering that I had only two days' notice of that role and had, as usual, perhaps overenjoyed the festivities the previous night, I think that I did a credible job.

The "Twilight Song"—one of Dartmouth's best-loved songs—calls students to "Come and gather on the campus, Make the gray old maples ring, With the songs of Alma Mater, With the songs we love to sing."[36] I answered this call in each of my four years at Dartmouth, missing only those Glee Club concerts that took place in the fall of 1965, when I was studying in France. "Song" is one of the several most significant words—perhaps with "fellowship," "nature," "skiing," "scholarship," and "poetry"—by which I characterize my college experience. Song cemented friendships, uplifted my spirit, acquainted me with wonderful alumni, and carried me to the far reaches of the United States. Hearing Dartmouth songs never fails to evoke magical memories. I loved singing under Paul Zeller at Dartmouth.

---

[36] Fred. L. Pattee, "Twilight Song," *Dartmouth Song Book*, 70.

House Parties Weekend bonfire on the Dartmouth Green, October 1964

White Church and Medical
School with Oak Hill Skiway
in the distance, January 1965

Sybil "Sis" Waterman with her
mother and brother (Glee Club
member) Dana Waterman, '68,
Saint Louis, March 1967

Dartmouth Row, January 1965

Baker Library and Webster Hall, January 1967

Dartmouth College Band, October 1966

Dancing at the Tri-Kap Winter Carnival party, February 1966

Chapter 7—Long White Afternoons

Familiar as I was with snow in Buffalo, New York, I was disappointed with the relatively small accumulations of snow in the Connecticut River's Upper Valley during my years there. As a child, I was used to annual snowfalls averaging about ninety-five inches—a result of the so-called lake effect in which winds pick up moisture from Lake Erie and dump extraordinary amounts of snow at the eastern end of the lake on Buffalo. I doubt that Hanover had much more than half this amount in each of my four years at Dartmouth.

But lovely snowstorms swept through the Upper Valley of the Connecticut River several times each winter. Dartmouth's already stunning campus with its central Green, surrounded on four sides by brick buildings, was simply exquisite after a snowstorm, as the snow clung to the sides of the buildings, etching rectangular patterns in the mortar lines and outlining in frostings of snow the senior fence on the Green's west side and the black iron railings that accent most of the college's buildings. Towering Baker Library on the north side of the central Green drew your eyes northward over the snowdrifts wherever you stood on the Green. It thrust its white-capped tower skyward, topped with a weathervane depicting the college founder teaching a Native American beneath a pine tree, as though punching a hole to spill snow from the storm clouds that drifted over the Green below the summits of the surrounding hills.

The historic row of white brick buildings with dark green shutters, constituting Dartmouth Row on the Green's east side, seemed to perfectly blend with the blanket of white cloaking the campus. Beyond the buildings ringing the Green, white pines and spruce gently swept up the slopes of the foothills on Hanover's outskirts. Standing on the balcony of the Hopkins Center at the south end of the Green looking north, you saw a perfect composition of green and white spread before you.

Just after Thanksgiving, a thirty-foot lighted spruce with a star on top magically appeared in the center of the Green, where the gravel paths crisscrossing the space converged in their own star pattern. On all four sides of the Green, fifty-four smaller lighted trees enclosed the entire space—one for each state, as well as Puerto Rico and the United States territories. As darkness fell and the trees' colored lights were reflected in the snow, the peace and beauty of the scene took your breath away. Months before, the exact spot had been lit with flames of prefootball frenzy, shadows had danced around a bonfire, and football rally shouts and songs had echoed over the Green. Now in the sublimity of winter, the only possible motion and song were the peaceful drifting of snow under the sparkling lights and the wind's rustling chorus.

The first substantial snowfall in November of my freshman year brought most of the student body to the Green for a huge snowball fight. I was in Baker Library in my favorite study alcove when the movement of students outside became obvious. Within minutes, hundreds of snowballs flew back and forth across the Green as students and even some faculty celebrated in the darkness-made-light by the starlight and reflected lights of surrounding buildings. Only the chiming of midnight by the Baker Library bells ended the traditional party to celebrate the first snow and sent me happily toward my bed in Topliff Hall.

The other huge snowball fight on campus that I recall happened in March of my senior year. Classmate and Tri-Kap brother Bill Bogardus and I, with hundreds of other students, bombarded each other and then took aim at Dean Seymour, who attempted to lure the surging crowd away from Main Street's shops by running in his T-shirt across the Green, inviting friendly fire.

There was not a lot of snow until just before Winter Carnival in early February of my first year. January was relatively snow-free to my great disappointment. After returning from the Christmas holidays at home, I began the job that was a part of my financial-aid package, earning two dollars per hour, two hours each day, as a member of the dish room crew at the Dartmouth Dining Association (DDA) in Thayer Hall. My daily shift began at six o'clock in the morning, which was a great time to work, allowing me to get up early at my favorite time of day and to finish my dining hall work before classes began at eight o'clock.

From Topliff Hall to Thayer Dining Hall was about one-quarter mile—an easy five-minute walk, even in the predawn cold when the temperature often was below zero. Every morning, I walked over to Thayer with Ted LaMontaigne, '66, who was a student manager at the Dining Association and lived on our hall in Topliff. The walk gave me a chance to enjoy the freshly fallen snow, sparse as it was that first winter. By the time the library chimes struck seven, the snow was crisscrossed with footprints and ski tracks.

The work at Thayer was easy. When we reported for work, we changed to a white coat, which was worn over our shirts and provided by Thayer. I was happy to find a friend from my previous summer's job with the AMC, Larry Goss, '66, already working in the dish room that first morning.

A thoughtful, older man—Norman Bueddeman—was the manager. He oversaw several student managers, who in turn supervised the about two-dozen members of the student dish room crew. Conveyer belts carried used trays, piled high with plates, glasses, and silverware, from the dining areas to the dish room. Members of the dish room crew had different tasks, and we rotated among these every twenty minutes or so. As the conveyor belts slid past, one worker picked paper off the trays, another glasses, another cups, and so forth. The items to be cleaned were stacked in special dish or glass racks or cutlery trays and fed through a large, commercial-style washing machine with very hot water, emerging on the other side, where a team stacked the air-dried items on carts to be wheeled to the dining hall for reuse.

Once a week or so, I was assigned for part of my shift to the "pots and pans sink," which was really the only difficult job in the dish room. The pots and pans in which food was prepared were very hard to clean and had to be carefully scrubbed at this sink. Mr. Bueddeman was careful not to assign a worker there for more than about fifteen minutes at a time, for it was a demanding task to scrub pot after pot, especially if food had been burned while cooking. It was actually a job that I did not mind. I was used to both cooking for huge crowds and cleaning up afterward, including scrubbing pots and pans, because my experiences as a hutman for the AMC during the summers of 1962 and 1963, mentioned earlier, had included both chores. I was told, furthermore, that Nelson Rockefeller had worked in the dish room as a student at Dartmouth and scrubbed pots at the very sink where I was occasionally assigned. If Rocky could do this, so could I!

There were three overlapping two-hour shifts for each meal. My shift (six o'clock to eight o'clock) was the easiest, because for the first hour there was hardly anybody having breakfast, so the dish room was quiet. At such times, we were assigned to scrub down the conveyor belts, mop floors, or to polish the steel doors of the refrigerated rooms in the basement. Sometimes we helped the student waiters clean up the dining halls as well. One of the trickiest tasks in that endeavor was cleaning butter pats off of the high ceiling. A student would place a pat of butter on a folded napkin in his lap and then jerk the napkin taut, rocketing the pat skyward where it often stuck to the twenty-foot-high ceiling. Lots of fun to launch such pats but hard to clean them off of the ceiling!

Several older women from the Hanover area worked at DDA in the kitchen, on the serving lines, in the front office, and punching meal tickets at the entrance to DDA. I recall especially a Mrs. Wilson, who was typical of these women—extremely friendly and helpful, who always asked students how they were doing. These women were among the few motherly types of women most of us saw for months between vacations. Their interest in us and their concerned inquiries about our lives were very much appreciated!

Another dining hall ritual attended the entrance of a young woman (usually a date) into the main dining hall, especially in the middle of the week when dates were uncommon. If the woman was attractive and there were not a lot of other women in the hall, someone would start tapping a glass with a spoon, and soon the entire hall would ring with these expressions of admiration, causing the date some consternation.

I had a lot of fun working with friends at Thayer. My roommate Pete worked there, as did many of my other classmates, such as Jay Boekelheide, Melvin Boozer, Brad Langley, Rich Weller, Wayne Johnson. Tim Armstrong, Fred Behringer, Mickey Beard, Xavier Mendoza, Bob Davidson, Victor Lyn, John Issacs, Dick Chu, Bob Burka, Sam Ostrow, Wayne Beyer, and later my Dutch roommate, Wim deHaas, to name just a few. At one time or another, probably a majority of the class of 1967 spent some time at Thayer, working either in the dining room as waiters or in the dish room, as substitute workers when regular workers could not work due to class conflicts, extracurricular activities, or road trips. Each student worker was responsible for arranging his own substitute in the event he could not work.

In my second, third, and fourth years, I worked as a manager in the dish room, which was even easier than my first year's work. Managers were responsible for making sure that each position was covered in each shift, for rotating workers among the various workstations, and for otherwise assuring that the dish room operation went smoothly. We also handled complaints and tried to promote harmony among the student crew and the nonstudent adults who operated the equipment and were responsible for repairs as needed. I never had to handle a complaint or dispute of any kind. It was a very laid-back type of job, and I spent most of the time either picking my nose or chatting with Mr. Bueddeman, student workers, and other nonstudent employees, such as "old Jim."

Jim was an older man with graying hair, whose face was weathered and usually unsmiling. He looked as though he had endured a very tough life. Pete and I tried to become friends with him, realizing almost immediately that he was lonely and did not have much of a life. He had operated the huge dishwashing machine in the Thayer dish room for three shifts, day in and day out, with no holidays, for thirteen years when we first met him in 1964. I recall his telling us that his wife had died and that he had no children, so he seemed to be alone in the world.

One winter day, quite unexpectedly Jim invited Pete and me to his house for dinner and the night. With some trepidation, we accepted, so one evening Jim drove us in his old Ford pickup truck along snow-drifted roads to his house in the mountains north of Hanover not far from Lyme. Jim lived in an old farmhouse that was falling apart. He heated it with a wood stove. I recall that we ate a type of simple stew that he had prepared. We talked until late at night, finding out more about Jim's life before we went to bed in the sleeping bags that Pete and I brought with us.

I don't recall much of the conversation that night. But the next morning, when Jim drove Pete and me back to Thayer for the morning shift, I remember that my respect for Jim and my awareness of the extreme poverty and hardship faced by most of the residents of Grafton County had tremendously increased. We later thanked Jim by buying him dinner at Lou's Restaurant on South Main Street. It was far too small a response to his needs. We had many subsequent conversations in the dish room and elsewhere when I met him in town or on campus. Mostly we discussed the need for Dartmouth to recognize a labor union to represent its employees, like Jim, and to provide better pay and benefits. (This finally happened in 1966, when the employees elected the Service Employees International Union.)

Almost every day of the next four years, I remembered that visit with Jim, felt helpless to do anything meaningful to help, and appreciated the luxury of the college life I was living. Later I realized that Jim's unexpected invitation and my brief experience with him that night presaged my experiences in the world community, beginning with my Peace Corps service, where I witnessed incredible poverty attending the lives of so many people overseas and yet was the recipient myself of unbelievable generosity and kindness from them.

Norman Bueddeman—my wonderful overall supervisor—also became a friend. He and his wife, Midge, lived out in Etna, a neighboring town, on Dogford Road. As their children were grown and no longer lived with them, the Bueddemans seemed to enjoy mentoring the Dartmouth students who worked at Thayer Dining Hall. On at least a dozen occasions in the next four years, I was invited with one or two other students for fine dinners with them at their home. Even more frequently, particularly in the winter season, Midge Bueddeman invited a group of students to their home in the evening for homemade pie and hot chocolate.

After finishing my work at Thayer each morning, I headed to classes. Work shifts sometimes ended about ten minutes early to allow students to get to classes on time, as needed. Whenever possible during the winter term, I chose classes and scheduled science laboratories so as to complete them by noon or early afternoon. The joy of long white afternoons outdoors then awaited me.

If you joined the Dartmouth Outing Club (DOC), you could partake in most of its activities for free or at very minimal cost. In the winter, the DOC's activities included winter hiking, ice climbing, snowshoeing, and skiing primarily. As soon as snow had blanketed the campus and surrounding mountains, I joined hundreds of my classmates and headed for the DOC's office in the basement of Robinson Hall to arrange to take skiing lessons and to rent skis. Every day in the winter term, buses stood by to shuttle students on a regular schedule from Robinson to one of the three skiing venues where lessons were taught by advanced and expert skiers.

The closest ski area was for beginners. About one mile straight north on North Main Street from Robinson Hall, just past Occom Pond, lies the Dartmouth Golf Course and the Dartmouth Outing Club House, which is a lovely stone building built in 1929, nestled on the shore of the pond. Just beyond the house and at the southwest corner of the golf course was a broad hill, several hundred feet wide and about one hundred feet high, with a small rope tow.

My first afternoon of ski lessons, after borrowing some skis and poles from the DOC, I climbed on a shuttle bus and was quickly driven north to the golf course's beginner slope—about a two-minute ride. Student instructors from the DOC taught us there how to navigate the rope tow to the top of the hill, where in small groups of four to five students with an instructor we learned the basics of skiing.

We first learned how to slide down a small slope slowly with our skis in a parallel position. Then we learned how to push our heels outward to bring the skis into a V position, creating a kind of snowplow, which allowed us to navigate down the full hill fairly slowly without crashing into too many people. After we had mastered this, we started learning how to shift our weight so as to place our weight entirely on the downhill ski and to traverse across the slope of the hill. Each lesson took about two hours. After about several weeks of twice-weekly lessons, I graduated from a beginner level to an advanced-beginner status and started skiing at Oak Hill. At the golf course, perhaps the most important aspect of skiing that I mastered was how to relax when I fell, so as not to injure myself! I quickly became an expert in this delicate maneuver.

The Oak Hill ski area was located about one and one half miles northeast of Hanover on the west side of a low mountain just south of Storrs Pond. The shuttle bus drove north from Hanover, out Route 10 in the direction of Lyme, past the Dartmouth Golf Course, and turned east onto Reservoir Road. About one-quarter mile up the road on the left was a dirt road leading to the nearby ski area. By bus it took about eight minutes.

Dartmouth constructed the ski area in the early 1930s and built there one of the first overhead ski lifts in the country. It was a J-bar lift that was possibly the first J-bar ski lift ever constructed, I was told. The lift stretched about 1,200 feet up the middle of the slopes to the top, from which there was a drop of about 350 feet over a 0.3-mile-long slope. Its capacity was about six hundred skiers per hour. One dollar bought a lift ticket good for twelve rides. When I first saw Oak Hill, the huge wooden poles supporting the lift marched ominously up the slope, I thought, seeming to dare me to try to use it.

Getting on the lift was not difficult, but getting off the J-bar at the top required some courage and agility at first. I recall falling down several times at the icy top of the lift before I mastered the technique of gently pushing the bar away as I slid off to the other side of the lift.

The main slope at Oak Hill faced almost due west. There were two trails: a novice trail, which you accessed by a short rope tow, and the intermediate-level trail from the top of the slope. Standing at the top of the intermediate trail, you could easily see Vermont's Green Mountains on the other side of the Connecticut less than a mile away, beyond the so-called Vale de Tempe ski jump on the golf course. Oak Hill was almost as crowded as the beginner's ski area at the golf course, but I loved the wide sweep of the slope, the incredible view to the west, and the speed that you could build up over a one-quarter-mile run. It was, however, a little discouraging to see so many three- and four-year-old local children whizzing down the slope, weaving in and out of traffic with ease, as though they had been born with skis on!

Hans Krichels, '66, my sophomore student adviser from Topliff Hall, to whom I have previously referred, was one of the instructors at Oak Hill. Hans told me that before the Dartmouth Skiway was completed about eight years earlier, most of the ski racing at Dartmouth had taken place at Oak Hill. With his help over the next month or so, I improved my skiing to a full intermediate level and was capable of stem turns, parallel traverses, and smooth C-turns, which were wide, semicircular turns for practicing carving techniques—leaning, shifting my weight, and pressing the upper edges of my skis into the snow to make turns with my skis parallel to each other.

I was seldom cold at Oak Hill, even when the wind was blowing. Because the slope faced west, the sun was full upon you as you swept down the slope, so that even in subzero temperatures you felt warm and comfortable. It was a friendly hill, where you knew most of the skiers (intermediate-level skiers were mostly freshmen) and could make dozens of runs each afternoon. And it was close enough to

Hanover to be very easily accessible within minutes. I took several dates there during my freshman winter term.

By the end of February, I was skiing at the Dartmouth Skiway, located on the AT about twenty minutes by bus north of the college in Lyme. Skiing there was a big step up from Oak Hill. At the summit on Winslow Mountain, the elevation was about 1,943 feet. From that point to the lodge at the base, the vertical drop was 968 feet, and the longest trail down was one and one-quarter miles.

I spent so much time at the Skiway—almost three to four hours almost every afternoon of the winter terms—I got to know its trails very well. It was an outstanding ski experience, offering five trails and a large, open slope, ranging from expert to novice. There was significantly more snow at the Skiway than there was on campus. For students, an afternoon of skiing cost about one dollar.

On most days at the Skiway, I wore a light parka emblazoned with a red-and-white patch on the sleeve proclaiming "Mount Madison Volunteer Ski Patrol (MMVSP)." During the summers of 1962–63, the crew of the AMC's Madison Spring Huts on Mount Madison in the Presidential Range, near Randolph, New Hampshire (where I was a hutman, as previously mentioned), founded the MMVSP, distributed ID cards, created patches and other identifying paraphernalia, and advertised the patrol extensively, although I was the only skier (then a novice) among the six-man crew and there were no ski trails on Mount Madison. Essentially, it was a social club, but its members had the privilege of skiing for free at most ski areas in New England, since volunteer ski patrol members were extended that courtesy. Within one year, we had over one hundred members. So I skied for free at the Skiway merely by wearing that parka.

I usually used the 3,700-foot-long Pomalift, which could carry eight hundred skiers per hour on a busy day to the summit of Holt's Ledge. On a clear day, the view from Holt's is extensive. Winslow Ledge, also part of the Skiway, is to the north. Smarts Mountain is behind Winslow, with Mount Cube behind and to the left of Smarts. Straight out to the east is the rocky summit of Mount Cardigan. Swinging to the south are Ragged Mountain, Mount Kearsarge, and Mount Ascutney. The other lift was a 1,600-foot-long T-bar, which serviced both the Green Pastures—a wide and gentle, open slope for novices and intermediates—and the lower half of the Worden Schuss—a steep, relatively narrow expert trail. From the summit of Holt's Ledge, you could access five of the six major trails. Of these my favorite at first was the Papoose, an approximately 6,000-foot-long trail for novices. It was an easy sweep down to the bottom on the Papoose, even for a novice like me. I remember especially my first run down—the swoosh of my skis on the snow, the wind on my face frosting up my goggles, my ski edges clattering on the icy spots, the bite of the cold on my neck and nose, the incredible view of the snow-covered mountains and evergreens on all sides, and the elation of the speed and freedom I felt on that slope. And all the time I thought to myself, *Damn, I've got three more winters of doing this. What could be better?*

When I got really cold on my afternoons at the Skiway, there was always a blazing fire in the fireplace in the Brundage Lodge, and for twenty-five cents you could get a cup of hot chocolate. From the lodge's balcony, there was a great view of the bottoms of all six trails, since they converged just south of the lodge. At the convergence, there was a steep and often icy drop of about twenty feet. On countless occasions, I skied beautifully down a trail only to wipe out on that little drop right in front of the lodge, prompting catcalls from the balcony.

Lessons continued several times a week for my first two years. I gradually got better, but I was a slow learner, although I considered myself a decent athlete. Our lessons were usually held on the Green Pastures trail. Eventually, I graduated to the Lyme Drop by the end of that first winter. It was a 4,900-foot-long trail for so-called top novices and bottom intermediates. The Lyme Drop became my preferred trail for the next year or so, but by my senior year I could navigate fairly well the Gauntlet, Sachem, and even the Worden Schuss.

The showcase for skiing at Dartmouth each year is the Winter Carnival, which has been a tradition at Dartmouth since 1910 and is the big winter weekend for students. Carnival is a version of a "field day" for winter sports. All kinds of winter activities are featured, including skiing, bobsledding, snowshoeing, skating, and hockey, as well as intercollegiate competitions in these and other sports. There are dances, concerts, plays, and parties galore. Every carnival has a theme. In 1964 the theme was "Snowbusiness." The carnival statue in the center of the Green was a fifty-foot-high Native American brave in the design of an Academy Award trophy.

Each year there was a contest for the best Winter Carnival poster design. My brother had several carnival posters on the walls of his room at Dartmouth when our family visited him in the 1950s, as well as several on the walls of his room at home. Each depicted a ski jumper in full flight. Some of the same posters were hung on the walls of the main room at the Moosilauke Ravine Lodge during my Camp Jobildunc years and college years, mentioned below. Mrs. Gilbert decorated the walls of her laundry with carnival posters, all of which showed a skier. The 1964 poster featured a downhill skier in tuck position.

For carnival weekend my freshman year, I invited a girl named Kaete from Swarthmore College, whom I had met the previous summer in the White Mountains. She was cute, spoke several languages, and had impressed me with her knowledge of literature. We had written to each other since the previous July. She turned out to be a fine companion for the weekend but not the romantic date I had been hoping for. My first Winter Carnival, however, was still very enjoyable and well worth the thirty dollars (a big part of my budget) I spent during Kaete's two-night visit.

Pete and I were determined to get tickets for our dates and us for a gala television show that was being filmed in Webster Hall during carnival weekend. We heard that three hundred pairs of tickets were going to be available for freshmen. So the previous weekend, we spent most of Friday night in front of Webster Hall to get those tickets. Pete was number 273, and I was 274 in line to buy tickets, and we got them!

Kaete and I attended the Glee Club concert (the Varsity Glee Club sang), watched the ski jumping events at the Vale de Tempe on the golf course, took a fine sleigh ride all over Hanover and the Dartmouth campus, watched Dartmouth overwhelm Harvard (7–1) in the Ivy League Championship hockey game, joined a dance at Alumni Gymnasium, and went to the "Hootenanny Saturday Night" taping for TV of a show in Webster Hall. The latter was a musical variety show filmed in a different location each week. At Dartmouth's carnival, the show featured host Jack Linkletter (son of Art Linkletter) and the following:

> "Hootenanny Saturday Night" (Everyone)
> The Serendipity Singers: "Sing Out"
> Orriel Smith: "The First Time Ever I Saw Your Face"
> Mike Settle: "Hey, Li-Lee, Li-Lee"
> Herbie Mann & His Sextet: "Harlem Nocturne"
> Lionel Shepherd Mime Troup: pantomime routines
> The Phoenix Singers: "Didn't It Rain," "Lovely Choucoune"
> Mike Settle: "Haul Away, Joe"
> The Brandywine Singers: "Columbus Stockade Blues," "Mandy"
> Jerry Shane: stand-up comedy routine
> Herbie Mann & His Sextet: "Down by the Riverside"
> Orriel Smith and Mike Settle: "Paul and Silas"
> The Serendipity Singers: "Sail Away," "Six-Foot-Six"
> Finale: "The Music Train" (Everyone)

I really liked that show! The championship hockey game and the show were the highlights of the weekend for both of us. Watching the ski events was fun, but we both almost froze to death in the ten-degree weather on the golf course and at the Skiway.

The weekend following carnival was Fathers' Weekend for our class, described already. My father was not a skier, so we were not able to enjoy a long white afternoon on the slopes together. Dad loved hockey, however, so we attended the freshmen hockey team game against Yale on Saturday night and watched Yale whip the 1967 team. The Yale star wings were both high school classmates of mine from Nichols High School—Warren Gelman and Jack Walsh. My father and I enjoyed seeing them. Their freshmen team at Yale was undefeated that year, and they went on to lead one of Yale's best varsity hockey teams in subsequent years.

When Dad left for home on February 23, there was a huge snowstorm, finally providing the substantial snow—more than ten inches—that would have been nice weeks earlier for carnival. Despite a warm spell in early March, when one day I was skiing in fifty-five-degree sunshine, the snow lasted long enough that I was able to ski until late March. That freshman year, I had more than fifty afternoons on skis—fantastic, long white afternoons.

Later winters were also filled with the exultation of snow on firs and mountains, crisp, cold mornings, and blissful runs down pine-scented, welcoming trails. In the next twenty years of my skiing life (before a back injury in the 1980s curtailed much of my skiing), I skied at bigger and more challenging ski areas with much better snow conditions. But I never again experienced the same rush of adrenaline and pure joy that infused me while dropping down ski trails at Dartmouth's temple to Boreas and Chione.

Mount Washington (6,288'), White Mountains,
New Hampshire, October 1964

Peter Thomas, '67, with New York state trooper on
the New York State Thruway, September 1964

Limnology Laboratory, Abisko, Sweden, with Lapp Gate in distance, July 1964

Leena Palm with Lapp Gate in the distance, Abisko, Sweden, July 1964

Torneträsk, Sweden, with Lapp Gate in the distance, July 1964

Uppsala Castle and Uppsala Cathedral at sunset, Uppsala, Sweden, July 1964

CHAPTER 8—ROAD-TRIPPING

"Anyone for a road trip?" The challenge rang out through the halls of the Topliff castle, the beery cellars of the fraternities, and the common rooms of other dormitories as though summoning Christian crusaders to the walls of Jerusalem. All who heard it stopped whatever they were doing and thought, *Am I up for this?*

The "road trip" was defined in the 1960s at Dartmouth as a leap of faith in which young men (a) jammed together in a vehicle without seat belts to travel treacherous mountain roads for hours under often adverse weather conditions, (b) trusted that at their destination they would meet girls whom they knew (or did not know) who would provide conversation and female companionship (or perhaps more) for a brief evening, (c) enjoyed (or not) a date of several hours always including alcoholic beverages, and (d) returned to Hanover in the same vehicle without seat belts to travel the same treacherous roads for hours under often adverse weather conditions, exhausted and suffering the results of overdrinking and (usually) frustration. Sometimes a road trip was by oneself, if you decided to hitchhike. More often than not, the anticipation and trust that motivated the considerable expenditure of time, energy, and funds associated with a road trip were misplaced. But as Alexander Pope recognized in his *Essay on Man*, "Hope springs eternal in the human breast ..."

My first road trip was to Boston in mid-November. Stan Brown, my Topliff and Glee Club colleague from Lexington, Massachusetts, had a grandmother who lived in Hanover on Park Road. He was dating a girl named Jane from Jackson College (sister school of Tufts University). Stan invited his roommate Bill Kirkpatrick, Pete Thomas, and me to drive with him—he borrowed his grandmother's car—to his home on a Friday evening, where we ate dinner with his parents and younger sister, Prudence, and enjoyed a lively evening of conversation with his father (Sanborn C. Brown, '35), a professor of physics at the Massachusetts Institute of Technology, his mother, and sister.

The trip took about three and one half hours on the (preinterstate) country roads of New Hampshire and Massachusetts as we listened on the car's radio to the popular music of the early 1960s, such as "Puff the Magic Dragon" sung by Peter, Paul, and Mary, Bobby Vinton's "Blue Velvet," the Motown hit "Heat Wave" by Martha and the Vandellas, and Andy Williams's rendition of "The Days of Wine and Roses," among others of my favorites. For a freshman, having a car at your disposal was against college regulations, which forbade both having a car on campus and driving one in Hanover. We all luxuriated in the delicious excitement of Stan's violating college rules.

Stan's girlfriend had arranged blind dates for us with her classmates at Jackson on Saturday night, and I recall that we ate together at one of the college's dining facilities before taking in the movie *Tom Jones* in Boston. My date was a talkative, well-informed, attractive girl named Mary with whom I had a fine evening—one of the few blind dates in my life with whom I got along well. The movie was fantastic—it later won the Oscar for best movie in 1963. After dropping the girls off at Jackson, we drove back to Lexington, staying again at Stan's home before returning to Hanover on Sunday afternoon.

This first road trip from Dartmouth was one of the best of the several dozen I undertook at Dartmouth. Because our dates were friends of Stan's girlfriend and this was our first such experience, we were all on our best behavior. No one drank heavily; no one boasted of "scoring" with his date. It was a fun, interesting, and relaxing weekend. I enjoyed it enough that in the ensuing months of my freshman year, I went on road trips to Mount Holyoke College in South Hadley, Massachusetts (117 miles; about three hours), to Skidmore College in Saratoga Springs, New York (113 miles; two and one half hours), to Yale University in New Haven (185 miles; five hours) to visit high school friends, and two trips to Simmons College, in Boston (130 miles; three and one half hours). (I mention the distances and travel times involved to demonstrate that road trips from Hanover were indeed arduous adventures, particularly in the years prior to the completion of interstate Highways 89, 91, and 93, parts of which opened in the next several years.)

At Simmons, I experienced perhaps the worst of my road-tripping experiences. I had met a Simmons freshman at a Simmons mixer in January in Boston. I recall that her name was Alice, and she was both very attractive and charming, I thought. We had a lovely evening together dancing, drinking in her dormitory room at Simmons, and talking frankly about our past lives and problems at college. It was a memorable road trip. Several weeks later, I wrote what I thought was a complimentary letter to her, because she seemed like such a kindred spirit. I hoped that the brief evening with her might turn into a deeper friendship and relationship, and I indicated as much in the letter.

Her responsive letter was lengthy and provided me with some hope that she was interested in becoming a closer friend. She said that she would like to see me in Boston again in the coming months. So in mid-March, without letting her know that I was coming, I joined a group of upperclassmen from Bissell Hall who were driving to Boston on a Saturday morning and returning the same night. They dropped me off near the Simmons campus, and I easily found Alice's dormitory. I had intended to surprise her.

As soon as I entered the main entrance to the dormitory, I saw a bulletin board in the front hall. On it was a familiar letter—the letter I had written to Alice several weeks before. She had posted it on the board, and it was covered with mocking, annotative comments from her Simmons dormitory mates. It is an understatement to characterize these statements as insulting and unkind, especially as my behavior with Alice had been completely respectful and benign.

I grabbed the letter, tore it up, turned and fled, confused and shocked. I don't remember how I left the campus or what I did until the late-evening rendezvous with my Dartmouth ride back to Hanover. I remember only being dazed and more humiliated than I had ever been before. That was it for Alice and for Simmons College, as far as I was concerned. I should have known better. (Simmons was not included in the Green Book's list of preferred women's colleges.) I also learned to be more careful in the future with candidly expressing my feelings.

Shortly after that disastrous weekend in Boston, a letter from my brother assuaged my wounded ego. He wrote to invite me to work with him during the coming summer at Uppsala University's Institute of Limnology, in Uppsala, Sweden. The invitation was totally unexpected but gratefully received. Instead of moping about my humiliation at Simmons, I was immediately full of excitement and expectation about a trip to Sweden! I had never before been to Europe or, for that matter, to any place outside of North America. This trip could be a road trip to top all road trips! Of course, I immediately accepted, and we started to plan when and how I was to join him, my sister-in-law, and young nephew.

John was a limnologist—the freshwater equivalent of a marine biologist. At that time, he was at the beginning of what turned out to be a brilliant career in science—begun as a student at Dartmouth—focusing on the ecology of Arctic and Antarctic lakes worldwide.[37] I had been his assistant several summers before on a research project at Lake Peters, Alaska, in the heart of the Arctic National Wildlife Refuge, so I was familiar with the research in which he was then engaged.[38]

Before my June departure for Sweden, however, the spring term held several more road trips. The first of these was a trip home after exams were finished in mid-March. I could not find a ride to Buffalo and decided to hitchhike home, despite the cold weather and an approaching storm. I mention this trip because it turned out to be quite an adventure and took me much longer than the fifteen hours I had anticipated.

I left in the early afternoon, catching my first ride south on US Route 5 in Norwich, Vermont, just across the river. I made it to Brattleboro, where a fierce snowstorm began, and then caught a ride west on Vermont Route 9 across the southern part of the state in the snow. The driver was going to the Skyline Restaurant near the Hogback Mountain Ski Area on Route 9 and dropped me off at the pass near the restaurant. It was dark, cold, and snowing heavily. I waited in the darkness and snow for over two hours for another ride and then gave up, taking shelter in the restaurant in the hope that someone would stop there and give me a ride toward Bennington. No vehicles were on that road

---

[37]   During his career, among many positions, he was the lead principal investigator of the Arctic Long-Term Ecological Research (LETR) project, president of the American Society of Limnology and Oceanography from 1984 to 1986, served on the board of directors for the Arctic Research Consortium of the United States from 1989 to 2001, and served on the US Arctic Research Commission from 1996 to 2004. At the end of his career, he retired as the director of the Ecosystems Center at the Marine Biological Center, Woods Hole, Massachusetts.

[38]   This incredible experience in the wilderness of Alaska is described in my memoir *Buffalo Wings*.

in the storm. A waitress there told me that I looked half-frozen—which I was—from the snow and strong wind. She let me sleep on a cot in the back room.

The next morning, I bought a rejuvenating breakfast and, as soon as the snow had stopped and plows had cleared the road, caught a ride on a tractor-trailer truck going to Syracuse. Somewhere between Albany and Syracuse on the New York Thruway, I fell asleep. Although I had asked the driver to let me off when he left the Thruway at the Syracuse exit, he forgot and woke me only when he had reached his destination, which was an industrial park in suburban Syracuse in the middle of nowhere. After thanking the driver, I held out my thumb at the nearest intersection, expecting to wait for a long time in the growing darkness. By this time it was about twenty-eight hours since I had left Hanover, and I was getting extremely tired of hitchhiking.

The second car to come along stopped. The driver was going to Rochester on the Thruway and offered me a lift. In the course of our conversation, I discovered that he had graduated from Dartmouth many years before. When he found out that I was a freshman heading home to Buffalo for spring break and that I had left Hanover more than a day before, he insisted on driving me all the way home, right to my house, although Buffalo was ninety miles west of Rochester and this was at least a five-hour detour for him. I learned that night a lesson repeated throughout my life thereafter—that members of the Dartmouth community have unbounded generosity, which manifests itself when least expected and often when most needed.

That long hitchhike home in March was well worth the effort. I was always happy to be home with my parents and other family members, and during this break in Buffalo, I reconnected with a girl I had dated in high school and had a wonderful time—such a good time that in April I hitchhiked home again for a weekend, mainly to see her again. This time, the trip by thumb took about ten hours in each direction. The second weekend also was a superb weekend, although I felt very guilty about missing classes on Friday and Monday! It is funny how a thumb could become an extension of my heart (or some other body part).

When I hitchhiked I always took with me a handheld sign, made of cardboard, indicating my destination in large black letters. I usually decorated the sign with a depiction of an eighth note (♪), which always prompted an inquiry from the driver who picked me up. It was a good luck symbol for me. I think I was unconsciously thinking of my mother in doing so.

My mother was an excellent pianist and taught piano for many years out of our home. Her favorite composer was Chopin, and she played his nocturnes and waltzes with such passion and finesse that even twenty years after her death that music brings tears to my eyes. She was also persistently eager to match me with young women whom she thought I should date. I learned over the years to view with great skepticism any girl whose smile, attractiveness, personality, or talent my mother touted.

Throughout high school, my mother had tried to interest me in the daughter of a violinist whom my mother had often accompanied on the piano in the past. "Janis is so attractive and such a skillful pianist that I know you will like her," my mother harped. I stoutly resisted her entreaties for over a year, using the excuse that my best high school friend—Bob Ramage—was already dating the girl in question that year. I finally conceded that my mother was right and dated Janis Terry in high school off and on until I met Lindsey, whom I mentioned above. During spring break, since Bob had written me that he was no longer seeing her, I asked Janis out again and remembered how talented, smart, fun, and (incidentally) pretty she was. Our reconnection prompted my second trip to Buffalo in less than three weeks, and Janis was my date for Green Key Weekend.

Green Key Weekend on May 9–10 was Dartmouth's celebration of the coming of spring. There were concerts and parties, sports events, and activities designed to spark enjoyment of the warmer weather outdoors. Although in many ways I loved winters in Hanover, by April the longing for warmer weather and spring flowers was excruciating. In early May, the mud season—with its plank paths across the muddy footpaths of the Green—was beginning to dissipate. The flowering plum trees next to Baker Library burst into their fragile pink blossoms, and daffodils and tulips bloomed in the campus's dozens of flower beds. The hill winds were finally a bit warmer. It was almost too wonderful to bear!

Janis arrived on Friday night with another girl from Buffalo, who was the weekend date of classmate Andy Mack from East Aurora. We spent a lazy, three-day weekend highlighted by watching the fuzzy green buds of the surrounding forest canopy leaf out, walking hand in hand through the awakening forests along the river, cheering the crew races on the Connecticut, laughing at the chariot races on the Green among the entries from dormitories and fraternities, and sleeping out on the college golf course with hundreds of other couples. I introduced her to Bartlett Tower, to the observation platform on the Baker Library tower, and to my favorite nooks and crannies of the library and Hopkins Center. We had a memorable weekend together—the first of several with Janis at Dartmouth.

In the period of emotional letdown after the big spring weekend, Pete and I caught "baseball fever" and spent hours playing catch on the lawn of Alumni Gymnasium across the street from our room. We also started to attend the films presented on weekends at the Hopkins Center by the Dartmouth Film Society. The first movie we saw in that year's series showcasing horror films was *Dr. Cyclops*—a 1940 Technicolor science-fiction horror film about a mad scientist who shrank people.

Three weeks after Green Key Weekend, at Sandi Ingalls's invitation, I caught a ride with a senior to White Plains, New York, and then from there hitchhiked to Dobbs Ferry, located in the Hudson Valley just north of New York City, to visit her. The entire trip took only six hours, and it was a lovely drive across Vermont and then down the east side of the Hudson Valley from Albany. I stayed three nights with Sandi and her delightfully welcoming parents.

We spent the first evening together at Coney Island Amusement Park. Sandi's father let me drive their new convertible to and from the park, where we went on dozens of rides and watched spectacular fireworks. Early the next morning, we left for the World's Fair, which had just opened in New York

City. Admission was two dollars per person, which I thought was outrageously expensive, but Sandi's father had free tickets and a parking pass, which he presented to us. The theme of the fair was "Peace through Understanding," and it was dedicated to "Man's Achievement on a Shrinking Globe in an Expanding Universe." For me, the most impressive single memory of the fair was a twelve-story-high, stainless-steel model of the earth called the Unisphere.

Exhibit after exhibit showcased American culture and technology. Sandi took me to the most popular exhibits early in the day before the crowds arrived. The General Electric pavilion had a revolving auditorium that rotated around cinematic scenes of the future, such as robots that walked, moved, and talked perfectly like humans, models of all-electric modern kitchens and homes, and finally a purported experiment in nuclear fusion that ended in a big explosion!

The Coca-Cola exhibit hall recreated scenes from various parts of the world that you walked through, hearing the sounds, smelling the odors, and seeing the sights as though you were walking in a Hong Kong street, a Swiss resort, an African village road, and a tropical jungle. In the Bell Telephone exhibit, you rode in moving chairs on a conveyor belt past scenes portraying the history of communications. The Ford Motor Corporation offered a ride in a Thunderbird convertible on a moving road through scenes of animated prehistoric monsters—life-size, growling, hissing, and clamping tremendous jaws—and through the streets of a futuristic planet's city.

Kodak and Johnson's Wax, I recall, also had impressive movies featuring the latest projection techniques. At the IBM pavilion, I saw for the first time demonstrations of the uses of mainframe computers, computer terminals with keyboards, Teletype machines, punch cards, and telephone modems. After hours of walking and gaping at some incredible exhibits of technology, for dinner we went to a restaurant called Little Old New York in the Rheingold pavilion, where Sandi insisted on treating me to one of the best meals I have ever had! I remember discussing our feelings about the fair over dinner and both agreeing that such events were extremely important in bringing people from different cultures together to promote mutual understanding and thereby to realize the fair's theme. In a significant way, I thought my college experience embodied the same theme—peace through understanding—on two levels: eliminating conflicts in the world through appreciation by all countries of other countries' history and culture and on a personal level enhancing my respect for the great value of diversity of gender, age, race, religion, and culture with respect to my classmates, women, and other contacts of my college life through a shared exploration of human relationships.

Except for my hitchhike home in June, this road trip to visit Sandi was the last of about eight road trips during my freshman year—a great finale to a year of incredible trips by thumb or by car with other Dartmouth colleagues. But the best was yet to come, thanks to the generosity of my brother, to the kindness of his wife, and to his invitation to work with him in Sweden.

Just before final exams, I attended a preflight briefing for the passengers on the Dartmouth charter flight that would be departing from New York for London on June 14: the ultimate road trip. We were shown how to fill out customs' forms, told what to expect at airports on departure and arrival, given our tickets, and provided general information, such as the flight's duration, meals served, and baggage limitations (fifty-five pounds). I met the four Dartmouth professors and many of the students who would be traveling on the flight, most of them heading for European universities as part of Dartmouth's foreign study program. Students from other Ivy League and other New England schools joined us.

After hitchhiking home on June 8 immediately after my last exam, I dove into my preparations for the overseas road trip. Packing and a series of farewell parties with high school friends, including a poignant good-bye with Janis, made the two weeks at home fly by. At last on Sunday, June 22 at noon I flew to Newark, New Jersey, and caught a helicopter shuttle to John F. Kennedy Airport. The shuttle's route was right across the New York Harbor in perfect weather. I saluted the Statue of Liberty and took lovely pictures of Manhattan in the late-afternoon sunshine. It was eighty-nine degrees in New York City, so we were all very glad to board the Boeing 707 and feel its refreshingly cool air. I remember how fast my heart beat as I climbed up the steps from the tarmac to the plane's open door, met the seven flight attendants who greeted us as we entered the cabin, and thought of my first trip to Europe!

The flight took about six hours on British Overseas Airways. It was a first-class flight, which included two dinners, a breakfast, and all the free champagne we could drink! The girl next to me drank a little too much, but as she was one of the only six girls on the flight, extremely intelligent, and very attractive, I was happy to have her as a companion.

We arrived in London at six thirty in the morning, where I was met by my mother's English cousin Vera Holden and given a royal tour of London—Buckingham Palace and the changing of the guard, Tower of London, Parliament Buildings, Westminster Abbey, Covent Gardens, and the London subway system ("Tube"). We met two more of my English cousins, whom I had not met before (John Eyres and his wife), and had a fine dinner with them at an English pub, before my train left at ten minutes past eight for Harwich on the coast. The weather was perfect—cool and clear—and my first and only day in England en route to Sweden was the first sunny day there in three weeks, I was told.

On the train, I met several other American students (four girls from the Universities of Michigan and Illinois) also heading for the Netherlands, as well as Jim Hughes, '65, who was a great traveling companion. Jim was going ultimately to Copenhagen. It was about a one-and-one-half-hour train ride from London to Harwich. I was delighted by the clean, comfortable, modern, and efficient train system in England and thoroughly enjoyed the English countryside we passed.

My maternal grandmother (Margaret Eyres) was English, and I thus had significant ancestral roots in England. I felt a tug at my heart from, and a close bond with, the lovely hedgerows and engaging rural landscapes the train sped through. From Harwich, we departed on the ferry S.S. *Avalon* at ten o'clock under a gorgeous full moon and had a quiet, smooth channel crossing, during which I had my first sleep in thirty-six hours notwithstanding the other four passengers sharing the stateroom.

After we disembarked at Hoek van Holland at six thirty on Tuesday morning, Jim and I boarded a train to Copenhagen. The ride through the Netherlands and West Germany featured old-world German villages, fields of undulating, ripening grain, and gardens full of every variety of flower you could imagine. As the weather still was clear with puffy clouds, the passing pastoral scenery was spectacular!

The companions in my compartment were extremely sociable. There were six of us: a Dutch man and his fifteen-year-old daughter, two lovely Swedish girls slightly younger than me, and sitting next to me with her sleepy head on my shoulder most of the trip, a gorgeous Danish girl named Helene, who had studied in the United States and amazingly knew a cousin of my former girlfriend Lindsey! Helene lived in Copenhagen and carefully plotted what attractions in Copenhagen I should see in my four hours between trains.

Jim Hughes and I met up again as we left the train in Copenhagen station around eight o'clock that Tuesday night. I remarked to Jim that the girls in my compartment had been some of the friendliest and most attractive I had ever met. He had experienced equally alluring women in his compartment. We agreed that, if our experience on this trip so far was any indication of the coming summer's enjoyment, it would be a wonderful nine weeks!

The daylight in northern Europe lingered at this time of year until close to midnight, suffusing the evening sky and the city with a soft, golden radiance. It was a warm, satisfying glow that spoke of happiness, peace, and pleasure. Colored lights, the smiling faces of Danes, and the contented gazes of arm-in-arm lovers surrounded us on all sides. The weeklong celebration of midsummer was in full course!

We soon saw that the celebration of the longest day of the year in Denmark (which had occurred two days earlier) was akin to the light-filled celebration of Christmas at home. People were singing in the sidewalk cafes, dancing in the streets, and luxuriating in the evening sunshine as they rejoiced in the beginning of summer. Jim and I only had time to visit Tivoli, which is a wonderful public park next to the train station filled with amusement rides, restaurants, and dance halls. We toasted the arrival of summer with steins of Tuborg beer and basked in the excitement and joy that engulfed the park. I will never forget that first great arrival in Scandinavia!

After Jim headed to his hotel, I boarded a midnight train to Stockholm. I awoke in my three-person sleeping compartment, as the train approached Stockholm, around nine o'clock in the morning on June 24, to the sight of hundreds of red Soviet flags on the buildings and streets of downtown Stockholm and thousands of policemen everywhere. Soviet Premier Nikita Khrushchev was also visiting Sweden!

My brother John, his wife, Olivann, and his young son, Lawrence, met me at the station. They gave me a fantastic, whirlwind tour of Stockholm in bright sunshine caressed by a brisk breeze off the Swedish archipelago. The straining blue Swedish flags everywhere with their gold crosses contrasted favorably with the yellow hammers, sickles, and stars on the red Soviet flags. We visited the imposing Stockholm City Hall with its exquisite, palace-like interior next to the harbor, from the city hall tower viewed the harbor and islands making up the city, took a ferry around the harbor and past Nikita Khrushchev's ship, and visited the wonderful amusement park and zoo called Skansen. I was tremendously impressed with the blue water everywhere, the cleanliness of the streets and buildings, the manicured perfection of the parks, the smartly dressed people, and the fact that everyone apparently spoke flawless English (as well as German and French). Stockholm was one of the most beguiling cities I had ever seen! My lifelong love affair with Sweden had begun.

On Wednesday evening, we drove in John's Volkswagen bus north for about an hour to Uppsala through an idyllic landscape of farms, fields of horses and cows, and quaint cream-colored houses with red tile roofs—a distance of just over forty miles. As we approached the old city, the twin spires of the thirteenth-century Uppsala Cathedral—Scandinavia's largest church—and the imposing outline against the sky of Uppsala Castle on a nearby hill welcomed us. Uppsala then was Sweden's fourth-largest city and the seat of the oldest university in the Nordic countries, dating from 1477.

The university was the eighteenth-century home of Carl Linnaeus—"father of modern taxonomy" and one of the founders of modern ecology. It seemed the perfect place to do research in limnology.

While Stockholm had just charmed me with its modernity and beauty, Uppsala quickly won my heart with its ancient museums, cathedral, and academic structures, intimate charm, student cafes and clubs, narrow cobblestone streets, and old-world aura.

As we entered the city, John pointed out that the Fyris River neatly divides the city into two different parts: the historic quarter to the west of the river and the modern administrative, residential, and commercial city center to the east. Most of the historical sights and university buildings are in the western part, with its medieval design of streets, river views, and parks, all of which are dominated by the cathedral. We headed for the west half of the city.

John and Olivann had a six-room apartment on the third floor of a small, new apartment building of about a dozen units located not far from the historic quarter (Tälstensvägen 14C). Woods filled with blueberries and strawberries separated the buildings from one another, and gravel paths wound through neatly kept lawns and clusters of evergreens and birches. I stayed in an apartment about one half mile away but in the same extremely attractive, newer section of the city. Friends of my brother were away for the summer and generously let me occupy their small apartment with its ultra-modern Scandinavian furniture, overlooking lovely woods.

I was very impressed with the utility, design, and comfort of the apartment's rooms and furnishings. They were small by American standards but more than adequate. The light switches, especially, struck

116

me as ingenious—in the entrances and hallways of the building, the lights were timed to switch off after a short interval sufficient to allow lighted access to and from each apartment's entrance. I had never before seen such an innovation, but this arrangement was common in every apartment and public building. Lights did not burn unnecessarily all night in Uppsala's buildings.

Several other common essentials in Sweden were completely new and very appealing to me. For example, I had never eaten the addictive, yogurt-like *filmjölk* (a type of buttermilk) before; all Swedes seemed to consume it in great quantities! New buildings were all built around a central tower and crane that facilitated the hoisting of building materials. How elegantly simple and practical this approach to construction was! Cranes were everywhere. Swedes also loved a type of flat, hard crisp bread, called *knäckebröd*, which was delicious when spread with lingonberry jam or covered with cheese.

John's office and laboratory were located in the brand-new Institute of Limnology on the university campus within walking distance of both of our apartments. His research project, which very generally involved the study of arctic lakes, was supported by the institute's facilities. I did what I could to help in his data collection from the water samples and other research. We walked or rode bicycles to work usually, as did most of the dozens of scientists/professors and laboratory technicians at the institute, but cheap, modern public buses ran frequently and on time, so they were available if it was raining.

Without exception, the institute's employees were friendly and anxious to help me in any possible way. In general, my living and working environments in Uppsala were among the best I had ever experienced, especially since my brother and sister-in-law were tremendously caring and made sure that I joined them in my free time, visiting fascinating nearby ancient castles, churches, and the Uppsala Cathedral, as well as gorgeous gardens and lakes! I was very fortunate to be living and working in Sweden's historic, cultural, and religious center!

I had just settled in to the research routine and begun to familiarize myself with the city by long bike rides and walks, when John and I left for a research station in the far north of Sweden located near the town of Abisko in the region known as Lappland. Our trip by train in a comfortable sleeping car took about twenty hours on July 6. We passed hundreds of sparkling lakes and deep forests, with brief stops in a dozen or so small, attractive cities and towns as we traveled 850 miles to the cluster of houses located 120 miles north of the Arctic Circle known as Abisko.

The research station at Abisko was situated in the snowcapped Scandinavian Mountains on the shore of a huge lake (about 124 square miles in area and forty-three miles long), the sixth largest in Sweden, known as Torneträsk. Across the lake, the so-called Lapp Gate—a pass through the mountains that was a larger, more spectacular version of Cumberland Gap in Maryland—dominated the surrounding mountains. The views from our dormitory and laboratory windows were of the lake, surrounding snow-covered peaks, and miles of scrub spruce and fir—absolutely spellbinding!

We were in and around Abisko for two full weeks, taking water samples from Torneträsk, hiking miles across snowfields and glaciers to collect water samples from remote lakes, and otherwise enjoying the amazing arctic environment—small evergreen trees, sweeps of tundra vegetation, glaciers, and midnight sun—and the fellowship of the Lapps and other Swedes living in Abisko and at the research station. Although we were extremely busy from early in the morning until dinnertime each day, we had some fine days off. On one of our free days, we took the train north and west to Narvik, Norway, where we rode a cable car to the top of a mountain overlooking the city and harbor and had a wonderful boat ride in the adjacent fjords.

My second day in Abisko, I discovered the large and well-equipped hostel/hotel "Abisko turiststation" at the train station of the same name, just over a mile further west. The "hotel" was staffed by about forty young Swedish men and women, all of whom welcomed me with open arms. Americans were rare visitors so far north—I was somewhat of a sensation. Every evening there was an informal dance after the buffet dinner at the hotel for guests and staff. Visiting hikers from all over Europe were staying at the hotel. Whenever I had a leisurely moment in the evening, I walked down the train track—or if a friend was with me we could "pump" a handcar along the tracks—to the hotel to visit my friends, particularly the twenty or so girls who worked there.

At the third dance I attended, I met a lovely, doe-eyed, blonde girl with freckles named Leena Palm. Leena was working at the turiststation for the summer. For the next two weeks, my leisure time was filled with her laughter, smiles, and passion. We both knew that our romance was to be a short one, but we made the most of the long arctic days, hiking, swimming, dancing, singing, talking, and holding each other until the sun briefly set just before midnight each day that I was free. Leena and I communicated in a mixture of English, French, and Swedish (which I was learning as fast as I could). She was such a natural, free spirit and so easy to get along with that she in many ways personified my ideal girl. Whenever I think of Sweden, I fondly remember her and our two-week long, intimate friendship.

On July 21, we boarded the train to return to Uppsala, arriving after a full day on the train. The sun was now setting about nine thirty—a full two hours earlier than when we left only weeks before. I soon become good friends with one of my brother's friends—a genial, Swedish graduate student named Staffan Holmgren, who was also working at the institute. Staffan introduced me to the student social scene in Uppsala during the summer. It was an incredibly fun and educational experience!

I had never before heard of the student "nations" at Uppsala University, which date from the fifteenth century. Student nations are regional corporations of students at a university from a particular region of Sweden. Once widespread across Europe in medieval times, such organizations are now largely restricted to the older universities of Sweden and Finland. At Uppsala, there were thirteen such student nations, representing the thirteen provinces from which students attend Uppsala University.

A student automatically belonged to the "nation" representing the province of her or his birthplace. Staffan took me to his nation, the largest at Uppsala, called the Norrlands Nation, which operated the Club Norrlandia for its members and guests during the summer. Its members—both girls and boys—were all from the northernmost province of Sweden. The nation was housed in a medieval-looking building on the bank of the Fyris River in the most ancient part of the university and had over one thousand members. In effect it was like a huge, combined fraternity and sorority that sponsored, among other activities, dance parties every Monday, Wednesday, and Friday evening during the summer. Admission to the dances was eighty cents.

Inside Club Norrlandia, there was a casino, a drinking hall with beer on tap and a small band accompanying student drinking and folk songs, a relaxing lounge, a fine restaurant, and most significantly a ballroom with high-quality dance bands and singers. On my first visit, there was a fashion show opening the evening with a dozen or so lovely models from Stockholm showcasing the latest Swedish dress styles. In the course of an evening, you could eat, drink, watch a fashion show, sing, gamble, and dance to your heart's content!

I particularly was struck by the Swedish dance etiquette, which I soon learned. The girls—in fashionable dresses and high heels—sat at tables talking with friends. Male students—in sport coats and ties—asked women politely to dance and were then by custom restricted to two consecutive dances with the same woman, following which you escorted the woman back to her table. You had to dance four dances (two two-dance sequences) then with other women before returning to a woman to dance again with her. Typically, in a two-dance set, the first was a fast dance (including swing and Latin dances such as rumba or cha-cha) and the second dance was a slow dance (including waltz, foxtrot, or tango). My ballroom dance lessons in Buffalo as a young teenager had prepared me well, which was very fortunate, for Swedish girls were excellent dancers!

Every seventh dance was a so-called Sadie Hawkins dance where the women asked the men to dance. Occasionally, all would join in circles to dance a traditional Swedish folk dance called the *Hambo*. It was a fine arrangement and made it easy to meet and talk with dozens of women in a typical evening. After dancing with a particular woman who stirred my interest, I could tell if my interest was reciprocated by seeing whom she chose to be her partner at the next Sadie Hawkins sequence.

Staffan and I went to almost all of the dances at Club Norrlandia after I got back from Abisko. Roughly four hundred students attended each dance, and over several weeks, I got to know about a dozen girls rather well. I found Swedish women tremendously alluring, with their lilting accents, European clothes, elegant but subtle makeup and hairstyles, and confident but innocent sexuality. Of these women—all of whom were charming, smart, and attractive—one in particular was a jewel. Her name was Anna Margareta Ahlström.

Anna was an eighteen-year-old mathematics major who had just begun her studies at Uppsala in the previous autumn. Her English was fluent, and she had an amazing knowledge of the world for someone who had never left her farming village before coming to the university. She was almost my height (six feet), slender, and strikingly beautiful with long blonde hair and blue eyes. We dated heavily for the remaining four weeks of my summer in Uppsala, usually meeting at Club Norrlandia at first and then walking arm-in-arm round the riverfront's parks to one of the many bakery-like *conditori* to enjoy the lingering twilight and sunset, coffee, and pastries.

I was at first loath to drive John's VW bus in Sweden, although he was generous in offering its use, because traffic drove on the left of the road then, as in England. I was very reluctant (and scared) to try driving under this system. At Anna's urging, however, I started to drive to the Norrlands Nation's dances, so that we could visit some of the places she wanted to show me after several hours of dancing. This meant, of course, that I could not drink any beer or other alcoholic beverages at the club. Driving after drinking alcohol was absolutely proscribed in Sweden, and violators went to jail and lost their vehicles. Anna was strict!

On one of these excursions, the local police stopped us—I had been driving briefly on the right (wrong) side of the road, forgetting where I was and what I was doing as a result of my fascination with the woman snuggling beside me. Traffic was very light most of the time and required little concentration. Anna advised me to remain silent and to let her do the talking with the two young officers. She also charmed the policemen, apparently, as after a brief exchange with her, the officers tipped their hats to us and left, smiling.

On our fifth date, Anna and I drove to Gamla Uppsala (Old Uppsala), a historic site dating from the third and fourth centuries, which is the ancient cultural, religious, and political center of Sweden. She showed me there the three huge burial mounds from the fifth and sixth centuries, which were thought to be tombs for royalty.

At a nearby restaurant, she ordered mead—an old Norse alcoholic beverage made by fermenting honey with water. It was served in traditional containers, which were long, curling rams' horns. You drank from the narrow end of the horn by raising the curved, larger part of the horn higher than the mouth to start the liquid coursing through the horn. Anna explained that it was important to lower the horn as soon as I heard the gurgle of the moving liquid. Of course, on my first attempt to drink from the horn, I did not follow her instructions quickly enough, with the result that the mead gushed from the mouth of the horn in a torrent, completely soaking me. Anna and I laughed until we cried.

On the way home, Anna invited me to go back to her place with her. I was so befuddled that I let her guide me to her apartment house on the outskirts of Uppsala, where she was living with a cousin, without noticing where I was going. The next morning, as I drove back to my apartment house guided by the cathedral's spires, I made a mental note of the route I would need to follow in the future to get to her apartment again, but I was in such a state of bliss that my mental note might as well have been written in hieroglyphics.

We had arranged for me to pick her up the next Saturday morning at her apartment for a sightseeing trip to Gavle—a small coastal city to the north of Uppsala. Several hours before I was supposed to pick her up, I decided to make a dry run so as to be sure that my memory was reliable enough that I knew where I was going and how long it would take me. I retraced the route based on my mental note and eventually came to the street leading to her apartment, I thought. But there was no apartment house on the street, and it dead-ended at the imposing gates of a psychiatric institution that I had no recollection of ever seeing before. This could not be the correct route. So I again retraced the route, with the same result. I began to worry that perhaps I was crazy or that Anna might be a patient.

Since neither Anna nor her cousin had access to a phone, and I did not even know her address, I could not contact her. I became increasingly frustrated. Finally, I approached a guard at the gates, who spoke English. I explained my predicament and bewilderment. When I described Anna to him, he immediately knew whom I was trying to reach and advised me that she lived with a staff member of the institution (her cousin) in an apartment complex on the grounds of the institution. Thereafter I became so familiar with the route to Anna's apartment that I could have driven it blindfolded.

The remaining few weeks in Uppsala were like a dream. It was delightful to be with my brother and his family, and pure heaven to be with Anna. When I left by train for England on August 27, I knew that I had just experienced the summer of a lifetime (and perhaps the romance of a lifetime)! The train trip back to Hoek van Holland was anticlimactic. I pined for Anna. No other woman looked attractive or interesting anymore, although once again there were lots of very enticing young women on the train.

The English Channel crossing was stormy. In the middle of the night, I went out to the forward deck to savor the lightning, thunder, and rough seas. It was deserted except for a young man at the rail wearing a Dartmouth jacket with whom I immediately struck up a conversation. He was Chan Newton, '66, and that night was the beginning of a fine friendship that lasted for several years after Chan graduated. Chan was returning on the same charter flight, having spent the summer term at the University of Freiburg, Germany. We talked all night during the crossing about our respective European experiences, which were remarkably similar in many ways. Both of us agreed that our summers had been wonderfully enlightening and tremendously enjoyable. I think that we also shared the nagging feeling and regret that we had perhaps been too preoccupied with European girls to have absorbed, as much as we should have, the history, culture, and life lessons that our summers had presented. In a sense, I guess, all road trips were like that.

Fyris River and Uppsala Cathedral, Uppsala, Sweden, July 1964

Anna Margareta Ahlström, Uppsala, Sweden, August 1964

Dr. John Hobbie, '57, and Dr. Charles Goldman crossing
stream near Torneträsk, Abisko, Sweden, July 1964

My best Swedish friend, Dr. Staffan Holmgren, with his date,
Uppsala University, Sweden, July 1964

Kappa Kappa Kappa fraternity, 1 Webster Avenue, Hanover,
New Hampshire, September 1964

Baker Library tower at sunset, September 1964

Chapter 9 —"Gay Young Sophomores"[39]

The second verse of the song "Pea Green Freshmen" refers to "gay young soph'mores." By this, I think the song means "happy" or "carefree" sophomores, derived from the Anglo-French "gai" of Germanic origin. I doubt that the early nineteenth-century anonymous author of the lyrics intended today's common use of the term (sexual orientation).

Some of my hundreds of classmates were undoubtedly "gay" in the new sense of this word, although I was not aware of their orientation. I only know of one who eventually "came out"—the remarkable Mel Boozer. My heart deeply regrets the frustration and discrimination that Mel and others must have suffered in the 1960s and later. I was undoubtedly quite naïve then, but I don't recall even thinking about sexual orientation, much less discussing it. It was simply not on my mind at all. Gay men did not exist. Invisibility can be just as hurtful as overt discrimination. With very few exceptions, awareness of issues of the racial, gender, and sex discrimination that had surrounded us in society all of our lives was just beginning to percolate into our granite brains in those years.

In a subtle way, my preconceived prejudices regarding people of different backgrounds were beginning to change by the end of my freshman year. Dartmouth provided that first year at least limited exposure for me to young men from many diverse countries and backgrounds, as well as to several Americans—African Americans and Chinese Americans—from equally foreign albeit native-grown cultures. My family in Buffalo had African American acquaintances, and one elementary school classmate whom I considered a friend was African American. I also had a friend from the Mohawk tribe in elementary school. My high school, however, was lily-white. Clearly, I had had little contact with people of diverse racial or ethnic backgrounds growing up in Buffalo.

Classmates like Mel Boozer, Stan Chang, Richard Chu, and Xavier Mendoza (Bolivia)—and later fraternity brother Roger Tung—were my first true racially diverse friends. Learning about Dartmouth's historic beginnings as a school for Native Americans and Samson Occom's role in those beginnings was also enlightening and fostered my appreciation for American Indian culture beyond the Dartmouth "Indian" and the Hovey murals. Although I had not quite fully appreciated then my shift in feelings regarding diverse peoples, looking back I am very grateful that my freshman year began my comprehension—now a foundation of my existence and worldview—that understanding creates friendship, and in friendship there is peace.

---

39 "Where, O where are the gay young Soph'mores?" Anonymous, "Pea Green Freshmen," *Dartmouth Song Book*, 7.

My sophomore year was "gay" in the old sense of this term. When I think about my sophomore year, three memories are especially vibrant. The first of these was the spring Glee Club trip that I have already described, crossing the nation. The next was my ultimate abandonment of my lifelong dream to become a physician, torpedoed by a combination of my laziness, ineptitude in chemistry, and fascination with the world of words. The last was joining a fraternity of outstanding young men.

At the end of my first year, my transcript evinced a "gentleman's C plus" average. I had greatly enjoyed the French, Greek and Roman studies, English, and history courses, with their small classes of about ten students, but my biology and mathematics courses with a hundred or more students in each were very difficult. Chemistry was impossible. No amount of rubbing the noses of the busts of either Warner Bentley (Hopkins Center director) in the Hopkins Center or of Craven Laycock, class of 1896 (former dean of the college), just outside the entrance to the Tower Room in Baker Library—which I did almost daily—seemed to bring me the required luck in chemistry. In retrospect, I wonder if the size of the class and the corresponding relationship (or lack thereof) with the professor directly correlated to my enjoyment and success or lack thereof.

As I began my second year at Dartmouth, I reflected on my meager academic accomplishments to date and resolved to do better. In a sense, the summer in Sweden reassured me that there were at least a few lovely women in the world who found me attractive and with whom I could find both friendship and intimacy. This reassurance, I hoped, would allow me to worry less about girls and focus more on my courses. With this resolve, I looked forward to twin decisions in the coming year—one academic and the other social—that would significantly alter my Dartmouth experience for the better.

I still had a ways to go, however, before it finally sank into my consciousness that I was killing myself in science courses and in mathematics, with dismal results, while in French, English, history, government, and psychology, I loved the classes, hardly broke a sweat, and had generally positive results.

Psychology 1 is a great example. It was a very eye-opening course—a general introduction to human behavior—that I enjoyed tremendously in the spring term of my second year. Emphasis was placed on the basic psychological processes of perception, learning, and motivation, as they relate to personality, individual differences, social behavior, and the behavior disorders.

One of the lecturers was Professor Chauncey (Chince) N. Allen, '24, who had taught at Dartmouth for over forty years. He knew how to capture your attention, and at the same time his casual banter made you feel comfortable in his lectures. I still recall his presentation on perception, in which he showed us a movie upside down to make the point that the brain is an amazingly adaptable system— within minutes, our brains had compensated, and we were viewing the movie as though the image was not reversed.

I often saw Dr. Allen on his bicycle around town after taking Psychology 1. I told him how much I had enjoyed his presentations in the introductory course, and he was always friendly and gracious. It turned out that we both a deep interest in stamp collecting. He was a famous philatelist and editor of a prominent philatelic periodical. Once, when we were discussing how local politics had changed over the more than half century of his life in Hanover, he recalled that he used to be on the town board that oversaw elections and counted ballots. Hanover was so uniformly Republican for so long, he chuckled, that the first time two votes for a Democrat candidate were cast, the election board threw them out as clearly invalid ballots. He and his wonderful wife, Margaret, later became my great friends until their deaths more than thirty years after my classes with him.[40]

As I mention above, I very badly wanted to study medicine and become a doctor eventually. This dream kept me plodding through the premed courses, in the face of my growing conviction that the sciences especially were my weak subjects—despite my great enjoyment of the summer limnological research with which I had assisted my brother in Alaska and Sweden and of the several biological field trips with Dr. Likens to Mink Brook. My resolve to focus on my studies notwithstanding, I ended my sophomore year with an overall grade point average identical to that of my first year: C plus.

Within this context, I had to select a major course of study. A student did not actually select a major formally until the second year. Dartmouth was helpful in doing what it could to assist me in evaluating what my major course of study—and perhaps my future career as a consequence— would be.

First, in this regard, were the results of the Strong Vocational Interest Test, which I had taken the previous autumn. I was very skeptical that a vocational test could be helpful in assisting me to decide what I wanted to study at Dartmouth. I received the results the same week I received an invitation for a meeting with the dean of freshman, Al Dickerson.

The test results and "profile" were presented in graph format and plotted to compare my results in each of ten categories with patterns of interests from studies of men successfully engaged in certain occupations. Of the ten categories listed on the graph, my highest score corresponded supposedly to success in arts-sciences (physician, dentist, psychologist, architect, artist, etc.). My second highest result indicated strong interest in words and ideas (advertiser, lawyer, author-journalist). My only other strong interests corresponded to success in social contacts (school superintendent, social science teacher, public administration, personnel manager, minister, vocational counselor) and in music (musician), respectively.

On the negative side, my results indicated a probable lack of future success in mathematical-scientific endeavors, production activities, accounting work (certified public accountant), and business detail (accountant, office worker, purchasing agent, banker). Although it did not occur to me at the time, the results actually predicted fairly well my academic performance and my career choices in the future.

---

[40] My reconnecting with Chauncey and Margaret Allen during my Peace Corps volunteer service in Korea in 1969 is recounted in my memoir *The Time of the Monkey, Rooster, and Dog.*

The format of the graph and my scores on it resulted in a distinctive side-facing W, similar to the Greek letter Σ, known as the "Dartmouth W," that was characteristic of most of my classmates, I was told.

Part two of the profile (Cooperative Reading Test percentile ranks) reported my reading scores in terms of Dartmouth freshman percentile ranks (i.e., the percent of my classmates' scores below mine): Vocabulary–79; Speed of Comprehension–79; and Level of Comprehension–94. These results suggested that my strength relative to my classmates (if I had one) was in my reading skills.

Unrelated to the Strong Profile, each freshman met with Albert Dickerson, dean of freshman, toward the end of the spring term, to discuss academic progress, a possible major, and life in general. My second formal meeting with the dean (my first meeting was after my adventure on the previous Columbus Day weekend date with Sandi) was pleasant, although Dean Dickerson stated that he thought I was spreading myself too thin among my academic courses and extracurricular activities. I mentioned my illnesses (mononucleosis and measles) during the term and told him that I had given up crew in order to improve my grades, which seemed to satisfy him. When I mentioned that I would be working during the coming summer at the University of Uppsala in Sweden, Dean Dickerson said that he envied me and would join me if he could!

I also had ongoing regular meetings during my sophomore year with Dr. Arnold, my faculty adviser, who counseled me to not give up yet on my medical school aspirations but to give science one more chance. By the end of the year, however, as I have mentioned, I was so discouraged by chemistry that I threw in the towel.

In many ways, Pete Thomas was on a track parallel to my own. Pete was also a premed student and having problems similar to mine regarding chemistry courses. To his great credit, he completed the premed curriculum and went to dental school after graduation. Besides singing in the Glee Club, he played trombone in the Dartmouth College Band, as well as in the Barbary Coast, which was a student jazz ensemble. Pete was extroverted, a skilled musician, and a fine athlete, as well as having a fantastic sense of humor! We laughed a lot together, often at ourselves and at our obsessions. I also recall that he spent a tremendous amount of time polishing his car. We decided to be roommates again in our second year at Dartmouth. He was a great roommate, and I was very pleased.

Pete picked me up in Buffalo in his Austin Healy on September 4 and gave me a ride to Hanover. I was trying to get back to Dartmouth in time to lead one of the freshman trip's hikes up Mount Moosilauke. After about three hours on the New York Thruway, we heard a siren behind us. Pete had been very careful not to exceed the speed limit, so I was initially sure that the state trooper behind us was not intending to pull us over. But it soon became clear that the siren was meant for us! The trooper gave Pete a ticket for "driving on the left" and "not keeping right," which was an infraction I had never heard of before. The fine was ten dollars, and because Pete had an out-of-state license, we had to appear immediately before a justice of the peace in Syracuse and pay the fine (I contributed half). With this unexpected delay, I barely made it back in time to participate in the hikes.

For our sophomore year, we were assigned a dormitory room on the western outskirts of the campus in one of the newest dormitories (in the so-called Wigwam cluster), overlooking the river. Our first-floor suite of two rooms in the southernmost Wigwam (2 South Wigwam) had large windows looking west toward the Green Mountains across the river. Between the dormitory and the edge of the steep embankment dropping to the river was only about thirty feet. On the first floor were a common lounge area with a television and a fine ski-lodge-type room with curved couches surrounding a huge fireplace. Except for the isolation (we were at least one half mile from the Green—about a ten-minute walk), it was a great dormitory and room assignment!

We decided to each take one of the rooms. We flipped a coin for the first choice, and Pete won, taking the bedroom as his room. I had the living room, which had the slight disadvantage for privacy purposes of having the entrance to our suite in my room. Each room was about ten feet by ten feet and had a modern desk, desk chair, and lounge chair. My lounge chair was orange. The college had provided colorful curtains already. The room was fresh and clean. A common bathroom in each wing of the dormitory served us and twelve other students on our floor.

With the help of a dozen or so freshmen, we collected our trunks, purple rug, and other furnishings from various storage locations on campus and soon were comfortably moved in. We cut the rug in half, so we each had a lovely purple carpet in our half of the suite. On my walls, I hung a Navajo rug and the green curtains that Pete and I had bought at auction the year before. Pete had a couch that he bought at White River Junction for nine dollars, and we also had a bookcase-bar and a coffee table, both of which we made and varnished.

A lot of my friends were also assigned to the Wigwams. Amazingly, five of the Nine Freshmen with whom I sang in the Freshman Glee Club were in South Wigwam. Chuck Novi, '66 (whom I knew from East Aurora, New York), and classmates Bill Moore, Mike Gfroerer, Gene Tabor, Jim Schlough, and Don Wehrung were in Middle Wigwam. Classmate Craig Kerins, whom I had played high school football against when he was at Shadyside Academy, was in North Wigwam. Our hall mates included classmates Harry Cramer, from Chambersburg, Pennsylvania, and Mike Darby, who was from Dallas, Texas, which was the capital of the universe according to Mike's daily reports. Mike was an interesting guy; he was very wealthy, president of his family's company in Texas (which made pottery kilns), and engaged to a Mount Holyoke student, whom he flew down to South Hadley, Massachusetts, to see each weekend.

Shortly after convocation, fraternity rush week began for interested sophomores. Each night for most of one week in September, the Dartmouth fraternities opened their doors for sophomores to visit. The fraternity houses were spotless, drinks and hors d'oeuvres were served, and pretty hostesses (girlfriends of current members) welcomed sophomores. At each house, you registered as a visitor. Dartmouth had twenty-four fraternities in 1964: Alpha Chi Alpha, Alpha Delta Phi, Alpha Theta, Beta Theta Pi, Bones Gate, Chi Phi, Delta Kappa Epsilon, Delta Upsilon, Gamma Delta Chi, Kappa Kappa Kappa, Kappa Sigma, Phi Delta Alpha, Phi Gamma Delta, Phi Kappa Psi, Phi Tau, Pi Lamda Phi, Psi Upsilon, Sigma Alpha Epsilon, Sigma Nu Delta, Sigma Phi Epsilon, The Tabard, Tau Epsilon Phi, Theta Delta Chi, and Zeta Psi. Pete and I decided to participate in rush week, hoping that we would be invited to join a fraternity, more for social outlet reasons than anything else.

We both visited at least a dozen houses during rush week. Pete decided he wanted to rush Chi Phi, which was located across from Alumni Gymnasium on East Wheelock, and happily was invited to join. I settled on three fraternities: Kappa Kappa Kappa, Alpha Theta, and Phi Kappa Psi. A lot of Tri-Kap's members and Alpha Theta's members were in the Glee Club, and I knew several members of Phi Kappa Psi from the Outing Club. My brother had also been a member of Phi Psi.

I was ultimately invited to join all three houses and selected Tri-Kap for several reasons. First, I liked the four brothers who were singing with me in the Glee Club, one of whom was the new president of Tri-Kap: Stephen L. Coles, '66, Robert E. Cowden, '66, Harry (Terry) M. Lowd III, '66, and Robert Y. Justis, '65 (Tri-Kap President). Chan Newton, '65, whom I have mentioned I met on the channel crossing just weeks before, was also a Tri-Kap brother, as was an extremely nice foreign student from Norway—Steinar Kottum—whom I had worked with at the Dining Association. The other members also seemed very likeable.

Second, I liked the Tri-Kap house itself, which was both impressive and comfortable. Tri-Kap's location was superb. It was the first fraternity on Webster Avenue (1 Webster Avenue), right on the corner at the top of Fraternity Row—the closest fraternity to Baker Library.

Finally, I liked the fact that Tri-Kap was the oldest local fraternity in the United States—founded in 1842, the second-oldest fraternity at Dartmouth, and the sole fraternity that specifically espoused the principles of democracy, loyalty to Dartmouth, and equality of opportunity. The last fact was brought to my attention during pledge week by a Tri-Kap alumnus whom I met during my visit. He was New Hampshire Supreme Court Justice Amos N. Blandin Jr. '18, and he looked like the quintessential Supreme Court justice with his wavy white hair and bushy eyebrows that gave him an extremely jurisprudential appearance. I was very impressed by his kindness and obvious devotion to Tri-Kap in that he had taken the time to come to Hanover from the state capital—Concord—during rush week.

The only downside to Kappa Kappa Kappa was the Greek letter for "Kappa." KKK definitely had a negative connotation. But after all, the Dartmouth fraternity had the name and the Greek letters a quarter of a century before the first Latin letters KKK appeared in connection with the white supremacist organization.

Twenty other 1967s joined me in becoming members of Kappa Kappa Kappa: William R. Bogardus, Duncan S. Ballantyne, Henry A. Budd Jr., David C. Davenport Jr., Philip N. Davey, William C. Doran, Robert Evans, William F. Fell Jr., Nathaniel Fuller, Albert C. Hine III, Michael Jones, Steven

G. Kurtz, William C. MacCarty, Jeff E. Maynard, William L. McCague Jr., David R. McMahill, Frederick J. Moore, Stanley E. Neill Jr., Richard D. Sellers, and William A. White III. Thomas E. Nelson III, Michael W. Seely, and Edward H. Truex IV later joined our 1967 Tri-Kaps. It was a great group of 1967s!

On the first and second weekends in October, the autumn colors of New Hampshire's glorious sugar maples, oaks, and other deciduous trees were at their peak at Dartmouth. On all sides of the Upper Valley of the Connecticut River were incredible ribbons of red, orange, and yellow woven amongst the green pines, balsams, spruces, and firs on the rolling foothills of the White Mountains. Pete and I climbed Mount Moosilauke—up and down in six hours—to savor the incomparable autumn colors. We also both spent long hours in the wood workshop in the basement of the Hopkins Center, crafting our ornate fraternity pledge paddles.

Janis Terry was my date for the homecoming festivities on the third of October. I still felt a very strong affection for Jan, despite my summer girlfriends in Sweden. She came up from Pembroke College, where she had just enrolled as a freshman. We had a fine weekend together, enjoying the first of the several autumn bonfires on the Green and the Glee Club's songs at Dartmouth Night (my first event as a member of the Varsity Glee Club).

As the brothers of Tri-Kap drove 120 miles north to Mount Washington very early on Saturday morning of the following weekend, our several cars cruised for two hours through scenery of indescribably exquisite colors and spectacular mountains. We were on our way to climb the highest peak in the northeastern United States (6,288 feet), where over 150 people have died in the past two centuries.[41] It would be my twelfth ascent of this majestic and often dangerous mountain.

Our group climb began at Pinkham Notch at the base of the massive Tuckerman Ravine. About twenty of us scrambled up the relatively steep trail that took us across the Cutler River on an old bridge then past a lovely waterfall after about one half mile—Crystal Cascade—and then upward to the base of the glacial cirque on the southeast side of the mountain. As we climbed, the trees became shorter and sparser, virtually disappearing as we reached the base of the headwall of the ravine and scrambled up the rockslides to its top. Amazingly striking views of Wildcat Mountain and Carter Notch, as well as of the cliffs of the Boott Spur to the south of us, opened up above tree line. It was a short hike from there to a convergence of trails on the shoulder of Mount Washington called Tuckerman Junction, where from a boulder-strewn landscape we could see miles across the majestic purple ranges of the White Mountains and the crimson valleys below.

Luckily, the weather was perfect. It was a sunny, mild day with almost no wind. The last half mile to the summit of Mount Washington led us onto a section of the AT that climbed upward to our goal. It became noticeably cooler as we got closer to the top. We broke out our parkas for the first time and were grateful that the hundred-mile-per-hour winds for which Mount Washington is famous were

---

[41]   Nicholas Howe, *Not Without Peril* (Guilford, CN: Globe Pequot Press, 2009).

not present as we celebrated the successful ascent. The entire climb took us about four and one half hours up an approximately four-mile-long trail, climbing 4,280 feet. After resting, we turned around and made a quick hike down the same route, making it to Highway 16 at Pinkham Notch in about three and one half hours. This was the first of many memorable hikes that my Tri-Kap brothers and I took together in the next three years in New Hampshire's ancient White Mountains.

Only one week later, Pete had heard so much from me about the climb of Mount Washington that we decided to drive north and to go up to the summit in his open Austin Healy on the so-called Auto Road or Carriage Road, which was built around the time of the Civil War. The narrow dirt road starts at the Glen House on state Route 16 at an elevation of 1,600 feet and winds slowly and torturously up twelve miles to the summit. It was seventy degrees and sunny at the start of the climb when we paid the seven-dollar fee and started up. At the top, it was eight degrees with zero visibility in the swirling clouds and eighty-mile-per-hour winds blowing a few flakes of snow around. After parking Pete's car, we had dinner in the Mount Washington Observatory with one of the men I knew there from my summers working for the AMC on nearby Mount Madison. Then in the dark and cold, we tried to start Pete's car, which was reluctant to show any signs of life. After ten minutes of fiddling and praying, the Austin Healy coughed into action, and we made it safely down the mountain and back to Hanover.

Just after we arrived, we heard the startling news that President Dickey had issued a statement of endorsement of Lyndon Johnson in the ongoing, controversial 1964 presidential election campaign. Senator Barry Goldwater—an ultraconservative Republican—was opposing President Lyndon Johnson. John Sloan Dickey may be fairly characterized as a staunch Republican and an unofficial leader of the Republican Party in New England. He had never before publicly endorsed any candidate for election, so his endorsement of a Democrat was astonishing news!

I was so amazed that I immediately thought the story was another fabrication of the *Dartmouth* in one of its bogus editions, like the February 4, 1964, edition ("All the news that's pfft we print."). That hilarious edition had the preposterous front-page headline "College Becomes Co-educational; Female Students Arrive This Fall," a byline on the front page stating "State Health Service Threatens To Force Thayer Hall's Closure," and a lead story on the last page crowing "Basketball Team Wins National Championship; Sixty Points In Last Half Defeats UCLA."

As enjoyable as the two October weekends had been on Mount Washington, the next weekend was even more wonderful! Stan Brown, Pete, and I reprised our 1963 road trip to Boston, staying again with Stan's parents in Lexington, Massachusetts. We spent the evening sampling the homemade mead, wine, cider, and beer that Professor Brown had concocted in his cellar. On Saturday, Pete and I had blind dates from Lasell Junior College arranged by Kathy Shed (a girl from East Aurora, New York, with whom I worked during my summers with the AMC). Our dates were a lot of fun!

On Saturday afternoon, we all attended the Harvard-Dartmouth football game in Cambridge. The game—which Harvard was favored to win—was simply amazing! Before thirty-two thousand fans in the stadium and twenty million television viewers, Dartmouth crushed Harvard, 48–0! It was the worst defeat in Harvard's history. The Johns only crossed the fifty-yard line once during the entire game. At halftime Dartmouth led 35–0, so our second team took the field with classmate Mickey Beard at quarterback. Mickey was fabulous enough to be named the sophomore player of the week by the Associated Press for leading Dartmouth to two more touchdowns!

After the game, we took our dates to the Dartmouth postgame reception, which was a wonderful victory celebration, and then to an AMC reunion on Beacon Hill, where I reconnected with many old crewmates from my White Mountain summers on Mount Madison. Both were the sort of parties where everyone is so deliriously happy that they go around kissing and hugging everyone else. They were two of the best parties I ever attended!

The postrush month involved a lot of activities at Tri-Kap. We had several dinners to welcome the new pledges, a movie night, and a program of pictures (slides) regarding my 1961 summer in the Arctic National Wildlife Refuge in Alaska's Brooks Range. There were also some unexpected attempts to kidnap me and Pete by our respective new fraternity brothers for purposes of hazing us.

I was visiting Mike Darby next door in South Wigwam when the first attempt to kidnap me occurred. We heard a commotion in the hallway outside of Pete's and my room, peered out, and, seeing ten Tri-Kap brothers in the hallway, locked Mike's door until the freshmen in South Wigwam had tossed my brothers out of the dormitory and secured the area.

The second time, Pete and I had just finished fortifying the door to our room by placing two-by-fours across it with much hammering and nailing. My four fraternity brothers' attempts to break down the door were futile, and the noise alerted South Wigwam's rescue troops, who soon expelled them.

The third and last time, I was walking with my new pledge brother Sandy McCague around Occom Pond, just before Halloween. We had just passed the Outing Club Lodge and were heading back along the west side road. Five brothers had apparently been tracking us. As soon as we saw them, Sandy and I took off, separating to sow some confusion. I sprinted several blocks to the safety of Baker Library, easily outrunning my brothers. Sandy disappeared and later told me that he had been captured.

In most cases, the hazing was little more than dropping a pledge off somewhere distant from campus and making him walk back to Hanover. I escaped any such indignity! And I also missed a group hazing—better left not described—that I heard took place one night at the fraternity house. But at the Tri-Kap Halloween costume party later that week, I felt that I needed to smooth the feelings of any brothers disappointed by my escapes, so I concocted an elaborate costume and appeared as a six-foot condom. My costume won the prize for best costume, as the brotherhood debated whether my costume was too small to fit any of them.

Shortly after Halloween, I had my first experience with a computer. On December 6, I stopped by the Kiewit Computing Center, located just to the north of Baker Library, and encountered the Dartmouth Time-Sharing System. Two professors in the Mathematics Department—John Kemeny and Thomas Kurtz—had developed and implemented the time-sharing system with the goal of providing easy access to computing facilities for faculty and students alike. We were told that this was a revolutionary system, among the first of its type in the world. It had been switched on earlier in the year. Several classmates in the Wigwams reported that the computer could tell you what your perfect mate would be like. I thought that I had better try it.

I was directed to sit down at what was called a computer terminal, which had a teleprinter that printed information, instructions, and results on a ream of yellow paper, which you tore off to read. After pushing a button, I received the following information:

THIS UNIQUE PROGRAM IS THE ULTIMATE IN FEMALE PROPORTIONING AND DESIGN. THE POTENTIAL GIRL WITH WHOM THE USER SHALL BE ASSOCIATED OUGHT BEST BE CONSIDERED WHENEVER THE MIND ROAMS FREELY INTO THE NEBULOUS WORLD OF DREAMLAND. SHE IS, IN SHORT, THE PERFECT GIRL.

DATA REQUIRED IN STEP 100 IS THE USER'S AGE, HEIGHT, WEIGHT, HAIR COLOR (1=BLACK, 2=BROWN, 3=LIGHT, 4=RED), EYE COLORING (1=BLACK, 2=BROWN, 3=HAZEL, 4=BLUE), AND AN ESTIMATE OF HIS PERSONALITY (0 TO 15: ABSOLUTE INTROVERT TO ABSOLUTE EXTROVERT) – IN THAT ORDER.

EXPLANATION OF THE VARIOUS BREAST MEASUREMENTS IS AS FOLLOWS: CLEAVAGE IS THE DISTANCE FROM NIPPLE TO NIPPLE IN MILIMETERS, BOUYANCY IS THE PERCENTAGE OF BREAST THAT WILL FLOAT WHEN THE NIPPLE IS AT WATER SURFACE LEVEL, AND HUMPHRIES EQUALS MOUTHFULS PER BREAST.

BEST OF LUCK.

I typed the requested information about myself on the terminal's keyboard and pushed the "run" button. The system printed out the following:

BROAD	19:08	6 DEC., 1964	
BUST	WAIST	HIPS	HEIGHT
33	24	32	64
AGE	FACE	PERSONALITY	INTELLIGENCE
17	… 10	12	12

TOO SMALL AN ASS. TELL HER TO SIT MORE.

SHE'LL DO.
  SCORE   81   PERCENT SEXY
TIME: 1 SECS.
AND THEN I RECEIVED ANOTHER RESULT:

A PERSONALIZED LITTLE WOMAN, ALL YOURS IF YOU CAN EVER FIND HER ...
BUILT TO YOUR DIMENSIONS.
** * * COMMENTS * * * *
LONG, BLONDE HAIR
HER EYES ARE BLUE-GREEN

BUST	CLEAVAGE	BUOYANCY	HUMPHRIES
37 IN.	205.1 MM.	44.1 P/C	4 M/F
WAIST	HIPS	HEIGHT	
24 IN.	37 IN.	68 IN.	
AGE	WEIGHT	VIVACIOUSNESS	
17 YR.	123 LB.	LIVELY	

THIS GIRL WAS DESIGNED ESPECIALLY FOR YOU
BY THE DARTMOUTH COLLEGE COMPUTER.
NO PROGRAM
TIME: 3 SECS.

I never figured out why I received two printouts with differing information about my "perfect girl," or understood some of the computer's statistical information or technical language, such as "buoyancy" and "humphries," and never found a woman who matched the design. (My confusion regarding this first experience with a computer has persisted with respect to my relationships with computers to this day.) I did, however, find women in the future—in particular, my wife—who were far better than what the computer designed!

In December, I made the decision to apply for Dartmouth's foreign study program after further discussions with Professors Gaudin and Richard Regosin of the French Department. Studying in France seemed as though it would be a worthwhile challenge, especially since I had not yet been to France and wanted to put my fairly fluent French to use there. I was tremendously enjoying my French classes with Professor Gaudin and doing well enough that I was hopeful my overall grade point average might improve.

The most difficult part of the application was writing a letter of introduction in French to the prospective French family with whom I might be living in the autumn of 1965, describing my American family, my interests, Dartmouth, and my hopes for the future. I also wrote that I was looking forward tremendously to getting to know them (although no matching of students with families would occur until September, so I had no idea who the family would be).

Over the Christmas holidays in Buffalo, I managed to get a temporary job as a mail carrier with the

US Postal Service, thanks to the influence of our longtime mailman in Buffalo, Art Markwardt. My work, starting at six o'clock each morning, entailed both sorting and then delivering thousands of Christmas cards and packages! In three weeks of lugging Christmas mail, I got to know most of the residents of a five-square-block area between our home on Buffalo's west side and the Niagara River. It was hard work, but it paid very well, and I enjoyed it tremendously! I had the same route over the Christmas holiday vacations of the next three years.

During the month of January, I spent a lot of time at the Skiway despite a cold spell that sent temperatures plummeting. In mid-January, I walked to my DDA job through a dark, snowy morning with a temperature of minus twenty-nine degrees! Bob Ramage, whom I have previously mentioned was my best high school friend, drove up from Yale to spend a weekend skiing with me, which we both enjoyed a lot, despite the bitter cold.

In the middle of the cold snap, one late afternoon at Thayer Dining Hall the fire alarm went off about a quarter to five. Within seconds, cascades of water began falling from sprinklers in the sophomore dining room where I was working as a substitute for a friend. A valve had blown out in the fire-sprinkler system, we were later told, setting off the alarm and the ceiling sprinklers in this one dining hall. There were at least six inches of water on the floor before the fire department arrived and turned the system off. We spent the rest of the evening manning pumps, mopping up the water, and drying furniture! I recall that a letter from Anna in Sweden, which I was carrying in my pocket, was one of the casualties of the downpour.

The theme of Winter Carnival in 1965 was "The Call of the Wild." The statue in the center of the college green was a standing wolf with a beer keg under one leg. Every dormitory and fraternity was also supposed to have a statue reflecting the theme. At Tri-Kap, after much deliberation among the brothers, a statue was sculpted of ice depicting two deer with crossed necks, entitled "Dear Harts." I don't recall that South Wigwam had a statue, since few people on campus ever came out to the campus fringe except for the Wigwam residents.

My date for Winter Carnival was a girl from Wells College in Aurora, New York, who was the daughter of one of my mother's good friends. Marty was a fine date, notwithstanding being under the curse of my mother's strong approval. The Glee Club's concert on carnival weekend was especially impressive, and Marty seemed to enjoy it, as well as the pajama party, great band, and dancing at Tri-Kap after the concert. We also watched the ski jumping and screamed ourselves hoarse as Dartmouth's hockey team creamed Yale 8–4, despite Yale goals by my former high school classmates Warren Gelman and Jack Walsh. It was a superb weekend!

In a last-ditch effort to tackle chemistry, I worked with a student tutor recommended by Professor Bowen in the Chemistry Department during the winter term. The student with the highest chemistry grades in the department over the past two years was a junior named Dick Jones, who had worked with me in the AMC Hut System in 1962 and sang bass with me in the Glee Club. Dick took me under his wing for the term (charging me only half the usual price for tutoring), but I ended up with a D in organic chemistry despite our combined best efforts.

On successive weekends in April, I hiked with Tri-Kap brothers and dates to several of the Dartmouth Outing Club's cozy cabins in the Hanover vicinity. These were typically accessible by a relatively short hike and were very simply constructed, one- or two-room structures of logs with an outside covered porch and an outhouse. Kerosene lanterns provided light, and a fireplace and wood stove furnished heat and the possibility of cooking hotdogs or hamburgers for dinner and scrambled eggs and sausage for breakfast. Often the cabins were located on a lake, such as Lake Armington, or at a site with a fine view. My favorite cabins were Hinman Cabin on Reservoir Pond, the nearby Fred Harris Cabin on the side of Moose Mountain, the Summit Cabin on the top of Mount Moosilauke, and Armington.

I loved the Outing Club! Its hikes and facilities were awesome. Crisp, cool air, exquisite sunsets, the murmur of the wind through the pines, and the luxury of simple living in a wilderness setting were matchless gifts presented to us all by the DOC's cabins. Not unimportantly, our dates usually loved these excursions … I always returned from a weekend at a DOC cabin spiritually refreshed and physically energized.

Another part of the DOC—the Ledyard Canoe Club—made canoes available for all students who wished to glide silently through New Hampshire's transcendent beauty on the Connecticut or on other rivers, lakes, or ponds. On several occasions, I took dates on canoe rides downstream from the Ledyard Bridge about one half mile to Gilman Island in the middle of the Connecticut River, where we camped at Titcomb Cabin—another favorite DOC cabin. In the spring, these short canoe trips were especially memorable, as you glided between banks filled with emerging ferns and the soft green of budding hardwoods. More than any other place in the Upper Valley, this cabin always prompted me to wonder about the bridge's namesake.

John Ledyard, a Dartmouth student in 1772, reportedly left Dartmouth from a spot near the crossing of the AT and the river in a dugout canoe, which he paddled to the Atlantic Ocean. His audacious departure from Dartmouth presaged his incredible future voyages with Captain Cook to the Hawaiian Islands and his treks thereafter around the world, including across Siberia. Although he was apparently only a Dartmouth student for several months, I was sure that his wanderlust was birthed on the Hanover plain. In an annual tribute to Ledyard each spring, Canoe Club members paddled two hundred miles down the river, riding April and May's surging waters from Hanover to Old Saybrook, Connecticut, at the mouth of the Connecticut. This trip was one of the many I regret that I did not experience during my college years.

By Green Key Weekend in May, my relationship with Marty had ended, so I invited an old friend from elementary school in Buffalo to visit me. Christine Benzow was a very smart sophomore at Cornell whom I had grown up with. She was almost like a sister, but I had always admired her red hair and trim figure in a not-so-familial way. She was fun, pretty, and a girl I felt no need to impress because she knew me so well. To my astonishment, we had a wonderful, romantic weekend together in the flush of spring's intoxicating spirit of rebirth and abandon.

The next weekend, I felt an urge to head north to Pinkham Notch at the base of Mount Washington, where I indulged in a weekend of partying with former AMC colleagues at the AMC's Pinkham Notch Camp there. Several dozen of us worked off our hangovers on Sunday morning by hiking a few miles up the icy Tuckerman Ravine Trail to admire the snow bridge at the headwall of the ravine, enjoying the warmth of the sun reflecting off the snow-filled ravine, where snow often lingered until midsummer.

At the end of the term, my French 21 seminar required a five- to ten-minute oral presentation in French about one of the novels we had read during the course. The presentations were recorded the first week in June. I was so nervous that I forgot the name of the book I was reviewing! But Professor Gaudin gave me high marks for my organization, grammar, and pronunciation, so I got a B on the presentation—highest in the class—and in the course. It was a good way to end my sophomore year.

In early June, I also attended a five-hour-long presentation about the foreign study program. I would be participating in the Experiment in International Living's home-stay program in the autumn while studying at the University of Montpellier in southern France with ten other classmates. We listened to presentations from the dozen or so students who had participated in the French program in 1963–64 and were very impressed with their stories and great passion for their experiences.

I also completed arrangements to take the Experiment's charter flight to Europe in late June from the Windsor Locks airport in Connecticut (Bradley International Airport). In March, brother John had invited me to return to Sweden to work with him again during the coming summer, making me deliriously happy! It would be great to work at the Limnological Institute, live with John and Olivann, and enjoy another European summer before going to France! I was still writing to Anna and to Staffan in Uppsala, and although I did not expect to resume with Anna the passion of the previous summer, I was looking forward to seeing her, Staffan, other Swedish friends, and my brother's family once more.

The Glee Club's spring vacation trip had been glorious, my first year as a member of Kappa Kappa Kappa had been very rewarding, and otherwise I had enjoyed my sophomore year enormously. I ended the term on a very high note, as I looked forward to foreign adventures in Sweden and in France in the next six months.

Brothers Bill George, '66, Graham Gerade, '65, Bob Justis, '65, Paul
Doscher, '66, Terry Lowd, '66, Tony Dambrava, '68 and dates at
dinner at Kappa Kappa Kappa fraternity house, October 1964

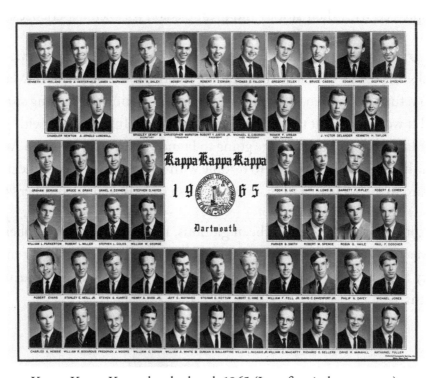

Kappa Kappa Kappa brotherhood, 1965 (I am first in bottom row);
photo courtesy of Fraternal Composite Service, Inc.

Tri-Kap brothers and Glee Club members during Glee Club
tour: Jim Mullins, '69, Dave Peck, '68, Hampton Rich, '69,
Eric Jones, '68, unknown alumnus, Mike Hermann, '69,
Loren Lortscher, '69, and Frank Couper, '68, April 1967

Tri-Kap brothers Phil Davey, '67, Chan Newton, '66, and Bill White, '67
at Moosilauke Ravine Lodge, January 1965

Tri-Kap Christmas party with brother Daniel Zehner, '66 as
Santa Claus with children patients at Mary Hitchcock Hospital and
brothers Sandy McCague, '67, and Bill Fell, '67, December 1964

Kappa Kappa Kappa brotherhood, 1966 (I am second from right in
fourth row from top); photo courtesy of Fraternal Composite Service, Inc.

Judy Castor, Al Hine, '67, with date, and Bill Hoyt, '68, with date,
on the Moosilauke Road, April 1966

Janis Terry, June 1964

Party at Kappa Kappa Kappa with Eric
Jones, '68, Ralph Woodman, '69, Ron
Weiss, '67, and dates, October 1966

Kappa Kappa Kappa brotherhood, 1967 (I am top row, third from left);
photo courtesy of Fraternal Composite Service, Inc.

Robert Lynn, '69, Ralph Woodman, '69, and Mike O'Connor, '68, at
Tri-Kap reception for parents, November 1966

Al Hine, '67, Dick Sellers, '67, and Hal Budd, '67, at a
Tri-Kap dinner, April 1967

CHAPTER 10—"TRI-KAP MARCHING"

As a pledge in Kappa Kappa Kappa, I was required to read a book that set forth the history of the fraternity and famous alumni of Tri-Kap. I recall very little about what I read in that book, except that Tri-Kap's first house was located where the Hopkins Center now stands, and that alumni and honorary alumni of our fraternity included many former dignitaries: four congressmen, six senators, seven governors, two United States ambassadors, a United States Supreme Court justice, a presidential nominee, and secretaries of the Departments of Treasury and State. Pledges were obliged to recite historical facts about Tri-Kap, and insufficient information was punishable by whacks on the bottom from your pledge paddle.

The whackers in 1965 were seniors Peter R. Akley; R. Bruce Cassel; Michael G. Ciborski (vice president); J. Victor Delander; Bradley Dewey III; Thomas D. Falcon; Geofrey J. Greenleaf; Mosby Harvey; Edgar Hirst; Kenneth C. Ireland; Robert Y. Justis Jr. (president); A. Arnold Lundwall; James L. Markman; Christopher Marsten (treasurer); Chandler Newton; David A. Osterheld; Kenneth H. Taylor; Gregory Telek; Roger F. Urban (rush chairman); and Robert P. Ziemian. My brothers in the class of 1966, equally prone to whacking, were Stephen L. Coles; Robert E. Cowden; Paul F. Doscher; Bruce H. Drake; William W. George; Graham Gerade; Robin G. Haile; Stephen D. Hayes; Rock B. Ley; Harry M. Lowd III; Robert L. Miller; William L. Parkerton; Barrett F. Ripley; Parker B. Smith; Robert M. Spence; and Daniel A. Zehner.

I became quite close friends with several of my brothers during my sophomore year and in subsequent years. Tri-Kap's members were outstanding—I liked every brother (at least until my senior year when an older brother, new to Tri-Kap, tried to prohibit some nonmember friends from frequenting our fraternity's events. Happily, he was unsuccessful in the face of the brotherhood's overwhelming affirmation of the principles of inclusiveness and equal opportunity when I demanded a vote.) The best part about belonging to a fraternity was the opportunity to get to know brothers who were either ahead of my class or in later classes. The Glee Club also promoted friendships with members of different classes. I had friends in the Wigwams, but after freshman year, most of my social activities centered around, and involved members of, either Tri-Kap or the Glee Club.

The fraternity house itself was a significant focus of my Dartmouth life, although I never lived in the house. As I have mentioned, its address was 1 Webster Avenue. The house faced south from its location on the north side of Webster Avenue. As you looked at from the sidewalk running east-west on Webster, it looked like a three-story brick house of imposing dimensions with a front patio in front of series of three French doors that opened from the living room onto the patio. It was three times the size of a normal Colonial-style brick house in Hanover.

You entered Tri-Kap through an impressive circular portico with six pillars. A large hallway by the front door opened to the right into a large living room with a lovely fireplace at the far end. On the hallway's right wall as you entered was a large portrait of the earl of Dartmouth. To the left of the hallway was a smaller room with a fireplace, called the library, off of which on the front side of the house was a small guest bedroom reserved for visiting alumni. The library was lined with bookshelves of old books and served as a repository of Tri-Kaps's historic documents and artifacts. On the first level, the floors were hardwood floors, somewhat the worse for wear from decades of use by young men and women.

At the far end of the hallway, a staircase on the right led downstairs to the basement level. The left stairs led upstairs to brothers' rooms and bathrooms on the second floor. From the second floor, a narrow stair led to the third floor's rooms, including several bedrooms and the "GOTE" where fraternity meetings were held in a sort of secret room lined with pictures of past Tri-Kap classes of brothers.

In the basement, there were three large rooms and a little kitchen. To the right or west side of the descending stairs (under the upstairs library) was a room with a fireplace and comfortable chairs and couches for lounging. To the left or east of the stairs was a huge, wood-paneled room with billiard and Ping-Pong tables, a bar with a large mirror behind, and built-in seats around the walls. On the south side of this large room was the imposing bar, from which beverages were doled out in massive quantities on party weekends, especially Dartmouth Night and homecoming in the autumn, Winter Carnival in the winter, and Green Key Weekend in the spring. The basement always smelled a bit of stale beer, despite the repeated mopping of the linoleum tile floor by the pledges.

To the left of the bar area, in the southeast corner of the basement, was the television room, also known as the "pit." It had a number of couches and mattresses arranged for comfortable viewing of the large TV at one end, as well as for relaxed engagement of other activities best performed on comfy surfaces. I don't recall that I ever saw a light in the "pit" in my half-dozen or so ventures into it with a date.

Tri-Kap was a superb place to go just to relax on a weeknight after a tough day of studying. It was also close enough to Baker Library, where I usually spent long hours daily in my favorite study spot high in the stacks, that I could break up the stress of studying or writing by a two-minute walk to the fraternity for a quick game of pool or Ping-Pong. There was always a brother available for a game.

On weekends with a date, or even on weeknights, the fraternity house presented a social venue where dinners, guest lectures by faculty, pre and postgame singing parties, and dance parties provided outstanding entertainment in a comfortable, intimate setting. Typically, our dinners were spaghetti, garlic bread, and salad repasts, with ice cream for dessert, served on long tables set up in the living room. You could easily seat thirty or more brothers and their dates at these events. Sometimes, they were formal events—"tails parties"—with dark suits and white linen tablecloths. More often the dress and table arrangements were informal. Sometimes we invited faculty speakers, or current or alumni brothers, to make presentations.

I recall that at the first fraternity dinner I attended, Professor Harold (Harry) L. Bond, '42, who was a Tri-Kap alumnus, faculty adviser to our fraternity, and chairman of the English Department, gave an excellent presentation after dinner regarding the Romantic Period in English literature, reading and explaining poems by Blake, Wordsworth, Coleridge, Byron, Shelley, and Keats. Professor Bond was both humorous and risqué!

In 1966, after he had won the Pulitzer Prize for poetry, Professor Richard Eberhart, '26, of the English Department was an after-dinner speaker, reading from his prize-winning collection of poems—*Selected Poems*, and generally discussing contemporary American poets and their poems. He was considered one of the foremost lyric poets of the twentieth century, and although I was at the time in one his classes and had often enjoyed his readings, it was always thrilling to hear him read poetry and discuss his life.

Another faculty visitor to Tri-Kap was Professor James Sykes of the Music Department. He presented a marvelous, condensed version of masterpieces of the Western music tradition, playing (on Tri-Kap's old upright piano) excerpts of works by Bach, Beethoven, Chopin, Verdi, and other great composers and explaining the evolution of the tradition. It was a hugely enjoyable evening of music.

Math professor John Kemeny, who had previously been an assistant to Albert Einstein at Princeton University, talked to us about the Kiewit Center, computers, and *Star Trek* (a television series that had just begun to air). He was a spellbinding speaker (later president of Dartmouth 1970–81) and made the absurd prediction that one day we would each have a handheld device with more computing capacity than the huge computer occupying the entire building known as the Kiewit Center.

Dean Thaddeus Seymour also spoke at a dinner. He later highly commended Tri-Kap at a weekend meeting at our fraternity house of the fraternity corporation officers, reportedly stating: "We are pleased to be able to hold this meeting here because we feel that Tri-Kap is a model house. A model not only in its physical condition, but also in all of its support from the alumni."[42] The dean also remarked that if all the houses could follow our example, there would never be a need to be concerned about any of the fraternities.[43]

Several other professors from the History, Psychology, Government, and Geology Departments joined us during my three years of Tri-Kap dinners. My favorite and the most fun presentation, however, was totally unexpected. A new associate English professor named Alan Gaylord gave a reading of

---

[42] *Kappa Kappa Kappa Newsletter,* May 1966, p. 2.

[43] Ibid., 3.

excerpts from Chaucer's *The Canterbury Tales* in Middle English, explaining the historical and literary context and significance. Readings in Middle English from Chaucer as entertainment? Knowing his audience, Professor Gaylord focused on the ribald aspects of the tales. As he read, he played the roles of each of the characters to our great delight and raucous laughter. Professor Gaylord was a fine actor and a great teacher!

There were also many memorable dances in the living room of the Tri-Kap house. On most big weekends, we had a band on Saturday night and sometimes on Friday night as well. I recall many dance parties with themes, such as a Halloween masked party, several Roman toga parties, pajama parties, and several square dances. The noise level at these dances was always deafening! Tri-Kap had a reputation for great parties, and many students who were not members participated in our dance parties and other activities because of it. That was a wonderful aspect of the fraternity system at Dartmouth—any student (except a freshman) was welcome to attend a social event at any fraternity—usually at little or no cost—and to drink, dance, or otherwise party to their heart's content. On several occasions, in fact, my dates and I ended up at other fraternities' parties when the music at Tri-Kap was too loud or the dance floor too crowded.

We also periodically held mixers with groups of girls from particular dormitories or sororities at other colleges. Sometimes we would jointly sponsor such an event with another nearby fraternity. On two occasions, I arranged for a square dance caller from Lebanon to come to the house to "call" square dances at mixers with the idea that it would be easier to meet girls and to get to know them in the less formal setting of a square dance.

At least one faculty couple, or sometimes an older alumnus and his wife, attended each of Tri-Kip's parties and dances. Our professors and their spouses were always welcome, of course, but we made an effort to invite certain faculty members and alumni to each house event to serve as *de facto* chaperones. I don't think that the college required this arrangement, but I thought at the time that it was a good idea.

The town of Hanover had no nightclubs, drinking establishments (it was a dry town), or dance venues other than the fraternity houses, so young and old faculty members enjoyed the chance for a night out in a relaxed and free social context. Additionally, the campus or town police were less likely to intrude on a party, searching for underage drinkers, if a Dartmouth faculty member, or an alumnus such as Supreme Court Justice Blandin, was in attendance.

I also recall with great fondness the sing-along parties at the house. On the evening before a big football, basketball, hockey, or other important game after the rally was over, or in celebration of a victory, alumni and brothers gathered at Tri-Kap to drink beer and to sing. Alumni whom I remember at these parties include Amos Blandin, '29, H. Hamilton (Ham) Chase, '47, Joe d'Esopo, '29, Jim Varnum, '62, Roger Wilde, '21, Charlie Widmayer, '30, Phil McGinnis, '36, and Jake Bingham, '18. Several alumni and brothers were excellent piano players and banged out familiar songs—Dartmouth songs in particular—on the upright piano, I have previously mentioned. The "Tri-Kap Marching Song" was always a favorite:

> We're Tri-Kap marching, here we go forward men!
> We're Tri-Kap singing, lift up your voice again!
> Marching along together, singing a song forever,
> To Dartmouth and to Kappa two in one forever!
> We're Tri-Kap marching, here we go forward men!
> We're Tri-Kap singing, lift up your voice again!
> Marching along together, singing a song forever,
> Hurrah for the pillar and the shield!

Another favorite was the "chug" song—an inducement to someone to chug his or her beer:

> Here's to [insert last name], he's true blue,
> He's a Tri-Kap through and through,
> He's a bastard so they say,
> He tried to go to heaven but he went the other way.
> So drink, chug-a-lug, chug-a-lug, chug-a-lug,
> Drink, drink, drink!

These sing-alongs would go on for hours and were tremendously fun! At least a half dozen of the brotherhood were members of the Glee Club, so the singing was quite passable.

Occasionally, our party weekends were held at the Moosilauke Ravine Lodge about fifty miles northeast of Dartmouth at the base of Mount Moosilauke. I have already mentioned this mountain and the lodge in telling about my camping experiences at Camp Jobildunc. Built in 1935 of huge spruce logs culled from the mountainside, the lodge was an imposing structure with spacious windows facing northwest and overlooking the Baker River and Mts. Moosilauke and Blue beyond.

The main building had a spacious common room and grand stone fireplace on the second floor with open outside balconies on each side. On one side of the common room was a small inside balcony accessible by narrow steps. On the opposite side was a two-story-high bank of windows providing gorgeous views of the mountains. Beyond the open outside balcony on the south side were a number of small bunkrooms, each with a second floor and each accommodating about a dozen people. On the north side was a kitchen and additional small bunkrooms.

On the first floor at ground level was the main entrance on the southwest side from which you entered a "ski room" and then a lobby with a large fireplace. Restrooms and showers were also located on this level. Underneath the stairs ascending to the second-floor common room was a linen closet in which blankets were stored on two large shelves. Underneath the kitchen area was a cellar with an old, temperamental oil furnace that provided steam heat to the lodge.

To the north of the main lodge snugly situated in a spruce grove was the Nate Emerson bunkhouse, which accommodated about fifty people in bunk beds three levels high. This bunkhouse had electricity but no running water or heat. Between the main lodge and the Emerson bunkhouse was a small structure, used for the crew's quarters, called the "Honeymoon Cottage" because a newly married couple that were crewmembers in the past had stayed there.

The lodge had been used historically as a ski lodge for both college students and members of the public. A number of ski trails were easily accessible by foot on the nearby slopes of Mount Moosilauke, and a small rope tow just beyond the Emerson bunkhouse had once been used to facilitate use of a ski slope for beginners nearby. During the 1950s and 1960s, the lodge was run by student crews and was only open to the public for meals and lodging during the summers. The rest of the year it could be used by members of the Dartmouth Outing Club for events or reserved by fraternities for weekends.

Of course, in early September it was used as a camp for the freshman trips. In the common room with a fire blazing in the hearth freshmen were told stories of Dartmouth's past, taught songs, and first greeted by college officials and faculty. For many students, as a result, Moosilauke Ravine Lodge was their first impression of Dartmouth and the venue in which they first met classmates and faculty—a special place.

One of the luminaries who often greeted freshmen at the lodge was Ross McKenney (a.k.a. Jean Baptiste)—an employee of Dartmouth whose first assignment in 1937 was to build the Ravine Lodge. In his French-Canadian version of English, Jean Baptiste regaled us with stories of how the lodge came to be and of his timbering, fishing, and hunting exploits in the north woods. He was a much-beloved and knowledgeable raconteur, filled with tall tales that he loved to spin by the fireplace at Moosilauke. My favorite was about how the huge old moose head in the lodge's main room had come to adorn the wall.

Returning to Moosilauke for a weekend of hiking and partying was always a great joy! On a typical Moosilauke weekend, the Tri-Kap brothers and our dates drove northeast early on Saturday morning for about an hour to the point, about six and three-quarter miles past the town of Warren, where the turnoff to the lodge met the Warren-North Woodstock Road (NH Route 118). We turned left onto a dirt road, which angled upward for one and one half miles to a turnaround area/parking lot just above the lodge. As you climbed out of the car and walked the short distance down the steps from the road to the lodge, the stillness and beauty of the mountain forest left you breathless. The scent of balsam, spruce, and pine and the freshness of the breeze exhilarated you beyond description!

The first order of business was always to store our sleeping bags and extra clothes in the bunkrooms. Since the lodge and outlying bookroom could sleep over one hundred persons, there was always lots of room. We unloaded our food, beverages, and cooking utensils and then prepared to climb the mountain.

The Gorge Brook Trail, which we usually chose for our ascent, provided a direct route between the Ravine Lodge and the summit of Mount Moosilauke. I knew that trail like the back of my hand, because I had climbed it several dozen times. The trail began by crossing the Baker River directly in front of the Ravine Lodge. There used to be a wooden dam across the river at the point of crossing, which created a fine swimming hole, when I was a camper there in the late 1950s. Later, after the dam was dismantled, you had to cross on a bridge comprised of several spruce trunks with a handrail.

It was a delightful trail. It ascended straight up the mountain initially, crossed the Gorge Brook, and then paralleled it on the right bank for a short distance before bearing right and climbing through fir and mixed hardwoods for about one-third of a mile. Eventually the trail bore left and slabbed up the left side of Moosilauke's East Ridge, presenting breathtaking views onto what was called the Pleiades (rock) slides and across to Mount Carr and Mount Kineo. A little further you passed the timberline and then a fine spring. Several hundred feet beyond the spring was a small Outing Club cabin with bunks and a stove used for emergencies (or for adventurous camping on the barren, boulder-strewn 4,810-foot-high mountain top).

Just after the cabin, the trail joined the Beaver Brook Trail, part of the AT—as the AT emerged above the Appalachian forest canopy for the first time in its northward path from Georgia to Maine—which led about one hundred yards to the summit. It was about three miles from the lodge to the summit and took about three and one half hours in good weather. It was always a superb hike! The view from the summit was known as one of the very best panoramic views in New England!

For the trip down, we usually took the so-called Carriage road that a half century or more before had allowed first horse and buggy then vehicular traffic access to the summit's stone Tip-Top House (a nineteenth-century hotel) built in 1860. The old road headed down the south ridge of Mount Moosilauke about 1.8 miles to the Snapper Ski Trail, where you turned east and dropped sharply down an extremely steep ski trail to the Gorge Brook Trail, about a half mile from the lodge. My legs would tremble for hours after making a fast descent down the trail's switchbacks on the Snapper!

The entire hike took about five hours. We would then flop, exhausted, onto our bunks with our dates to cuddle for an hour or so before we prepared the usual fraternity spaghetti dinner. On the north balcony of the lodge, an old circular saw blade, about five feet in diameter, had been hung to serve as a sort of bell to call people for meals. When struck with a sledgehammer, that blade made a terrific racket audible for miles—a noise our dates always enjoyed.

Dinner was followed by square dancing, admiring the night sky with its millions of stars from the lodge's balconies, and curling up with our dates in the bunkhouses or, if the weather permitted, under the spruce trees surrounding the lodge. If a brother did not have a date, faculty chaperones were usually available to hang out with.

One faculty couple in particular was generous in volunteering on many occasions to be wonderful chaperones at several Tri-Kap Moosilauke events and at our parties at the house: Joyce and David

Hanlon. Dave taught at the Dartmouth Medical School, and his attractive wife, Joyce, was filled with the joy of living, laughter, and fun—a treasure. They became my good friends. I loved dancing with Joyce! We had many exceptionally enjoyable weekends at Moosilauke Ravine Lodge!

The seniors left Tri-Kap and Dartmouth in June 1965. President Bob Justis, Vice President Mike Ciborski, Treasurer Chris Marston, and Secretary Brad Dewey were sorely missed for their many contributions to the fraternity. In September, while I was in France, a new class of pledges from the class of 1968 brought renewed vitality to our membership: Allan D. Ackerman; Richard G. Anderson; John T. Baker; Robert S. Block; Steven L. Calvert; Ginteras A. Dambrava; Paul A. Fitzgerald; Philip E. Freedman; David B. Hoffman Jr.; William C. Hoyt; Chris W. Hyvonen; Tracy L. Johnson; Robert H. Lynn; William A. Marshall; Jonathan D. Noon; Michael D. O'Connor; David B. Peck Jr.; Roger K. Tung; and Peter Zack.

In the spring of 1966, Tri-Kap was one of the outstanding fraternities at Dartmouth. Our house was considered to be modern, clean, and the best-kept house of all the fraternities. An extensive house renovation program costing $22,000 had been completed in time for the opening of classes. Tri-Kap was the first fraternity to provide both dormitory equipment and a sprinkler system to its brothers.

The previous autumn, the brothers had been ranked fourth academically among the two-dozen fraternities and won the college golf championship as a result of outstanding efforts by Ted Neill, '67, and Pete Zack, '68. In the winter term, the Tri-Kap hockey team, led by Bill Bogardus, '67, finished first in its league, and the basketball team—with league-leading scorer Ken Taylor, '66—finished with a fine 9 and 4 record. In skiing, Barry Ripley, '66, and Bruce Drake, '66, brought home a fifth place in the inter-fraternity competition. Our carnival statue called "Footloose" featured a cross-country skier in full stride and won first place in the carnival statue competition, thanks to the hard work of Ken Ireland, '66, and Bill Parkerton, '66. In the intramural athletic competitions Tri-Kap teams had excelled in each of the three terms, finishing fourth athletically overall among fraternities at the end of the year. Most surprising of all, Tri-Kap ended the nine-year reign of rival Alpha Theta as the king of the Hums competition on Green Key Weekend.

Each spring the fraternities held a singing competition known as "Hums" in which three songs were performed by each brotherhood in concert on the steps of Dartmouth Hall. One of the three songs had to be a Dartmouth song, but the brotherhood selected the other two pieces. Faculty judged the competition. Members of the participating fraternities were usually dressed uniformly in black pants and white shirts. Alpha Theta had won the contest every year for almost a decade and seemed unbeatable with a high number of Glee Club members among its brotherhood. Among other factors considered by the judges, besides the quality of the singing, were the percentage of the brotherhood participating, the appearance of the singers, the difficulty of the pieces, and the enthusiasm of the performance.

At Tri-Kap in 1966, every brother was required to sing in the concert. Terry Lowd, '66, was in charge of putting together a program of songs, organizing practices, and conducting the concert. From the beginning, Terry emphasized how much he wanted to beat Alpha Theta in the Hums competition. We practiced daily for several weeks. Brothers who could not read music or carry a tune were required to memorize the words and to mouth them without making a sound while the rest of us sang. The five of us who sang in the Glee Club—Terry, Eric Jones, '68, David Peck, '68, Ginteras (Tony) Dambrava, '68, and me—were expected to help the others learn the songs and execute them as well as possible.

Happily, thanks to Terry's hard work, we managed to dethrone Alpha Theta on Green Key Weekend. As Hums champions, Tri-Kap was invited to sing at the college's Alumni Officers Weekend on May 15 and continued to dominate the Hums competition in 1967 under David Peck's outstanding leadership and for many successive years afterward.

I also recall with great pride the efforts of the house to contribute to the Hanover community. At Christmas, for example, we arranged parties and a visit from Santa Claus for the children patients at the nearby Mary Hitchcock Hospital every year. With several other brothers, I spent autumn weekends splitting logs, chopping firewood, and stacking cords of wood at the homes of elderly residents of Grafton County, who relied on wood stoves to heat their homes in New Hampshire's cold winters. I only did it once, but other brothers visited nursing homes regularly in the Hanover area, sharing songs, stories, and laughter with the elderly residents. Tri-Kap was not unique in these activities—other fraternities were engaged in similar good works throughout the year.

The high quality of Tri-Kap as a fraternity was a credit to the senior leaders who graduated in the spring of 1966: Steve Hayes, president; Terry Lowd, vice president; Paul Doscher, treasurer; and Bill George, secretary. They had overseen the impressive house renovations and the rise of Tri-Kap's reputation. In 1966, the autumn rush was one of the most successful in many years at the fraternity, bringing a welcome, talented group of new brothers: John W. Allen; Durward P. Brandis; Robert T. Cole; Lee G. Demas; Bernard B, Ducamp; Garrick M. Giebel; Russell T. Granik; Jared O. Haynes; Michael O. Hermann; Dale L. Kessler; William H. Kinschner; Loren C. Lortscher; Robert Lynn; James M. Mullins III; Nick P. Perencevich; R. Hampton Rich; David S. Wakelin; Richard W. Walden; Douglas W. Webber; Laurence D. Wiseman; and Ralph R. Woodman Jr.

Our new officers of Tri-Kap's class of 1967 were Al Hine, president; Rich Sellers, vice president; Bill Fell, treasurer; and Dunc Ballentyne, secretary. They continued the excellent leadership of the past three years at the house and were genuinely talented and kind young men. The May 8, 1967 edition of the *Dartmouth* eloquently capped a great year for Tri-Kap, featuring a front-page story and picture of the brotherhood with the byline "KKK Wins Hums and Overall," noting: "The brothers of KKK hummed their way to victory on the steps of Dartmouth Hall Friday afternoon and in the process captured the award for overall inter-fraternity competition."

I felt extremely lucky to be a brother of Kappa Kappa Kappa not only because it was such an excellent fraternity but also because of its past and the many outstanding Tri-Kap alumni who had preceded the class of 1967. Although I was not aware of him when I was an undergraduate, one such alumnus is now especially noteworthy for me, and discovering his story—and much later learning that he was a Tri-Kap brother—has made me particularly proud of being a Tri-Kap.

In this regard, Tri-Kap celebrated its one hundredth anniversary with a huge celebration at the house in 1942. Tri-Kap's archives contain a record of the festivities and of the attendees. On the list of alumni in attendance at the celebration is the name of Homer B. Hulbert, who may have been among the most prescient, respected, and devoted men in the history of American involvement in the Far East.

Mr. Hulbert first came to my attention in 1969, when I reported to teach English as a Peace Corps volunteer in Korea at Kyungpook National University. My first day at the university in Daegu, Korea, I met the dean of the liberal arts college there, who became a mentor and close friend. In our initial conversation, he asked me about my background and particularly about my educational credentials. When I mentioned that I had graduated with a bachelor's degree in English from Dartmouth College, he surprised me by saying that he knew about Dartmouth. (None of the Korean language teachers in our training program had heard of Dartmouth. Most educated Koreans knew about Yale, Harvard, Princeton, and Stanford but not Dartmouth.)

Then he told me that the first English teacher, and probably the most beloved of the first Americans to come to Korea, had graduated from Dartmouth. He couldn't remember the name of the teacher or when he had come to Korea, except that it was a long time ago in the nineteenth century. That was news to me.

Much later, after I had left Korea, I discovered that the Dartmouth graduate to whom Professor Kim had referred was Homer B. Hulbert (1863–1949), who graduated from Dartmouth in 1884. Hulbert played on Dartmouth's second and third football teams of 1882–1883. He came to Korea first as an English teacher in 1886 and later as a Methodist missionary.

His accomplishments included founding the Korean branch of the YMCA, writing the first books in English about Korean history, culture, and the Korean alphabet, becoming a close friend of the Korean Emperor Kojong, and acting as Emperor Kojong's personal and most trusted emissary to Washington in 1905 and to the Hague in 1906 in unsuccessful efforts to thwart Japanese imperialism (almost half a century before the world awoke to this threat). Emperor Kojong invited Mr. Hulbert to live with him in the royal palace, which he did for several years—his presence as an American guest shielded the emperor from being assassinated by the Japanese, as the empress had been in 1895.

After Japan formally annexed Korea without objection from the rest of the world, brother Hulbert remained a steadfast ally of, and articulate advocate for, Korea—in Japanese-imposed exile in the United States—over a period of more than four decades.

Following Korea's liberation from Japanese rule in 1945, brother Hulbert returned to Korea in 1949 to receive Korea's highest civilian award from Korea's first modern president, Syngman Rhee, who had been one of his English students. Hulbert died there, at the age of eighty-six, after only one week on Korean soil. On a later visit to Korea, I discovered his gravesite in the Foreigners' Cemetery in Seoul. This memorable phrase—what he often told his friends during the forty-two years that he was forced to live far away from his beloved Korea—is inscribed on his tombstone in Korean script: "I would rather be buried in Korea than in Westminster Abbey."

Because my wife's homeland is Korea, and because I have come to love Korea and its people as a consequence of my Peace Corps service there, I was delighted (but somehow not surprised) to discover that Korea's most beloved early American friend was long ago a Tri-Kap brother.

Wim deHaas, '69,
September 1966

Anna Margareta Ahlström,
June 1963

Wim deHaas, '69, and me, January 1967

The University of Montpellier foreign study students: (from left) David Brooks, '67, Xavier Mendoza, '67, George Konikowski, '67, Craig Ordway, '67, James Henderson, '67, Robert Edwards, '67, Jack Harris, '67, unknown, Rich Weller, '67, Patrick Maddox, '67, David Sclove, '67, Tom Vosteen, '66, William Norrington, '67, and me, September 1965

Leena Palm, Abisko, Sweden, July 1964

My French brother Alain Lévère, Montpellier, France, October 1965

Carcassonne, France, September 1965

Jim Henderson, '67, Professor Richard Regosin, and Rich Weller, '67,
Montpellier, France, September 1965

Madam Réné Lévère, French cousin Nikole, French cousin Jean,
French brother Alain Lévère, Rich Weller, '67, and friend, Montpellier,
France, September 1965

My French home, 12 Rue Marcel des Serres.
Montpellier, France, October 1965

CHAPTER 11—"DRUNKEN JUNIORS"[44]

As one of his three pieces of advice to me as I prepared to enter college, my brother advised me not to get drunk, as I mentioned earlier. For the most part, I followed his advice, with rare exceptions. But I was often drunk with pleasure during my junior year, reeling through college life in Hanover and Europe with an intoxicating brew distilled of mountains, friends, cathedrals, medieval cities, family, romance, and the elixir of literature. I admit that, like Emily Dickinson, I was a debauche and an inebriate![45]

As my second year ended, with Professor Gaudin's assistance I selected the topic of my foreign study project, which was to be generally a fifty-page paper written in French, exploring love and passion in *La Comédie Humaine* of Honoré de Balzac. I had already read the first of the five Balzac novels that would be my subjects and had enjoyed it tremendously. *Le Père Goriot* (*Father Goriot*), set in Paris in 1819, is considered to be Balzac's masterpiece. I looked forward to reading and analyzing Balzac's additional works, but I had some reservations as to whether I could complete the paper during the term abroad. It seemed a daunting project! Consequently, I started to read *La Fille Aux Yeux D'Or* (*The Girl with the Golden Eyes*) as soon as I arrived home after final exams, hoping to get a quick start on my thesis and resolving that while I was in Sweden I would finish as much of the paper as possible before I even arrived in France.

At the same time, I prepared for my second Swedish summer. The last week in June, Sandi Ingalls met me at my aunt Kate's home in Oneonta, New York, for several days of relaxation together, before my aunt and my twin cousins (Molly and Kitty Craig) drove me to John F. Kennedy Airport in New York for my departure on June 27.

I left New York at three o'clock on Sunday afternoon on Icelandic Airlines. We refueled in Gander, Newfoundland, and again in Reykjavik, Iceland, which was lovely in the early light of Monday morning. The flight had been chartered by the Experiment in International Living for college students heading for Europe to live for several months with European families.

Soon after takeoff from Iceland, we circled a new volcanic island named Surtsey that had emerged

---

[44]   "Where, O where are the drunken Juniors?" Anonymous, "Pea Green Freshmen," *Dartmouth Song Book*, 7.

[45]   "I taste a liquor never brewed, From tankards scooped in pearl; Not all the vats upon the Rhine Yield such an alcohol! Inebriate of air am I, And debauchee of dew, Reeling, through endless summer days, From inns of molten blue …" Emily Dickinson, "I taste a liquor never brewed" in *The Oxford Book of American Verse*, 418.

from the ocean off the coast in late 1963. It was my first encounter with an active volcano. We had a clear view from the safety of the plane of the lava, rocks, flames, and steam spewing from the volcanic cone below. On one side of the plane, distant mountains with glaciers of white-and-blue ice were visible in the distance. On the other side was a sea of fire. I thought of the contrast between the icy creative power of glaciers, which had slowly formed so much of the New York and New England landscape that I loved, and that of the fiery volcanic fury below, which almost overnight had created a new island. Each power was also equally destructive. Robert Frost's poem "Fire and Ice" came to my mind as an apt description of the tableau beneath me.[46] I took this awesome spectacle as a positive harbinger of new sights and experiences awaiting me in Europe!

Our flight arrived in Amsterdam early on Monday afternoon. With several of the other students, I spent the afternoon and evening exploring the museums, streets, and canals of the city! We visited the Rijksmuseum to feast our eyes on masterpieces by Rembrandt, Vermeer, and others and took a canal boat that introduced us to the "Venice of the North." The Dutch were exceedingly friendly, spring flowers were in every window box, and we all agreed that Amsterdam had to be one of the most enchanting cities in Europe!

Early on Tuesday morning, I boarded a train for a trip across the Netherlands, Germany, and Denmark to Copenhagen. If anything, the trip north this summer was even more enjoyable than the previous year's wonderful trip! Of the seven students in my compartment, with whom I sang and talked all afternoon, a Dutch girl and a Swedish girl were going on to Stockholm with me by train. The three of us had an evening together in which to explore the amazing park—Tivoli—adjacent to the train station that had entranced me the previous year. After a few beers in a beer garden, the girls whispered together and then insisted on introducing me to Tivoli's famous roller coaster.

Most, if not all, of the roller-coaster ride was in a pitch-black tunnel. I sat between the girls and was quite terrified because in the total darkness I could not anticipate the ride's swoops, dips, and careening turns! The girls were equally petrified and almost squeezed me to death between them, holding on to me for dear life! The best part was that quite unexpectedly both girls kissed me at the same time in the darkness, as they had apparently secretly planned, while I simultaneously fought to keep my stomach from the churning engendered from the ride and responded with some fervor to both passionate kisses. I will never forget that ride or the total joyousness of that evening with two girls whose names I have forgotten …

My sister-in-law and my two nephews met me in Stockholm, and together we drove to Uppsala. It was so fantastic to be back in Sweden! My work at the Institute of Limnology was much more intense this summer than before, as my brother was frantically trying to wrap up his research before his return to the States in late August. The staff of the institute, which previously had been politely friendly,

---

[46] "Some say the world will end in fire, [s]ome say in ice. From what I've tasted of desire I hold with those who favor fire. But if I had to perish twice, I think I know enough of hate [t]o say that for destruction ice [i]s also great [a]nd would suffice." Robert Frost, "Fire and Ice," in *The Oxford Book of American Verse*, 567.

greeted me like a long-lost relative this summer! My good friend Staffan was at the institute, and several other male friends were back in Uppsala for the summer. With them I religiously went to the dances at the Norrlands Nation, met dozens of friendly girls, and generally had a terrific time. Anna, however, was nowhere to be found. Her cousin advised me that she was working for the summer in northern Sweden.

With my brother and his family, I visited several of Sweden's most historic and impressive historical sites, including Gripsholm Castle, Uppsala Castle, and Drottningholm Palace—the ornate and garden-ringed residence of the royal family. We also created a bit of history ourselves by playing Frisbee each evening after supper in the empty street in front of our house at 4 Walleriusvägen.

Swedes were not familiar with Frisbee. On the third night of our street flings, there were dozens of fascinated neighbors watching and asking to try it! Most of the institute's staff, as well, were soon watching John and me spin the Frisbee back and forth during lunch breaks in front of the institute. By the end of the summer, my parents had mailed a dozen or so Frisbees that we distributed as gifts.

As my Swedish improved, I got to know several of the laboratory technicians and supporting staff at the institute quite well and dated some of them. One was a particularly good friend. Her name was Anna Tolstoy, and she was the granddaughter of the great Russian writer Leo Tolstoy. We had several delightful dinners together.

Another good friend was a nurse named Siv Holgersson, whom I met at one of the dances. Siv and I became quite close. She was very patient in teaching me both Swedish language (she spoke little English) and culture. I owe Siv, with her beautiful green eyes, a tremendous debt of gratitude.

One day, after I had reached the point at which I could read Swedish fairly well, I saw an article in the Uppsala newspaper about a student at the university—Eva Sandahl—who had just been awarded a scholarship to study in Buffalo, New York. She was going to leave in September. I thought that perhaps I could tell her something about my hometown and help her prepare, so I wrote her a letter of introduction, providing her with my parents' names, address, and telephone number in Buffalo, in case she needed help, and asking her to contact me at the institute.

Eva never contacted me, but as luck would have it, when she arrived in Buffalo in the fall, no one was at the airport to meet her—the university had forgotten about her arrival. So she called my parents. My sister-in-law had just returned to the States from Uppsala and was visiting my parents in Buffalo. Olivann was then fluent in Swedish after having lived in Uppsala for several years. She answered the phone, recognized the Swedish accent, switched to Swedish, remembered my summer letter, and arranged for Eva to live with my parents until her situation at the university had been straightened out. I met Eva at Christmastime in Buffalo, and she was very grateful for our family's help. I told her that her countrymen had done so much for me in Sweden that my family and I could never repay them adequately.

The summer passed too quickly. Dozens of evenings at Club Norrlandia blend in my memories with visits to beaches, picnics with student friends, and excursions with my brother's family to Sweden's many lovely gardens, parks, and historic sites. Above all, I remember the Swedish students with whom I became close friends.

Throughout the entire summer, they discussed with me the Vietnam War and the racial problems in the United States. Some evenings we would talk for hours until the sun set well after midnight. Without exception, my friends were extremely antiwar and pro civil rights. They queried me as to why the United States was fighting what to them was an immoral war and at the same time discriminating against African Americans at home.

Although I shared their strong feelings of outrage regarding both subjects, I often found myself unexpectedly on the defensive, never justifying my country's failures but trying to explain that they were more complicated than Europeans understood. I pointed out, for example, that Sweden was unique in its historic and perhaps immoral political neutrality in times of conflict, as during the Second World War. Additionally, even though its population was extremely homogeneous (I seldom saw any minorities at all in Uppsala or even in Stockholm), I asked my friends about the discrimination manifest in the Swedish treatment of the northern Lapps as second-class citizens. Despite my instinctive efforts to defend my country and its weaknesses, I generally agreed with my friends that the war in Vietnam was appalling and that discrimination against African Americans was even worse.

These discussions about the Vietnam War and civil rights with my Swedish friends opened my eyes to two issues that previously had been easy to ignore in the relative isolation and frenetic pace of life at Dartmouth. Studying, skiing, work, and social activities had consumed me for the past two years. Thanks to my Swedish friends, I began to awaken to the world's problems that President John Sloan Dickey often referred to as "your" problems—meaning my classmates and me. I was not an "activist" at all by the start of my junior year, but I recognized the immorality and injustice of both the war and the continuing racial discrimination in the United States. Seeds of discontent and anger had been planted in Sweden, but my poor inadequate action to nurture those seeds would have to wait until I returned home at the end of the year.

At Norrlandia, perhaps my most exciting evening in my second Swedish summer occurred when the incomparable singer Eartha Kitt performed. She was amazingly talented. I heard that she was then having difficulty finding work stateside because of her antiwar campaign at home. During the intermission of her performance, when she was relaxing at a table, I asked her to dance. I think that she thought that I was Swedish or she otherwise might not have accepted. While dancing, I explained how I came to be in Sweden and how much I admired both her singing and her antiwar public statements. To dance with Eartha Kitt was an unexpected honor!

I met dozens of fantastic girls in the course of the summer, spent a weekend in Stockholm with an exquisite girl I met at the Norrlands Nation—Bodil Backström—and enjoyed several days visiting the gorgeous country home in Ånge of another lovely girl who had studied at Mount Holyoke for a year: Ebba Wikander.

Ebba's father was the director of Svenska Cellulosa Aktiebolaget—one of Sweden's premier companies. Their incredible manor-style home was located on six acres of manicured lawns and gardens that sloped to a forest lake. During my three-day visit, we had a typical Swedish summer picnic on the shore of the lake in the glow of the midnight sun, eating crayfish and a Swedish delicacy called *surströmming*, which is fermented herring. The smell of the latter is so overpoweringly awful that it is illegal in Sweden to open a can indoors! I noticed that the can of surströmming was actually throbbing before we opened it, and my hosts taught me that each bite must be preceded by a shot glass of aquavit, which is a vodka-like drink (about eighty proof), distilled from grain and flavored with spices and herbs, that helps the herring swim to the stomach (and makes the stench bearable). Ebba and her sister Barbro were marvelous hostesses!

In mid-August, while John was away at a conference, I traveled by train with my brother's wife and young children to Oslo, Norway, where they boarded the MS *Oslofjord* to return to the United States with an astonishing amount of baggage. I remember that when we had to change trains in Stockholm en route to Norway, Bob Richmond, '57, a Phi Kappa Psi fraternity brother of John, who was then assigned to the US embassy in Stockholm, met us at the station with his family to help us with the luggage. We never would have made the connecting train without Bob's help! Dartmouth to the rescue!

On the return trip to Uppsala by myself, I stopped for a brief visit in Stockholm. I explored the old quarter of the city—Gamla Stan—for several hours. When I returned to the train station and got in line to buy a train ticket to Uppsala, I noticed a tall, blonde-haired girl just ahead of me: Anna—my girlfriend of the previous summer! I felt as though I had just experienced divine intervention in this incredibly coincidental meeting in a city of more than half a million people! We had a joyous reunion and ate dinner together before her train left for her home. I never saw her again, to my deep regret.

At the end of August, my Swedish friends arranged a series of farewell parties at the institute and at the Norrlands Nation. I was so sad to leave Uppsala, which I had come to love deeply. In my wildest dreams, I had never expected to enjoy my Swedish experiences so fully—under the warm glow of the midnight sun—the wonderful friendships and joyous dances, celebrations, visits, picnics, and other events of my second summer in Sweden. As I departed Uppsala on September 1 by train for Paris, I vowed to return before too many years had passed.

It rained the entire train trip from Stockholm to Paris. I spent one night in Paris and managed to visit the Eiffel Tower and the cathedral of Notre Dame despite the pouring rain. Paris under stormy skies did not have her best face on for my first visit, so I was not very impressed. From the City of Light, I took a train to Avignon where the sun came out just as I joined my Dartmouth classmates, whom I called the "lucky thirteen"—the dozen besides me who had elected to study in France at the University of Montpellier for a term—on the train from Avignon to Montpellier.

My extraordinary Dartmouth colleagues were David Brooks, Robert Edwards, Jack Harris, James Henderson, George Konikowski, Patrick Maddox, Xavier Mendoza, William Norrington, Craig Ordway, David Sclove, Thomas Vosteen, and Richard Weller. Of the group, the only three I previously knew well were David Brooks, Xavier Mendoza, and Richard Weller, all of whom had worked with me at the Dartmouth Dining Association. Facing a new adventure together had a way of fostering relationships quickly, so we were all good friends in a matter of hours, it seemed.

We were met at the station in Montpellier by Professor Regosin and by a representative of the Experiment in International Living, who took us to our dormitories at the University of Montpellier in the so-called student men's city, which was located about one mile from the student women's city (we all immediately noted). Each of us had a separate room in one of eight modern, six-story dormitories comprising the student city of Triolet. My single room on the fourth floor had a bed, desk, closet, lamp, two chairs, and a cupboard-like partition that separated a mirror and small sink from the rest of the room. The bathroom with showers was just down the hall, shared by about twenty students. My new address: Pavillon C #84, Cité Universitaire du Triolet, Chemin des Brusses, Montpellier (Hérault), France.

All of the approximately 1,300 foreign students ate together in a student dining hall, cafeteria-style, using meal tickets, just as at Dartmouth. The dining building was located halfway between the men's and women's dormitories. The food was excellent! About 30 percent of the students were women, and a majority in September were English or American. Practicing your French at meal times was not easy, as everyone was speaking in English!

The university's rules for students were explained to us, and we were admonished that two of the rules were strictly enforced: girls were forbidden in the men's dorms at any time, and we were not allowed to take the blankets from our rooms to the beach!

After two days, our group compared notes regarding the women at Montpellier. The regular French students had not yet arrived to begin classes, so most of the women we met in the cafeteria were foreign (non-French) students. The initial consensus was that American women were generally prettier, although the other foreign women at the university were more stylishly dressed than their American counterparts. I thought to myself that very few of the girls I had met so far in France could compare in beauty or elegance with the vast majority of the Swedish girls I had just left in Uppsala!

We began classes almost immediately, attending four to five hours daily, Monday through Friday, but there was no homework! These were special classes for foreign students, focusing on French language, history, culture, and literature. Regular French students did not join us in classes or on campus until mid-October. I buckled down immediately to my Balzac paper, hoping to finish it before the end of October. My procrastination was cause for great concern—I thought I was way behind on my project—until I discovered that most of my Dartmouth colleagues had not yet even started to work on their papers!

With no homework, I had lots of time to explore Montpellier. It was a fascinating city and much more like what I had imagined as the typical European city before visiting Amsterdam, Copenhagen, Stockholm, and Uppsala. The university itself was awesome. Established in 1289, it was one of the oldest universities in Europe, and its architecture, gardens, and ancient courtyards and passages were a constant source of amazement.

The section of the city where the university was located for the most part was centered around a huge park on a hill from which to the northeast vineyards and orchards were visible for miles, spreading across the rolling terrain to distant purple mountains. To the south, the city stretched to spacious, clean, sandy beaches bordered by the ever-so-blue, sparkling Mediterranean Sea.

Several wide boulevards lined with palm and cypress trees led from the central hill to the city's quaint main squares where shops, cafes, and restaurants were clustered. Most of the streets, however, were very narrow and twisting, like the old quarters in Stockholm and Uppsala.

I found the people in Montpellier were generally much friendlier than the Swedes, probably because I was speaking their language. They were more shabbily dressed and smaller in size than Scandinavians, as well, but they laughed, argued, and cried with more passion than my northern friends!

Everything was quite expensive, with the exception of food and wine. The Beaujolais wine that cost two dollars per bottle in Sweden cost less than fifty cents in France. On the whole, however, the cost of living was much less than in Hanover.

The land around Montpellier was quite arid with hundreds of orchards and vineyards supported by an extensive system of irrigation canals. One of the landmarks that caught your eye immediately was the half-mile-long seventeenth-century aqueduct—the St. Clément Aqueduct—that still carried water from a spring in the mountains to the center of the city. It was a constant reminder that, as we were instructed, it was important to conserve water in the dry south of France.

Perhaps the best features of the area were the Mediterranean Sea's beaches! The university was about one half hour by bus or train from the nearest beach, which was clean, spacious, and usually filled with students from all over the world, particularly since we had a long string of sunny days in September. Our first weekend four of us from Dartmouth took an old train—like something out of an old Western cowboy movie—to the beach, which was called Palavas-les-flots. The train looked to be about one hundred years old. Its top speed was about twenty miles per hour, as we passed by vineyards, orchards, small farms, and very medieval-looking hamlets.

I took a Frisbee, which we flung at each other over a distance of about thirty yards in the midst of dozens of umbrellas, couples making out, and hundreds of bikinis (all the women wore tiny bikinis).

Frisbee thrilled the young French children at the beach, and our game turned into a keep-away game, with a French kid pouncing on the Frisbee every time one of us missed. Like the Swedes, the French had never seen a Frisbee before. By midafternoon about seventy people were sitting outside our playing area, watching and encouraging us. It was great fun!

One of the German students took a special interest in Frisbee and asked to join in our game. Nadia Bobbert was from a town near Hannover, had spent the summer at the University of Montpellier and was about to return to Germany. She was an extremely attractive, dark-haired beauty and spilled out of the tiniest bikini I had ever seen! For her remaining two weeks in Montpellier, we went to the beach together as often as we could.

On our second Sunday in France, we left with sixty other foreign students on a bus excursion to Béziers and Carcassonne. From six o'clock in the morning until ten o'clock at night, we rode along the gorgeous French coast and up into the mountains, stopping at Ensérune, where we visited lovely Greek ruins and pre-Greek relics dating from about 700 BC, we were told, as well as several ongoing archaeological excavations of ancient cities. In Béziers, we stopped at the cathedral—famous as the site of part of the massacre of 1209 when twenty thousand people were killed—whose Romanesque architecture and rose window were quite impressive, but it was at Carcassonne that I was completely astonished. We came over a ridge and saw before us in the valley below, rising from the coastal plain, a plateau on which was built an incredible walled city from medieval times, complete with turrets, gates, moats, and flags flying. Simply amazing!

Carcassonne was just as it was in the Middle Ages—many series of huge walls, towers, narrow streets with overhanging houses and shops, and countless secret passages and nooks. We also visited the castle and cathedral set amidst the splendor of the ancient walled city. I skipped lunch and beat our group to the cathedral, where I sat enthralled for almost an hour during a fine organ recital. The organist was excellent and played the Pastorale and Final of the "Six Pieces" by César Franck, which I have always liked. We spent several more hours walking around the city, climbing the towers, and exploring the walls. Visiting Carcassonne was one of the highlights of my life!

During the week, we focused intensively on French language. Each day I had two hours of language laboratory, four hours of "conversation supérièure," and one hour of casual conversation in French with Madame Abouyé, who was a professor at the university and in charge of the Dartmouth program. Twice each week, I also met with Professor Regosin, who was the project adviser for our foreign study program and a wonderful man.

In our other classes, we studied everything from history to Bridgette Bardot movies, which led us into spicy discussions of love and sex in France. Concerning the latter, I still recall our first language laboratory, where we were pleasantly astonished to find that our language teacher was a lovely blonde student about twenty-five years old with one of the sexiest voices I have ever heard. Throughout the lab session, there were many hushed exclamations and remarks of the type that you might expect from Dartmouth guys, until finally the instructor purred over the earphones, "Really, messieurs, we must get to work. There will be plenty of time for love after you have learned her language!" That shut us up!

In the evenings, we frequented the hundreds of sidewalk cafés and student nightclubs in the city—often in ancient cellars and wine vaults. My favorite of these was a café called La Puce Qui Pleure (the Crying Flea) where I had endless discussions with Indian, Pakistani, and other Southeast Asian students, as well as with a lot of Spaniards, Germans, and Italians. I was quite surprised at how fearful of China and the Soviet Union, and how pro-American, almost all of these students were in their comments. The then French president, Charles de Gaulle, was quite anti-American in his policies and speeches and was universally disliked by virtually all of the foreign and French students I met.

One evening, two French girls spent hours teaching me and two Norwegian students local French songs at La Puce. We had a fantastic time! As the other students and I walked home afterward down a nearby street, suddenly we heard giggles from above us, and our French friends splashed a tub of water on us from their balcony, all in good fun.

Six weeks passed in a flash. Before we knew it, our two-week vacation had begun on October 13, just as dozens of French students were trickling into Montpellier to begin classes. After debating whether we should try to travel to Italy and Switzerland, Xavier Mendoza (my Bolivian classmate) and I decided to hitchhike north together to Copenhagen and back, if we felt that we could accomplish this trip in the fifteen vacation days. So we stuck out our thumbs, painted a Bolivian and American flag on a sign reading "Stockholm," and headed north through Switzerland, Germany, and Denmark. We made it to Copenhagen in four days, visiting Basel, Hamburg, Hannover, and Frankfurt on the way.

The autumn colors were superb, and the weather cooperated with sunny, pleasant days during the entire trip. Europeans were uniformly friendly and hospitable in giving us rides and treating us to gripping conversations and delectable food along the way! Because we had reached Denmark so relatively quickly—thanks in large part to the speedy German autobahns (on which we played cat and mouse with the German police at several hitchhiking spots)—we decided to go further north to Stockholm, where Xavier wanted to visit a Swedish girl he knew there. In the late evening of the next day, we arrived in Stockholm. As it was too late for Xavier to contact his friend, we went to the train station to inquire about a cheap place to spend the night.

Then we had an encounter that was typical of the generosity and hospitality we experienced throughout our two-week journey. At the station, we met a watchman named Martin Oskarsson with whom we talked in broken English and Swedish for over an hour. When he went off duty at twelve thirty in the morning, he invited us to his small apartment for the night, where we shared a simple dinner and slept on cots in his spare bedrooms. The next morning, he directed Xavier to his friend's residence, and I left for Uppsala. I wrote to Martin after we returned to Montpellier, expressing our deep gratitude for his thoughtfulness—so characteristic of all the Europeans whom we met.

I stayed in Uppsala for several days at the apartment of a friend. Of course, I visited my Swedish friends and basked in the sights and sounds of Uppsala University amidst cooling temperatures and the red, gold, and orange leaves of a Swedish autumn. I even made it to one dance at Club Norrlandia!

Our return trip south was generally as delightful as the trip north had been but a little more frustrating and less efficient. On the trip north, we had covered 1,550 miles with six rides in four days. Going south, it took us twenty rides and five days. We had one further noteworthy and unusual adventure as we approached Hannover on our second day of the return trip.

A middle-aged German man named Paul picked us up on the autobahn and drove us into the city where I hoped to meet and crash with my German friend Nadia, whom I had met and dated in Montpellier. He helped me try to call her from a telephone booth. When I discovered that Nadia Bobbert was in Paris and we had no place to stay as a result, Paul offered to take us to dinner and to let us spend the night in his apartment in the city. As it turned out, Xavier and I had dinner with him at a fabulous restaurant and then at his invitation went to several lavish German nightclubs before going to his luxurious apartment, where we continued drinking.

At some point during the evening, Paul said that he had a surprise for us. He got up and went to a closet, as Xavier and I apprehensively looked at each other. In a few minutes, Paul returned, carrying what he said was his World War II uniform—a black German military uniform with swastikas on the arms and emblems (two lightning symbols) identifying the wearer as an officer in the Schutzstaffel or SS. So our friend had had an interesting past. I never thought that I would ever meet an SS officer, and I will admit that Xavier and I were both a bit shaken with his previous identity.

The next morning, our German host dropped us off at the nearest autobahn ramp after telling us that he had not enjoyed an evening so much in a long time, and thanking us, even though he generally did not like Americans, Paul said.

It took us three more days to get back to Montpellier. We arrived finally back at our dorms about four o'clock on Sunday afternoon, two hours before we were scheduled to meet the French families with whom we would be living for the next seven weeks. After shaving, showering, and changing our dirty clothes, we headed to the rendezvous point at the station.

I was met by a warm, welcoming lady of about forty years old—Madame Réné Lévère—and her nineteen-year-old son Alain. I liked them both immediately. Madame Lévère was a typical French mother with her black hair, small frame, and dark eyes, which alternately snapped and twinkled. Monsieur Lévère, who had been a lawyer, had died just before Alain was born, I soon discovered, and Madame had raised Alain by herself, struggling at first to make ends meet. She had brought him up well. Alain was friendly, helpful, and anxious to teach French language and culture to his older American "brother," as he called me.

Madame was the director of social welfare for all of the hospital employees in Montpellier, numbering about three thousand members of the staffs of the four city hospitals. She was also the elected Montpellier representative of the French branch of the Soroptimist Club, which is a global, voluntary women's organization working to improve the lives of women and girls through programs leading to social and economic empowerment. She had just returned from a meeting of the French Soroptimist leaders in Paris. Every major city in France had a branch of the club, which in each city consisted of a member representative from each profession. It was an honor to be asked to join the Soroptimists and even more of an honor to be elected as your city's representative. She was a live wire and felt very strong compassion for people who were unhappy or struggling in any way! She was also very gracious, warm, helpful, and a terrific cook, I soon discovered.

Alain was an only child. He was a bit shorter than me, with dark hair and brown eyes, and very talkative and lively! He liked sports, classical music, and girls very much (even more than me)—my first night with the Lévère family he invited three lovely French girls over for a fine dinner, which he prepared himself. Alain talked so fast and slurred his words so much—almost spitting his words out—that at first I had great difficulty in understanding him. But he was invariably helpful and patient in teaching me French—particularly French slang—and painstakingly guided me through the pitfalls of studying in Montpellier and romancing French girls! He also did an amazingly perceptive and lifelike imitation of French President de Gaulle, which always prompted gales of laughter from any witnessing family or friends.

I helped Alain with his English, and he helped me greatly with my French. It was a fantastic arrangement! I felt very fortunate to have him as my French brother.

We lived in a comfortable apartment of three bedrooms, a kitchen, a bathroom, and a large central hall that doubled as a living room, on the second floor of an old, two-story smallish building in the center of the city (12 Rue Marcel de Serres), just below the central park. Madame Lévère collected antiques, so the furniture was all old and handsome from the seventeenth and eighteenth centuries. I had my own bedroom, overlooking a side street on one corner. It was quite cozy and comfortable.

Madame had come from a once quite wealthy family, but during my stay, I discovered that she was working extremely hard to pay for private tutoring for Alain, who was in his second year at the university, and to support her elderly parents, who lived nearby in the city. Her life now was both hard and busy. A nursing student named Annie, who lived in a small apartment owned by Madame Lévère adjacent to ours, provided another source of income, and Madame also had a small vineyard in the countryside about 150 miles from Montpellier—a family property—from which she got wine and fruit every week.

French cuisine was fantastic! We usually were up by seven o'clock and had a breakfast of *café au lait* or hot chocolate with bread and butter. It was my daily job to get out to the local bakery before breakfast and buy the long, narrow loaves of French bread—freshly baked and delicious!

We had our largest meal of the day in the early afternoon. Typically it consisted of several courses: an hors d'oeuvre of fish, sausage, or canned meat; a salad; a main meat dish, such as chicken, pork, or beef; vegetables such as beans or cauliflower plus potatoes (often french fries); a plate of cheeses with bread; and finally a dessert of fruit or cake. We drank wine with the meat and cheese courses and water with the other courses. For the evening meal, which was quite late for me (usually around eight thirty) we usually had a bowl of soup and the leftovers from lunch. I ate extremely well as a member of the Lévère family!

In early November, we read about the blackout that hit the northeastern United States on November 9. The French were quite pleased, I think, that a disaster of such magnitude could occur in America! We talked about it for days!

My sister, Cecilia, who had lived in Paris and was fluent in French, wrote several lovely letters to Madame Lévère, thanking her for opening her home and family to me and passing along the news of our family in Buffalo. Her letters, written in French, always caused a sensation! Madame Lévère read my sister's letters to all of her friends and members of our huge family, took them to her work, and otherwise was overjoyed to have a correspondent in the United States. Ceci's letters were a huge reason that my relationship with the Lévères blossomed so quickly and fully.[47]

My two months with my French family passed very quickly, filled with several enchanting excursions to the family's country estate (dating from the fifteenth century) on the back of Alain's motor scooter or in Madame's old Citroën "Deux Chevaux" (smaller than a Volkswagen Beetle), dances such as the International Ball at the university around Thanksgiving, Alain's guided tours of the university's oddities (such as the medical school's collection of medical anomalies) and intriguing ancient buildings, and dinner parties with countless relatives of the family living all over southern France. At one of the latter, I met the "child genius" of France, who at fifteen was studying at Montpellier for his PhD. I also met three of Alain's cousins who were extremely attractive and coquettish, although slightly younger than us. Madame took me aside before I met these beauties and warned me never to be alone with them in a room—the strict Huguenot traditions that infused our family would not tolerate any indiscretions with young women ... Even a kiss would be unthinkable!

My coursework at the university went extremely well. I enjoyed the classes with various French professors and with Professor Regosin, reading and discussing works of Stendhal, Claudel, Montherlant, Giraudoux, and Sartre, and surprisingly took a great deal of pleasure in reading Balzac's novels, discussing his work with the Lévères, and writing my paper. I spent countless hours at the dining room table in our apartment writing and rewriting the Balzac thesis. I think that Madame and Alain were impressed with how hard I worked on Balzac!

---

47 Ceci went to Mount Holyoke College and finished her graduate work at Cornell University, first majoring in Romance languages and then becoming a family therapist in Modesto, California. She has always been a bulwark of support for me.

Toward the end of my stay with the Lévères, I realized that Madame tightly closed the shutters on the windows of our second-floor apartment every afternoon at five o'clock exactly, despite the fact that the sun did not set until about nine o'clock. I finally asked her why she did this, since it would have been pleasant to have the late-afternoon sun brightening the apartment's interior. Madame thought for a moment, then laughed, before she told me that her family had gotten into the habit of closing the shutters so early when the Germans occupied Montpellier. Her family had sheltered and protected a young Jewish girl for four years, and the closed shutters assured that prying eyes would not detect her as darkness fell and it was easier to see into the lighted apartment.

When she told me that, I realized that the war had shaped France and the French in many ways that were difficult for Americans to appreciate, since for us the war had been "over there." Even French President Charles de Gaulle, in his hostility to Americans and the English, seemed to be still suffering from war-related trauma—the perception that the Allies' generals Eisenhower, Montgomery, and Marshall had ignored him during the war, when he was in exile in England.

As I prepared to leave my French family, I took a short trip to the French Alps to visit the family of my French pen pal in Grenoble—Dominique Buffard—with whom I had corresponded throughout high school and college. My sister had set up the pen pal relationship between us when she had worked in Paris a decade or more before, so Dominique and I had written to each other in broken French and English over many long years. It was fantastic to finally meet her and her family, as well as to recognize so many of the things in Dominique's life that her letters had described.

My course work was completed in early December, as I presented two half-hour oral reports in French and turned in my Balzac paper, which ended up being sixty-five pages long. I received a B for my oral reports, a B for my literature courses, and an A for my paper, which tremendously pleased both Professor Regosin and, ultimately, Professor Gaudin.[48]

I had a tearful farewell with my French family, who had been so supportive and caring for almost two months. We wrote each other regularly for the next five years, until I returned to visit them in 1971 on my way home from Peace Corps volunteer service in Korea. They will never be forgotten. My term in France was a high point of my life!

The year 1965 may aptly be described as my "European year" at Dartmouth, because I spent almost seven months in Sweden and France combined. It was good to be home when I returned in mid-December, resumed my holiday job with the postal service, and prepared for the start of the winter term. Pete Thomas, Chris Light, '67, and Pam Austen (Pete's girlfriend from Buffalo) drove with me from Buffalo to Wells College in Aurora, New York, where we dropped Pam off before crawling for fifteen hours through a blizzard back to Hanover.

---

[48] The Balzac paper was good enough to be accepted in graduate school at the University of Wisconsin in 1968 as a substitute for my master's thesis, allowing me to earn an MA in English in about eight months, before I left for Korea.

I had dated Pam when she was a junior in high school and I was a senior. She attended a suburban high school and was a classmate of several girls I had dated, including Janis Terry. Pam was a special woman—intelligent, generous, sensitive, and an attractive blonde. I had such a high opinion of her that I fixed her up with several Dartmouth classmates when she became a freshman at Wells College, not far from Buffalo. On one of the weekends that Pam visited Dartmouth as a classmate's date, she came over to see me, met Pete, and the rest was history. They married after graduation.

On that wintry January night, several hours after leaving Pam at Wells, about one o'clock in the morning in Saratoga Springs the local police ticketed Chris for going through a yellow light at about ten miles per hour in the driving snow. At the police station in the early morning, we pointed out that the traffic light was defective in flashing a green light at the same time as the yellow light, so the ticket was reduced from twenty-five dollars to ten dollars. A lawyer at the station told us that a judge would throw out the charge if we could wait until nine o'clock when the court opened, but we decided to pay the ticket and continue to Hanover, rather than waiting out the blizzard in Saratoga.

After arriving at Dartmouth at five thirty, we moved Chris out of my room (where he had roomed with Pete while I was away) and moved me into 402 Middle Wigwam, which had changed its name to McLane Hall. I was delighted with the new dormitory! From the windows in Pete's and my rooms, we looked down onto the blue Connecticut River with an even better view, since we were on the fourth floor, than we had in South Wigwam the previous year. The next day, I began my three courses, all of which I enjoyed greatly: Economics 1, English 61 (Shakespeare), and English 82 (American poetry).

The economics course was essentially an introductory course with about fifty students taught by a revolving cast of the professors in the department, all of whom were fine teachers. I enjoyed the course, but I realized almost immediately that I would never be a businessman! Professor Tom Vance taught the Shakespeare course, and he was enthusiastic, clearly in love with his subject, and brilliant! But the jewel of my winter term was the English seminar with Professor Richard Eberhart!

I was the only junior in a class with ten seniors. The seminar met on Tuesday evenings for four hours at the Eberharts' home on Webster Avenue, overlooking the river. His wife, Helen, always served hot chocolate or coffee and brownies or cookies, as we met in the Eberharts' living room in front of a crackling fire, discussing the poems and poets assigned for the week. Early in the term, I made a fifteen-minute oral presentation on the poetry of Robinson Jeffers, contrasting Jeffers to Frost (both of whom were favorite poets). Visiting poets, such as Robert Lowell, occasionally joined us to read their poetry and help with our analysis and enjoyment. It was pure heaven and probably the most agreeable course I ever took anywhere! I became irrevocably hooked on American poetry!

While taking Professor Eberhart's course, I became aware of an enchanting tradition of the English Department. Every afternoon at four o'clock, afternoon tea was served in the library of the Sanborn House, next to Baker Library. The Sanborn House was the home of English faculty offices, seminar rooms, and most significantly a lovely library filled with Oxford editions of literally all the major works of American and English literature. Thousands of books lined the bookshelves of the stacks on the outside walls of the main room and on the second floor balcony on three sides of the room. Under imposing brass chandeliers, comfortable chairs and reading tables with brass lamps were strategically placed in nooks on the balconies or in the main room in front of the large fireplace. It was a gorgeous room! The flickering light of the fire seemed to dance on the books in winter months as though coaxing them to slip from the shelves into the embrace of a caressing hand. I often imagined that the library had been modeled on some seventeenth-century library in a stately English castle. Whenever I could, I enjoyed an afternoon break at Sanborn, where for ten cents you could sip Earl Grey tea, munch cookies, and talk with faculty and students of the English Department.

During the winter term, several huge snowstorms resulted in the greatest accumulation of snow in Hanover since the winter of 1938. The skiing was terrific at the Skiway, although at night the temperatures plunged to about minus twenty degrees. The contrast with my life in warm, sunny Montpellier, just two months before, could not have been greater in terms both of the weather and of the pace of life. At Dartmouth, with four Glee Club rehearsals each week (as we prepared for five February concerts and for the spring trip), my job at DDA, classes, and skiing each afternoon, my life was extremely hectic!

In the midst of my readjustment to life at Dartmouth, Mel Boozer mentioned an intriguing visitor to campus. Malcolm X, a well-known African American civil rights advocate, was visiting the college. He spoke at Spaulding Auditorium on January 26, 1965, and met with dozens of students over breakfast before being interviewed on WDCR—Dartmouth's radio station. At Mel's invitation, I joined the group that met with him. I expected to meet an angry, radicalized individual. On the contrary, although I did not speak to him personally after our introduction, I found him to be engaging, inspirational, and reasonable. I was impressed. When I heard of his murder, one month after his visit, I was shocked and saddened.

On Winter Carnival Weekend, I was in charge of the decorations at Tri-Kap for the dances each night. The carnival theme was "Winter Wanderlust" (I wondered how some genius had artfully contrived to arrange for the last syllable to be a part of the theme). My date was Madelyn Pert—a very smart, tender, and cute freshman from Mount Holyoke College. She helped with the decorations, and we had a great weekend together. Pete's date was Pam, of course, so we double-dated to the hockey game and skiing events in the afternoons before Pete and I sang in the two Glee Club concerts.

In February, as well, for the first time I made the dean's list due to my grades during the autumn term in France. I was very happy about that! My GPA was beginning to climb very slowly.

The mud season always began in late March or early April. Boards were laid on the Green's paths, which resembled quagmires, waiting to trap the unwary in pools of mud. As spring blossomed on the campus in mid-April, I was on my way to a class on the day after my birthday (April 13) when I noticed a group of protesters with signs demonstrating in front of Dartmouth Hall. Antiwar protests were very rare at Dartmouth. In fact, this was the first one I had seen. Members of the Students for a Democratic Society (SDS) were protesting the visit to Dartmouth of General Lewis Hershey, the director of the Selective Service. Several hundred students had gathered, and I surprised myself by joining in the shouts against the war. I was beginning to feel that the American government's involvement in Vietnam could not be justified at all.

Before the spring Glee Club trip, I decided to invite a close friend of my cousin Kate up for a weekend. Jan Green was a lovely girl I had known from childhood visits to my uncle Tom's family in Sodus, New York. I was pleased that Jan accepted my invitation for a weekend, and it was a lot of fun to be with her. Her stories about my six female cousins and their secrets were enthralling! I especially remember a romantic evening at the Occom Inn—one of my favorite places to take a girl I was trying to impress—and a lingering farewell kiss when she left. I had intended to pursue a relationship with Jan further, for I liked her immensely, but another nearby romance intruded shortly after I returned from the Glee Club's spring tour.

After he had tried on several occasions to hook me into a blind date, I finally reluctantly agreed to let fraternity brother Phil Freedman, '68, fix me up with a freshman nursing student from the Mary Hitchcock Nursing School, which was attached to the Dartmouth May Hitchcock Hospital. Phil's girlfriend—Donna—was a very sweet woman who persuaded me that her friend—Judy Castor—would be an ideal date.

As it turned out, Judy was not only a wonderfully fun, intelligent, and interesting woman but also one of the prettiest girls I had ever met, whose exotic face and long, dark hair completely enchanted me. She was part Choctaw and part Cherokee, which added to her mystique. Judy's dormitory was also only three blocks from Tri-Kap, so it was relatively easy to meet her for dates and weekends.

We went on many hikes, spent many nights at the Moosilauke Ravine Lodge and nearby Dartmouth Outing Club cabins with Phil and Donna, and canoed on the Connecticut to Gilman's Island and back often, enjoying the extraordinarily compelling arrival of spring in the Upper Connecticut Valley with its soft green leafing-out of the maples, oaks, birches, and other hardwoods in the forests and surging whitewater in the creeks.

Two weeks before Green Key Weekend, I was in charge of Tri-Kap's Moosilauke weekend, when the entire brotherhood with their dates spent Friday and Saturday nights at the lodge. It was a lot of trouble! The snow was so deep on the mountain roads that the road to the lodge was impassable. We had to shovel out a parking area on the side of the highway and then pull toboggans—laden with bedding, food, and beer kegs—from the road one and one half miles to the Ravine Lodge. Phil Davey and I cooked a chicken dinner for about sixty people the first night and spaghetti the second night, with help from Judy and other dates. On Saturday night, we had a square dance caller from

Etna (who hiked in from the highway) and danced until two in the morning. It was one of the best Dartmouth weekends of my life!

Judy was my date for Green Key Weekend. After watching the crew races and dancing until early morning at Tri-Kap, we spent the night on the golf course and had a special Sunday brunch at the Norwich Inn.

I was getting quite serious about my relationship with Judy. With Professor Eberhart's help, I was writing a lot of poetry (not part of any course but just for fun), and Judy was an appreciative audience. I called her my muse. April, May, and early June were blissful months with her. But suddenly Judy unexpectedly and mysteriously returned to her home in Rutland, Vermont, for the summer in mid-June and never came back to the nursing school. I was devastated! I later heard that she had gotten engaged to, and later married, her high school sweetheart … My anguish was palpable.

Tri-Kap brother Bill Fell rescued me from my misery with a generous offer. Bill had a pilot's license and one day in June asked me if I would like to go with him on a flight around the Presidential Range in a small plane. We took off from a nearby airport on a grass runway (it seemed like a cow pasture) in a two-passenger very small plane—probably a Cessna. It was a beautiful day. We flew north over Mount Moosilauke and then around the entire Presidential Range, from southwest to northeast, passing low over Mount Webster, Mount Jackson, Mount Pierce, Mount Eisenhower, Mount Franklin, Mount Monroe. Mount Washington, Mount Clay, Mount Jefferson, Mount Sam Adams, Mount John Quincy Adams, and Mount Madison. We flew directly over the Madison Spring Huts, where I had previously worked, on the shoulder of Mount Madison. It was a clear, sunny, and calm day, and I could see from a stupendous new perspective the White Mountains, trails, lakes, and rivers of northern New Hampshire that I had come to love. I will always be grateful to Bill for that fantastic, spirit-uplifting flight!

In the spring term, I had three tough English courses, each of which was enthralling in a different way. English 67 with Professor Harry Bond examined the Romantic Period and poems by Blake, Wordsworth, Coleridge, Shelley, Byron, and Keats. English 76 was a survey of American poetry (Poe, Longfellow, Emerson, Whitman, Melville, Dickinson, Robinson, and Frost) with Professor Eberhart. English 78 (modern American novel) with Assistant Professor Noel Perrin studied the fiction of Dreiser, Hemingway, Fitzgerald, Faulkner, and others. Again, the course with Professor Eberhart was particularly beguiling, as we enjoyed many evenings of his hospitality and poetic wisdom at his home before a cozy fire.

Early in May, one morning I bumped into Professor Eberhart at the Dartmouth Bookstore. He invited me to join him for breakfast at Lou's Restaurant on Main Street, where he was a frequent customer, for he was celebrating some good news, he said. When we entered the restaurant, everyone in Lou's shouted congratulations! The *Boston Globe* had just announced that Professor Eberhart had won the 1966 Pulitzer Prize for poetry! This was an even bigger honor than receiving the Bollingen Prize for poetry, which he won in 1962.

The other good news for me that week was a letter from Baker Library stating that I had been appointed as an assistant librarian in the Stefansson Collection of Arctic Exploration for the coming summer. My summer term at Dartmouth was to begin in mid-June. By working at DDA and at the library, I could cover all of the costs of the summer term.

So my junior year at Dartmouth came to a close with the sweet tastes of Swedish *aquavit*, Beaujolais wine, and Helen Eberhart's hot chocolate still fresh in the memory of my palate, and the writings of Balzac, Wordsworth, Jeffers, Frost, Dreiser, Hemingway, and Eberhart reverberating in the cadences of my heart. Despite losing Judy, it was a very good year!

Mts. Washington and Adams, Presidential Range, New Hampshire, above Madison Spring Huts in flight with Bill Fell, '67, June 1966

Sandra Ingalls, April 1967

Sanborn House and Baker Library, June 1967

My German friend Nadia Bobbert and Scottish friend
Joyce Fairley at beach near Montpellier, October 1965

Reserve Officer Training Corps on football field in front
of Leverone Field House, May 1967

CHAPTER 12—"GRAND OLD SENIORS"[49]

I was very pleased when Janis Terry told me that she would also be studying at Dartmouth during the summer of 1966. Our romance was over, but she was still a valued friend. So in late June we drove together to Hanover from Buffalo. I helped her move into her room in North Wigwam (newly named Hinman Hall) and then moved into my summer dorm room at 312 Topliff Hall—back in my former freshman dormitory! My year at Dartmouth as a grand old senior had begun!

Pete Thomas was also attending Dartmouth's Summer 1966 Festival. Pete elected to stay in his fraternity, Chi Phi. I missed Pete as a roommate, although my summer roommate was a very amiable Jewish boy from Queens (who had never before lived away from home) named Rich. We got along very well and were soon settled into our two rooms with all of my old furniture. Rich amused me by keeping a baseball bat next to his bunk in case he ever had to fend off an intruder!

That baseball bat became significant later in the summer. There were two entrances to Topliff Hall— the back entrance entered directly onto the second floor. The rooms were numbered so that room number 312 (our room) was directly above room number 212. Floor plans were identical on each floor. If you entered Topliff by the front entrance, you had to climb two flights of stairs to get to our floor, or one flight of stairs to get to the second floor. If, on the other hand, you entered by the back door, it was one flight up to our floor, and room 212 was on the entry level.

One weekend when I was climbing in the Presidential Range around Mount Washington, Rich was alone in our room. The occupant of room 212, late at night and in a drunken stupor, entered Topliff Hall from the back door (thinking it was the front entrance), climbed up a flight of stairs to our floor (thinking it was the second floor), and somehow entered our room and flopped onto what he thought was his bed. Rich clubbed him with the baseball bat! I heard that there was quite a furor! But no one was seriously injured.

During the summer, I had decided to study German! To this day I don't know why. It may have been Paul's influence (our scary "friend" from the hitchhiking adventure in Hannover, Germany, the previous October). I had classes each morning from eight o'clock until noon with two language laboratory sessions squeezed between two one-and-one-quarter-hour classes. Rich was in another German class. My outstanding German teacher was Professor Werner Kleinhardt,

---

49   "Where, O where are the grand old Seniors?" Anonymous, "Pea Green Freshmen," *Dartmouth Song Book*, 7.

who had a droll sense of humor and whom I liked immensely. Twenty-four of the 450 students on campus were studying German, eight in each of the three classes, and more than half of them were women. We ate together at a German table at Thayer Dining Hall and were supposed to speak only German!

From noon until four o'clock every day, I worked in the Stefansson Collection at Baker Library, cataloguing books, a job that was both easy and interesting. I spent more time reading the books—mostly about Arctic exploratory expeditions—than cataloguing them! I helped Janis get a similar job in the regular Baker Library collections, so we saw a lot of each other at work, at least, at the card files. Three afternoons each week, from about four o'clock until six o'clock, I was a French language laboratory assistant in the French Department, monitoring Peace Corps trainees who were learning French and otherwise preparing to serve in the Ivory Coast as volunteers. Since we had several hours of homework each night and I also worked at DDA each morning from six o'clock until just before classes began, I was extremely busy!

One of the other summer students living on our Topliff corridor was John Glasser from Princeton, with whom I had worked at Madison Spring Huts in the summer of 1963. John was also an avid hiker. We had a dozen or so great hikes on weekends, introducing Janis and Rich to New Hampshire's gorgeous mountains. The last weekend in June, several of my other prior crew mates at Madison drove over to see us—Tony MacMillan and four others—so we had a fine reunion. Seven former AMC hutmen I knew from my AMC work were studying at Dartmouth that summer.

The Dartmouth campus and the enveloping Upper Valley of the Connecticut River were covered with forests and flowers in the summer! Under a warming sun, puffy clouds drifted over the college Green, dragging long cool shadows across the students—including hundreds of women—stretched out on the grass amidst the elms with books or simply napping. In Thayer Dining Hall or in the Hopkins Center for the Arts, the unfamiliar and alluring sounds of women's voices and laughter—almost birdlike in their higher register notes—danced in the soft hill winds drifting through open windows. And in classes I found that their observations and comments were usually much more perceptive than the males in the class. If Dartmouth's summer campus was prophetic at all of what a coed college would seem like, I thought, Eleazar should have enrolled the women with the men in his school for Native Americans from the beginning. The other classmates on campus that summer would have wholeheartedly agreed with me, I am sure.[50]

I got to know three of the women enrolled in the summer classes quite well. Marjorie Bedrick from Pembroke College, Mary Lamb from Wellesley, and Patricia Johnstone from Ball State University all were good friends and fun partners for hiking or canoeing. I also dated for a while a very nice girl named Connie Darby, who was from White River Junction and worked as a secretary in the

---

[50]   Besides Pete and me, there were twenty-one other 1967s at Dartmouth for the summer term: Robert Dressler, Jonathan Gill, Ronald Hanson, Gerald Harris-Smith, John Hodgson, Craig Kerins, Ralph Kirmser, Jonathan Knight, Bradford Langley, John Manaras, John Meck, Merritt Meyer, Robert Morton, John Norris, John Parthemore, Wallace Ratliff, Donald Schwartz, William Thomson, Robert Webster, Willet Whitmore, and Kurt Wendelyn. There were also a lot of other Dartmouth classes represented.

Financial Aid Office. She had the prettiest blush I ever saw! Janis and I also occasionally dated. I was desperately searching for a girlfriend like either Leena or Anna of the Swedish summer in 1964, but I never found her at Dartmouth.

Throughout the summer term, the artistic face of Dartmouth was displayed at its best in what was called the Fourth Congregation of the Arts at Dartmouth! At the Hopkins Center, I attended with Janis or other dates several plays and symphony concerts. The plays included Shakespeare's *Julius Caesar*, Goldoni's *The Servant of Two Masters*, and *Take Care of Amelia* by Georges Feydeau, and I was extremely impressed with the high quality of the productions. I also enjoyed the concerts and recall that the Hop's film series had some excellent French movies as well.

One of my favorite singing groups visited Dartmouth that summer and sang at Leverone Field House to a packed house. The Mamas and the Papas were terrific, singing "California Dreamin'" and "Monday, Monday," as well as several other great songs. Leverone was not the best musical venue and always had a musty, dusty smell to it because of the dirt floor, but Mama Cass and company were spectacular.

I had one memorable adventure in the library on a humid summer evening. A very attractive and engaging older Swedish woman named Eva was also working late in the Stefansson Collection, cataloguing books. We talked a lot during the summer about Sweden and became good friends. Eva was married and very, very pregnant—she was so big that it was difficult for her to walk.

One evening we were both working quite late, about eleven o'clock, as I tried to make up some work hours missed in the prior week. I noticed that she seemed to be crying. Eva confessed that she would give anything to be able to move quickly again. Her condition and lack of mobility were depressing her. I asked her if she would like to move very quickly, if only for a minute, and she agreed.

I settled Eva comfortably into one of the library's large moveable chairs with coasters and started to push her down the deserted card catalogue hall that ran the length of Baker Library. We actually got going pretty fast! It was lots of fun, and Eva was laughing so hard that I thought she would have her baby on the spot! On our last run of three down the entire length of the hall, the west door to Baker Library opened just as we got there and were slowing down.

In strode President John Sloan Dickey, who was apparently out for a late-evening stroll around the campus. We were all startled. My heart was in my throat, and Eva looked thunderstruck. President Dickey smiled.

"Can I have a ride too?" he joked. "How much is a ticket?" And then, when he noticed how pregnant Eva was, "Be careful with that precious cargo!"

Eva had her baby two days later and afterward told me how much she had loved that ride and our encounter with the president!

My sister, Ceci, was also pregnant that summer. When she visited me in Hanover in late July, it was unusually hot and humid with temperatures in the low nineties. We went swimming in True's Brook to escape the heat, just off state Route 12A south of Lebanon, at a local swimming hole known as True's Ledges. A series of small waterfalls in the brook, dropping about fifty feet overall, form enticing pools for escaping hot weather. It was a favorite place to go swimming, especially since the Connecticut was considered too polluted from upstream urban waste and foul paper mills to be safe. My sister loved that natural swimming pool! We had a fantastic time together!

At the end of the summer, Janis and I attended a symphony concert together in the Spaulding Auditorium at the Hopkins Center. That afternoon I had had a lot to drink with her, which was very unusual for me on a date with Janis. As far as I know, this was the only occasion at Dartmouth when I got so soused that I have no recollection of anything that happened after dinnertime. Janis claimed that we attended the concert together, sat next to a young faculty couple named Gaylord, and conversed pleasantly and intelligibly with them all evening. I have no recollection of either the concert or of meeting the Gaylords. Professor Gaylord, however, confirmed Janis's report when I later took his class in the fall.

Toward the end of the spring term, I had been asked if I would volunteer to room with a foreign student during my senior year. Pete was going to continue to live in his fraternity in the fall, and my Tri-Kap brothers had repeatedly asked if I would live with them in our fraternity house. Although I liked my fraternity brothers immensely, the thoughts of living in the cramped quarters of Tri-Kap with the delicious scent of stale beer and vomit sometimes permeating the air, and of the noise of weekend bands making it impossible to sleep some nights before two in the morning or later, persuaded me to pursue other lodging.

Seniors had their pick of dormitory rooms, including single rooms, and I was hoping to get a room with a fireplace. But the thought of getting to know yet another foreign friend and of being able to teach him about the United States and American culture (as I had been so kindly taught about Swedish and French culture in the previous two years) was very appealing. I agreed, and in late August, after I had been finally told his name and address, I wrote the following letter to Willem deHaas, from Eindhoven, Netherlands, who would be my foreign student roommate:

Dear Willem:

I am to be your roommate next year at Dartmouth, so I thought I would write you a short letter just to introduce myself and to see if there is anything I can do to help you when you arrive in the U.S.A. I know nothing about you, except your name and your address, but I am looking forward very much to meeting you and getting to know you. A year at Dartmouth is really a tremendous amount of fun, as well as hard work, of course. I think you will like Dartmouth, and I hope you will have a marvelous year in my country!

This year will be my fourth and last year at Dartmouth College. I was "pre-med," that is, studying in preparation for medical school; however, my major studies recently have been in literature, both English and French. At Dartmouth I am an avid skier, although I am not very good, and I sing in the "glee club"—a sort of men's chorus which each year makes a concert tour of the United States. Most of the time, I am afraid, I am either studying hard or else I am preoccupied with some girl … the universal problem!

I live in Buffalo, an industrial city situated near Niagara Falls at the eastern end of Lake Erie, and I am writing to you from my home where I am passing a short vacation before returning to Hanover about September 15. My father is a pharmacist, and my mother works for the American Red Cross, so I don't get to see much of either of my parents, even when I am at home. I am the youngest of three children in our family— my brother, 31 years old, is married and teaches at North Carolina State University; my sister, 27 years old, is married also and lives with her family in Ohio. So I am the only one at home now, and my visits here are few and unfortunately short.

Not knowing when you will leave the Netherlands or when you arrive in this country, I can only hope that this letter will reach you before you do leave. If you need any help in any way, or if you would like to visit us in Buffalo before going to Hanover, please write, or call us after you arrive. My family and I would love to have you visit us! My address and telephone number are below.

Wishing you a pleasant trip, or if you are already in the U.S.A. perhaps, a good visit now.

Sincerely,
Chuck (short for Charles)

The summer term's eight weeks went by in a flash, and before I knew it, we were taking final exams on August 19–20 and preparing for a brief vacation before the start of the fall term's classes. I got two Bs in the German 1 and German 2 courses and liked German enough that I took German 3 in the autumn on a pass/fail basis.

My Dutch roommate met me at Dartmouth on September 10. He wanted to be called "Wim" and was eighteen years old, six feet six inches tall, and a tremendous soccer player! We got along very well right from the start. He became a "social member" of Tri-Kap at once, so that we could enjoy the house's social activities together. Like Pete, Wim had a great sense of humor. We laughed at the same things, appreciated good music, loved the outdoors, and talked incessantly about women. He also brought a European perspective to the discussions about Vietnam and civil rights that were mushrooming on campus among all the students. I was very lucky to have a second wonderful roommate in Wim!

My new "dormitory" was the Nathan Lord House, located at 41 College Street. Lord was a former president of the college, serving for thirty-five years (1828–63) and accomplishing a great deal in expanding the number of buildings and student enrollment and enhancing Dartmouth's reputation. His Bible-based literalist theology, however, supported the institution of slavery, as a result of which he prevented Dartmouth from giving an honorary degree to President Abraham Lincoln. He thereafter resigned in disgrace.[51]

Despite the notoriety of its past resident, the Lord House was a wonderful place to reside. It was located just north of and across the street from the Church of Christ on College Street.[52] From the outside, the Lord House looked like a typical, two-story white colonial home with green shutters. Our room on the first floor was eighteen feet by fourteen feet, had large windows on the north side and one large window on the west side with a large, ancient fireplace on the north wall between the two windows. We shared a bathroom across the hall on the first floor with the other ten students in the former home of President Lord.

As soon as Tri-Kap had chosen its pledges, I corralled several of them for a wood-gathering excursion across the river to the Vermont woods. With Wim and me, in about five hours pledges Michael Hermann, '69, Hampton Rich, '69, David Wakelin, '69, and Russell Granik, '69, cut up enough fallen timber—mostly cherry and birch—to provide plenty of firewood for our fireplace in the new room. We stacked the split wood behind the Lord House. That fireplace and its cheery fires had an awesome romantic effect on even the most heartless of dates and gave both Wim and me—and some special women—enormous pleasure during the cold winter months.

There were four other classmates in the Nathan Lord House; Timothy Armstrong, William Gerber, Robert Purvis, and Kurt Wendelyn lived on the second floor in room 204. I knew Kurt from Glee Club and Tim from freshmen crew. Next to our room on the first floor were a couple of sophomores: Jonas Johnson and Peter Notier. Rounding out the Lord House's denizens were Cornelis Van Vorst, '68, and Robert Haslach, '68, whom I knew from DDA.

My mother had made blue-and-green curtains for our three windows. We also had a couch, several comfortable chairs, dressers, a small table, and our bunk beds, which we kept stacked to save space. With my thick purple rug on the floor, it was a tremendously comfortable and attractive living arrangement—probably the best I ever had at Dartmouth!

My courses—German 3, Chaucer 1, and the English Novel—all entailed a tremendous amount of work. By far, Chaucer was the best of the three. I had signed up for the course with great trepidation.

---

[51] Hill, ed., *The College on the Hill—A Dartmouth Chronicle*, 76–77.

[52] The attractive little house has been moved twice since my college days and originally stood on Wentworth Street, where the lawn of Baker Library is today. Ibid. *1864 Prospect of College and Village*, endpapers.

Chaucer had the reputation of being one of the most difficult courses in the English Department, especially since Chaucer's language was generally characterized as Middle English. I went to the first class with great apprehension.

I was pleasantly surprised. Assistant Professor Alan Gaylord—whom I have already mentioned—was a visiting professor from the University of Michigan, reportedly *the* Chaucer expert in the United States, and a fantastic teacher. His lectures placed a great deal of emphasis on the spoken, as well as the written, language of Chaucer. We studied Chaucer as a literary artist and critic of his age based on readings from *The Canterbury Tales* and materials describing the medieval world of the late fourteenth century. But our focus was on the oral recitation of Chaucer's works—in Middle English. It was great fun! I got a B to my great surprise.

German 3 was extremely time-consuming and difficult, mainly because I did not have the strong background of vocabulary that others in the class had from their three to four years of high school German. Although Professor Kleinhardt—whom I liked a lot from the summer classes—taught us occasionally, other faculty of the German Department taught most of the classes. I struggled! I was glad that I took the course on a pass/fail basis and received credit!

The English novel course required me to read two lengthy novels each week by such writers as Defoe, Richardson, Fielding, Sterne, Smollet, and Austen. Assistant Professor Charles Terry, like Professor Gaylord, was new to the faculty but was a fine teacher. I was reading an average of nine hundred pages per week—such novels as *Moll Flanders, Tom Jones, Joseph Andrews, Pamela, Clarissa, Tristram Shandy, The Adventures of Roderick Random, Pride and Prejudice,* and *Sense and Sensibility*—and enjoying the course greatly! I fell in love with Jane Austen's novels! With an A in the English Novel course, I ended the term with a B plus average and again made the dean's list.

My social life during my senior year began on September 24. Tri-Kap held a mixer at the house with girls from Green Mountain Junior College on the weekend before classes started. I met a very lovely student by the name of Diana with whom I danced all night and then took to breakfast on Sunday morning at the Occom Inn. Diana had a very distinctive and attractive voice, as well as a unique, charming way of laughing that had the cadence of the love song of a chickadee. I was tremendously attracted to her. Before she returned to Green Mountain, we made arrangements for her to return to Hanover as my date the following weekend. I bought tickets for a play at the Hopkins Center and rented a bed for her on both Friday and Saturday nights at a local Hanover family's residence on Kingsford Road. I thought about being with her again all week.

On the Friday morning of her expected arrival, I got a telephone call from Diana, apologizing for having to cancel our weekend plans because she was sick with the flu. I was disappointed but understood that sometimes these things happen. Wim left with his date on a hike for the weekend, leaving me alone and somewhat morose, so on Friday evening I decided to take my camera and climb to the top of one of my favorite spots on campus—Bartlett Tower—to take some sunset pictures.

I walked up Observatory Hill and along the path to the entry to Bartlett Tower, where the heavy iron-barred gate to the tower steps was open. There was no one else around, and the surrounding pines were fragrant and still, waiting for the sunset. I started up the stairs. About three-quarters of the way up the steps, I heard a male voice coming from the top of Bartlett Tower and then a distinctive and attractive girl's voice followed by her laughter, which had the cadence of the love song of a chickadee. There was no doubt that Diana was with a date at the top of the tower. Apparently, her flu had been miraculously cured …

I turned and sadly retraced my steps. I was not about to confront her. As I walked down the path away from the tower, a campus policeman came up the path toward me, heading for the entrance of the tower.

"Got to lock her up early for the night," he said, and asked me if I had seen anyone in the tower. I replied truthfully, "I didn't see anyone, Officer," and a minute later heard the squeak and clang of the iron-barred gate in the distance as he shut and locked it. I almost returned to the tower that night after sunset to make sure that nothing tragic had occurred, but I didn't. Happily, there were no reports in the *Dartmouth* of sexual assaults, murders, or deaths due to exposure on campus that weekend.

On the weekend of October 14, I spent three days at Moosilauke with the Tri-Kap brotherhood. It was the peak of the fall colors. Mount Moosilauke and the surrounding peaks were stunning in their crimson-and-gold cloaks, and the weather was perfect—cool and sunny with no wind the entire glorious weekend. I was in charge again of the dinners and other arrangements, and I led the hike to the summit of Moosilauke and back. My date was a very nice sophomore from Wellesley, whom I had met at our Glee Club concert. It was Wim's first visit to the Ravine Lodge and Mount Moosilauke. He loved it, although he missed most of the weekend because he had a freshman soccer game.

Wim was an incredible soccer player! He made the freshman team and was quite frustrated for the first four games because the coach did not play him at all. Finally, in the fifth game he went in as a substitute and scored the winning goal! Thereafter he started and averaged a goal per game!

The lecture series for seniors known as the Senior Symposia—successor to the Great Issues lectures—began the last week in October. Our first speaker was the poet Archibald MacLeish, who spoke on man's essential worth. He was an excellent speaker. I recall that Supreme Court Justice William O. Douglas also gave an impressive lecture later in the year.

It may have been the lecture series that prompted a series of antiwar rallies in October and November. There were long lines of student demonstrators on the college green and peace vigils held by the bravest and most dedicated of the antiwar activists on a daily basis at noon. I rarely joined in the shouting lines, but early in November, I stopped by the Peace Corps' recruitment table in Hopkins Center, near the student mailboxes, and talked with a young recruiter about joining. She was extremely persuasive about the value of serving overseas as a volunteer, pursuing the Corps' mission of world peace. Because I was familiar already with the substantial Peace Corps presence at Dartmouth, I filled out an application and submitted it on the spot.[53] Perhaps I could start addressing the world's problems in my own little way.

House Parties Weekend was on November 5–6. My date was a cute second-generation Swedish American student from Vermont College, named Jeanne Peterson, who was also from Buffalo. Jeanne and I had a lot of fun together! She was extremely smart and caring and reminded me very much of both of my Swedish friends, Leena and Anna.

Tri-Kap had three bands, punch parties each day, a football rally complete with torches we made, and a lobster dinner at the house. We all went to the game and watched Dartmouth overwhelm Columbia 56–14. The game would have been somewhat boring except for the action in the last quarter. First, it was announced that Princeton had beaten Harvard, so that our only loss so far—to Harvard—would not prevent Dartmouth from at least sharing the championship.

More importantly, with two minutes to go in the game, one of our Tri-Kap sophomore pledges, Bill Kinschner, went into the game as Dartmouth's third-string quarterback for the first time in the season. On his second play, he seemed trapped in the backfield but suddenly broke loose up the middle of the field for a thirty-two-yard gain. Then, on Bill's fourth play he lofted a thirty-six-yard pass for a touchdown! Class of 1967 Tri-Kap brother Phil Davey then kicked the extra point—his first of the season. Phil subsequently kicked off to Columbia and made the tackle on the kickoff, as the game ended. Of course, the Tri-Kap crowd went wild! Final score: Dartmouth 56 (Tri-Kap 7), Columbia 14. Dartmouth ended up the 1966 season with a 7–2 record, having lost to Holy Cross and Harvard—both games we should have won! In the Ivy League we were 6–1—cochampions with Harvard. Classmate Wynn Mabry was picked as an all-American defensive back later in the year.

On December 1, I wrote to my parents to remind them of my upcoming tuition payment for the winter term of $320 ($640–$320 scholarship) and of my sixty dollars for fraternity dues for the next term—both due on December 15. I worked for my board at DDA, as I have mentioned, and usually was able to pay for my room with monies earned from summer work or from my postal service jobs during holidays at home. My parents paid for my other expenses, such as books, clothes, travel expenses, and social costs in addition to the tuition and dues.

During the winter term, my three courses were Comparative Literature 6 (the Medea theme), Chaucer 2, and English 83 (modern verse drama), which was a seminar. The largest of these had seven students, so all three courses were intimate and very interactive.

---

[53] Dartmouth's cooperation with the Peace Corps was unsurpassed by any other college or university. In the four summers 1963–1966 Dartmouth trained 715 Peace Corps volunteers, initiated with the Corps a two-year training program between students' junior and senior years, and produced sixty-six Peace Corps applicants from the class of 1966 (about 10 percent of the class compared to 1 percent, on average, of other colleges). Charles E. Widmayer, *John Sloan Dickey – A Chronicle of His Presidency of Dartmouth College* (Hanover, NH: Dartmouth College, 1991), 239–240.

Professor Kleinhardt taught the comparative literature course, which studied the Medea theme in literature from Euripides to Jean Anouilh and Robinson Jeffers. Once again, he was an inspiring teacher, and I thoroughly enjoyed his course.

Chaucer 2 continued the delight of my first Chaucer course with Professor Gaylord, as we examined *Troilus and Criseyde*. By midcourse I was reading and speaking Middle English rather well! The Tri-Kap brotherhood had found his Chaucer recitation at the fraternity house so entertaining in the fall that we invited Professor Gaylord back for two more dinners, and he and his wife later chaperoned several of our dances!

There were only five students in the verse drama course with Professor Eberhart. I was really fascinated by this course in which we each had to write a play in verse. Many evenings at Professor Eberhart's house, reading plays by T. S. Eliot and Christopher Fry and discussing the structure of modern drama in preparation for writing our own play, seemed to pass in a flash!

I worked hard to write a play and was delighted that Professor Eberhart was very happy with my work—so much so, as I have mentioned, that in March he presented me with a Citation "for excellent work on Eliot and Fry and for an original verse play." Dean Seymour wrote me a thoughtful note when I received the citation: "It gives me genuine pleasure to send you the enclosed Citation Report which has been added to your permanent record at Dartmouth. Such citations are rare, and you can take justifiable pride in the hard work and the achievement which this one represents …" I was thrilled to receive the citation and Dean Seymour's note, which was much better than the "first strike" that he gave me my second month on campus as a result of my rum adventure involving Sandi.

In mid-January—as skiing was difficult due to a succession of rainy, warm weeks—I attended a concert at the Hopkins Center with Jeanne that was memorable. Betty Jean Hagen, a marvelous violinist from Toronto, was the featured soloist in a program of the Dartmouth Symphony that included Brahms' Tragic Overture, Piston's Prelude and Allegro for Organ and Orchestra, Mendelssohn's Italian Symphony, and my favorite violin concerto, Tchaikovsky's Violin Concerto in D Major, opus 35. Miss Hagen was splendid, and the orchestra was also in fine form! Jeanne seemed to enjoy the concert as much as I did, and I began to think of her as a true kindred spirit.

The theme of Winter Carnival was "A Midwinter Night's Dream," which was captured in the statue in the center of the green—a thirty-foot-tall maiden in sixteenth-century attire. Jeanne was my date for the weekend, and Wim's date was Molly Howard from Buffalo. We finally had some significant snow just before carnival weekend, so the skiing events were amazing to watch, even in the subzero temperatures. The two Glee Club concerts went extremely well, and Paul Zeller immediately plunged into a frantic round of rehearsals to prepare for the spring concert tour in March (including a concert in Buffalo, as I mentioned earlier) and the later concerts scheduled at Expo 68 in Montreal.

Tri-Kap had a huge late-winter weekend party at Moosilauke before exams and the end of the winter term. Due to the snow, as in 1966 we had to park our vehicles on the side of the highway and trudge one and one half miles through more than two feet of snow to the lodge, pulling toboggans heavy with food, beer, and sleeping bags. On Saturday night, about fifty of us plus four faculty couple chaperones had an awesome time square dancing until midnight, and then I was prevailed upon to tell the Doc Benton ghost story, with some help from brother Jack Noon, '68.

The story in full took about one hour. At strategic points in the story, various sound effects were required—such as scratching on the outside of the windows facing Mount Moosilauke, the scream of a young girl being kidnapped, the clanking of chains in the cellar of the Ravine Lodge, and the thud of a child's body hitting the ground after being hurled off of a cliff in Jobildunc Ravine (the latter provided by a sack of potatoes or flour dropped from the balcony overlooking the lodge's main room before the fireplace). In brief—as I recall from hearing the story dozens of times (remembering that this is a greatly shortened version), the story went like this.

> Thomas Benton was born in the early 1800s in a town named for his family, located on the other side of Mount Moosilauke. The son of a prominent family, Tom was sent to the University of Heidelberg, Germany, to attend medical school. Although Tom excelled as a student, he felt like an outsider among the Germans and formed a close friendship only with one elderly professor.
>
> Although he was kindly, there was something strange about the professor. The other faculty members shunned him, and the students whispered about "blasphemous experimentation." But he took Tom under his wing, and the two spent many nights discussing medicine, science, and theology.
>
> When the old professor died, he left Tom some arcane books and a small locked chest, which Tom brought back to New Hampshire after graduation.
>
> Tom quickly became the most respected doctor in New Hampshire and could heal any patient who came to him. But in 1816, he learned the limits of his medical skills. His beautiful fiancée, the daughter of a wealthy landowner, came down with typhoid fever. Tom was unable to cure her, and she died in his arms.
>
> The shock was more than he could take. Tom abandoned his home and medical practice and retreated to a ramshackle cabin on Mount Moosilauke. The only possessions he brought with him were the books and the small locked chest given to him by his mentor in Heidelberg. Townspeople muttered under their breath that the old professor had been working on the secret of eternal life and suspected that, while Tom's fiancée may have died, the locked chest contained secrets that Tom was using to try to defeat death itself!

Weird things began to occur around the mountain in the 1820s. Over a period of ten years, six cows and ten horses were found dead, their corpses unmarked except for a single small wound behind their left ears. The body of a young man was stolen from the undertaker, only to be discovered on Mount Moosilauke—with a small wound behind its ear.

Although the locals pitied Tom for his broken heart, they didn't support livestock killing and grave-robbing. A group of officials trekked up the mountain to confront Tom, but when they reached his cabin, it was empty. Tom had run off into the woods, driven mad by grief and by his experimentation, it was supposed. Had he discovered the secret of eternal life but at the cost of his sanity?

In the 1840s, a young girl disappeared from her parents' farm not far from Mount Moosilauke. Tracking dogs were used to follow her scent. They led the searchers up the mountain to the headwall of Jobildunc Ravine. It was a cloudy, dark night, but just as the moon poked through the clouds, the men heard a faint noise above them on the cliff. As they watched in horror, a dark figure with long white hair, carrying a screaming bundle in its arms, raced to the edge of the headwall and threw it over the cliff. The child's lifeless, broken body had a strange mark behind its left ear.

Over the next century, many more animals and people mysteriously disappeared in the vicinity of the mountain. Local people learned not to be out at night near the mountain. Fear of the ghost of Moosilauke was so great that in 1860, when the Prospect House was built on the summit of Mount Moosilauke, construction workers refused to stay the night at the project. It was later known as the Tip-Top House of Mount Moosilauke. In 1870, a well-made carriage road (it was a state-chartered toll road and collected tolls until 1919) was built up the mountain and many more visitors were attracted. But no visitors dared to stay the night, so the owners' profits were limited.

In the early twentieth century, the Tip-Top House owners hired a team of five adventurers to stay nights on the mountain to prove once and for all that there was no danger to guests. The men stayed for two weeks. On the last night, something strange happened, and in the early morning one of the men was found on the outskirts of Benton, stark raving mad and blubbering about a mysterious stranger. The other four men's bodies were found later that day on the summit, each with a strange mark behind one ear.

At the beginning of the Second World War, the Tip-Top House was used by the army for top-secret communications projects. Heavy guards were posted. But one night without explanation in 1942 the structure burned to the ground. The army never returned to the summit, and the official report of the incident has always remained classified. But a surviving log of events that later surfaced had recorded that a guard had seen an old man with long white hair in the vicinity.

In the mid-twentieth century, for a time Dartmouth used the mountain as a ski area. Vestiges of trails, such as the Snapper Ski Trail, may still be seen. The ski team used to run up the mountain and ski down for conditioning and practice until two members of the team mysteriously disappeared in the early 1950s. Their tracks in the snow indicated that someone had pushed them off the headwall of Jobildunc. Their bodies were found at the base of the cliff with little marks behind their ears.

In the past ten years or so, the strange deaths seem to have ceased. Nevertheless, as implausible as it may seem that old Doc Benton still lurks in this area 150 years after his birth, Dartmouth cautions you to be on alert at all times and to report immediately any sighting of a haggard figure dressed in black with long white hair.

The ghost story had the desired effect. No one wanted to sleep alone in the suddenly creaky and cold lodge in the ominous shadow of the winter mountain. The chaperones warned that no more than two people per sleeping bag would be allowed.

When Jeanne and I looked for a place to settle down, all of the bunkrooms were filled. We finally found a linen closet on the first floor, under the stairs, which provided acceptable though somewhat cramped accommodations when the shelves and blankets were removed. We were cozy and safe from Doc Benton, who never would have found us under the stairs.

The next morning at breakfast, Jack Noon told the famous "Maple Syrup Story," to many groans from the brotherhood and their dates. I had heard and told this tale of two New Hampshire farmers many times when I worked as a hutman for the AMC at Madison Spring Huts:

Two farmers, Emmet and Newt, met on their monthly trip to town to buy supplies.

> "Mawnin', Emmet," said one.
> "Mawnin', Newt," replied the other.
> "What did you say you fed your hoss when it twas sick?"
> "May-pil syrup."
> "May-pil syrup?"
> "Ay-yup, may-pil syrup."
> "Mawnin', Emmet."
> "Mawnin', Newt."
> A month later, the two farmers greeted each other again.
> "Mawnin', Emmet," said one.
> "Mawnin', Newt," replied the other.

"What did you say you fed your hoss when it twas sick?"

"May-pil syrup."

"Y'say may-pil syrup?"

"Ay-yup, may-pil syrup."

"Kilt my hoss."

"Kilt mine, too."

"Mawnin', Emmet."

"Mawnin', Newt."

Jeanne was a real trooper to have endured without complaint both the Doc Benton tale and the story of the two farmers in one weekend. She was becoming a special girlfriend!

Winter term exams were right on the heels of the Moosilauke trip, but somehow I managed to do well: a B (Comparative Literature) and two As—my best term grade-wise at Dartmouth.

After Wim and I returned from the spring break Glee Club tour, I was exceedingly busy with two jobs (DDA and Baker Library), Glee Club practices, three demanding courses, making graduation arrangements for my family, and finalizing plans for another summer in Sweden and thereafter for graduate school. At the end of March, I received the reassuring news that I had been accepted for graduate programs in English at the Universities of Michigan, Wisconsin, and Washington—three large northern universities at one of which I hoped to experience coeducation in a more urban setting. I opted for Wisconsin.[54]

In my last term at Dartmouth, I took English 64 (the age of Milton) with Professor Schultz, English 74 (American and British poetry from 1914) with Professor Vance, and English 86 (seminar on Alexander Pope) with a new assistant professor named Peter Saccio. I struggled to keep my head above water in my last term but managed to enjoy my final English courses with the three fine teachers and receive three Bs from them. At the same time, I was frantically reviewing all of English literature—from Chaucer to Eberhart—in preparation for the comprehensive exam.

The latter pleasantly surprised me. Probably as a result of my having taken so many English literature classes in the past one and one half years, most of the material on the comprehensive exam was quite fresh in my mind. I ended up with a B plus.

Just before Green Key Weekend, an alien from another world visited the campus. In the 1967 presidential primary run up, Governor George Wallace chose to reprise his Dartmouth campus tour of 1963 when he had been cordially received and even applauded. He came to speak at the college on the evening of May 3, 1967, at Webster Hall. I decided to hear him, even though I despised his outspoken racist policies.

Inside Webster Hall, Wallace was interrupted repeatedly during his speech and left the stage several times

---

[54] My graduate school adventures in Madison, Wisconsin, are recounted in *The Time of the Monkey, Rooster, and Dog.*

as police dispersed students trying to get onto the stage. When he finished his talk, there was almost no applause. The student and faculty audience was mostly silent and, it seemed to me, disapproving.

I was at the back of Webster Hall and quickly exited. I found myself immediately in a group of several hundred students encircling his car. There was a mob mentality building among us, and for about ten minutes we jostled and rocked Wallace's car. I was not sure then that he was in the car, which had dark windows, but I was angry. There were some very large men trying to get us away from the car, but I never saw or heard any police.

Regarding the mini-riot after Wallace's speech, Dartmouth administrators did not see this as a proud day for the college, editorials across the country were uniformly negative, and most of the journalistic coverage was critical in tone. Dean Seymour hastened to publish a lengthy apology, and President Dickey followed with a short statement blaming "a few irresponsibles." I guess he meant me and other 1967s, such as car-rocker Bob Davidson.

The *Dartmouth* carried a host of letters, condemning or praising our treatment of Wallace. My favorite letter was from Professor Gaylord, who wrote in part, commenting on Dartmouth's official apologetic response to Wallace:

> … I wish to offer my small voice of protest. Dean Seymour, and all others who (I think presumptuously) "apologize for the whole College," please note this: although I am not at all ashamed, I would be willing to "regret" the excesses of the demonstrations you lament IF ONLY you had included in that fulsome telegram some other words like these:

> Your extraordinary rudeness to the Dartmouth community has been met in kind; the racial violence in the nation which you have hypocritically sanctioned with evasions and euphemisms inspired last night a small comic token in reply. Your refusal to allow meaningful answers to your lies provoked loud voices and actions which testify not only to rashness and unreason, but also to a deeper rage which cannot stand to see demagoguery flattered with politeness. I wish to apologize for these excesses, sir, both yours and theirs, and to regret that your outstanding impudence had not been met with better manners. Some lessons are learned harder than others. Let us agree to learn this together: self-control in the face of outrage is the gift of a greater maturity than was demonstrated last night. But also: some men, when lies are thrown in their faces, will not smile in peace.

> We regret the response; but we deplore the provocation.[55]

---

[55]   Alan T. Gaylord in the *Dartmouth,* May 8, 1967, 2.

I think that Chaucer would have applauded Professor Gaylord.

Green Key Weekend followed the excitement of Wallace's visit. Jeanne and I cheered Tri-Kap's entry in the chariot races on the green until the hastily constructed vehicle fell apart! We also watched the crew races and played golf all night on the golf course, under the light of billions of stars, in accordance with Green Key traditions.

My entire family came for graduation weekend. Wim was part of our family by now, having spent Thanksgiving and Christmas in Buffalo with the Hobbie clan. My parents, brother, and sister and their families, as well as my aunt Kate, stayed at the Pine Crest Motel. It was glorious weather the entire weekend! On Friday afternoon, the 1967s filed in our robes to the Bema where we ceremoniously smoked our clay pipes and then smashed them on the stump of the Old Pine on the hill above near Bartlett Tower. Classmate Jerry Zaks, in a Native American headdress, delivered a stirring address as we symbolically broke our ties to Dartmouth.[56] In the evening, we all attended a reception at the president's house, and then Jeanne and I attended the senior dance in Alumni Hall.

Already exhausted, on Saturday we slept late but got up in time for the commencement luncheon at Leverone Field House followed by a reception at Professor and Mrs. Regosin's home and a dinner at Tri-Kap.

Graduation ceremonies were held on Sunday on the lawn next to Baker Library under the guardian elms. We lined up on East Wheelock Street, and the academic procession to the commencement and baccalaureate exercises started at ten thirty. We were all extremely happy but a bit apprehensive about the future, particularly of the military draft that was then conscripting young men to fight in Vietnam.

As I walked across the lawn with my classmates, I never anticipated that within two years I would be serving in Korea as a Peace Corps volunteer or that within weeks of my return from Asia, I would be called for service in the US Army. Nor did I imagine that dozens of my classmates would serve in the armed forces—classmates Bill Smoyer and Duncan Sledge giving their lives for their country—or

---

[56]   Jerry later became a well-known actor and director on Broadway, winning four Tony Awards for his directing.

that forty would eventually become Peace Corps volunteers with me,[57] serving in twenty-two different countries—probably the highest number of volunteers (as opposed to applicants) produced by any Dartmouth class.

I was pleased to have finished college. At the same time, I was disappointed that I had not done better academically. Although my degree was awarded "with distinction in English," overall I was barely in the top half of my class. Yet I had learned how to live, and as it turned out, I had also developed analytic and writing skills that furnished the foundation for the legal career that provided a means to make a living and brought me great satisfaction.

[57] List of Dartmouth class of 1967 returned Peace Corps volunteers:

Ron Arps	Thailand	1968–70	Jack Kornfield	Thailand	1967–69
Blaine Bjornstad	Samoa	1967–69	Frank Lagay	Korea	1970–72
Jay Boekelheide	Chad	1967–69	David Levitt	Micronesia	1969–71
Melvin Boozer	Brazil	1967–69	Dick Lyczak	Thailand	1967–69
Dave Brooks	Morocco	1967–71	Gunnar Malm	Ecuador	1967–68
John Burns	Venezuela	1967–69	Brian MacNeary	Venezuela	1967–69
Fred Cowan	Ethiopia	1967–69	Mike Merenda	Ivory Coast	1969–70
Dave Davenport	Thailand	1967–71	Bob Miller	Afghanistan	1967–69
	Thailand	2005–05	Cary Moore	Malaysia	1967–69
John English	Micronesia	1967–69	Tom Moore	Cameroon	1967–69
Larry Fabian	Iran	1969–71	John Nunley	Bolivia	1967–69
Chuck Geisler	Colombia	1967–69	Dave O'Connor	Nepal	1967–69
Jim Gibb	Philippines	1967–69	John Pierpont	Philippines	1968–70
Jack Gramlich	Nepal	1967–69	Jeffry Pond	Iran	1971–73
George Grover	Colombia	1967–69	Herb Schneider	Iran	1969–71
John Hager	Chile	1968–71	Fred Schroeder	Samoa	1967–69
Chuck Hobbie	Korea	1968–71	Saul Spatz	Colombia	1967–69
Jim Humphrey	Morocco	1967–70	Michael Wilson	Cameroon	1967–69
Mike Jones	Malaysia	1967–69	Tom Wilson	Sierra Leone	1967–70
Cresson Kearny	Sierra Leone	1967–71	Bob Wood	Thailand	1967–69
Paul Killebrew	Peru	1968–70	Marty Zimmerman	Chile	1968–70

In learning *how* to live, however, I discovered the road to emotional and physical well-being. The honing of my appreciation of the joyfulness of music, the beauty of the still north woods in snow, the ecstasy of crimson-and-purple sunsets, the jubilation of sports competition, the intellectual elation of talking with learned teachers, and the exultation in the friendships and experiences with the people of my college years—these were the gifts provided by Dartmouth that have nurtured every day of my life.

Steve Guch Jr. was our class valedictorian. Robert Henry Winters, Canadian minister of commerce and trade, delivered the commencement address. President Dickey delivered the valedictory to the seniors. Hank Paulson Jr. '68, head usher,[58] did not say anything. By one thirty, we were no longer "grand old seniors."

---

[58] Henry "Hank" Merritt Paulson Jr. later served as the seventy-fourth US secretary of the treasury.

Classmate Jerry Zaks in a Native American headdress regales the class of 1967
at the site of the Old Pine near Bartlett Tower, June 1967

Dartmouth football team, October 1964

Chariot races on the Dartmouth Green, Green Key Weekend, May 1967

Snowstorm on Rope Ferry Road, Hanover, New Hampshire, January 1964

Cherry blossoms near west entrance of Baker Library, May 1967

Walking with classmates and clay pipes, June 1967

Chapter 13—Dartmouth Undying

The spirit or sense of the place where the Connecticut and the AT cross may not be captured adequately in the few pages of this memoir. No one who has visited Dartmouth may deny that a genius loci lurks there—the protective and alluring spirit of the place—perhaps best depicted in the iconographic weathervane topping Baker Library in the center of the campus, above the college green, buildings, trees, and humanity, pointing to the hill winds that cleanse, nurture, and cloak Dartmouth.

The unique and cherished aspects of the college may be partially captured in stories like "Doc Benton," celebrations such as House Parties Weekend and Winter Carnival, athletic and cultural events, and rituals such as bonfires and campouts at DOC cabins. But for me this entrancing spirit was even more manifest in the invisible weave of Dartmouth's culture, such as its history, songs, and symbols—a weave that encompasses as well both the tangible physical elements of the college, such as the White Mountains and Connecticut River, colonial brick architecture, and vast splendid vistas, and its interpersonal aspects, such as close relationships with mentoring teachers and the incomparable friendships of classmates and visitors arising from being together in this place. Most of all for me, the phenomenal beauty of the place of the crossing shaped the spirit of Dartmouth.

In his address opening my brother's senior year, President John Sloan Dickey discussed "place … the other pervasive influence that gives Dartmouth her individuality and character … I have concluded that probably more than any other American college Dartmouth's character flows from the place … of her founding … on the northern frontier."[59]

Ernest Martin Hopkins, Dartmouth's eleventh president, once linked the Dartmouth educational odyssey with the beauty of the Hanover region:

> I would insist that the man who spends four years in our north country here and does not learn to hear the melody of the rustling leaves or does not learn to love the wash of the racing brooks over their rocky beds in spring, who never experiences the repose to be found on lakes and river, who has not stood enthralled on the top of Moosilauke on a moonlit night or has not become a worshiper of color as he has seen the sun set from one of Hanover's hills, who has not thrilled at the whiteness of the snow-clad

---

[59] Widmayer, *John Sloan Dickey,* 109.

countryside in winter or at the flaming forest colors of the fall—I would insist that this man has not reached out for some of the most worthwhile educational values accessible to him at Dartmouth.[60]

Any lover of the poetry of Robert Frost, class of 1896, Richard Eberhart, '26, Richard Hovey, class of 1885, and Theodor Geisel, '25 (Dr. Seuss), knows that these Dartmouth poets recognized and "reached out" for—and in their writing sublimely expressed—the love of the natural beauty of the northern Appalachians described by President Hopkins.

Another Dartmouth poet, Franklin McDuffee, '21, won the Oxford Newdigate Prize for English verse in 1924 and taught thereafter at Dartmouth until his death in 1940. He never attained the acclaim of the four poets just mentioned but wrote the poem at President Hopkins's urging, which became the lyrics for one of the great college songs of the United States—"Dartmouth Undying."

McDuffee's lyrics describe the "soft September sunsets" that all graduates remember, as the golden and then rosy glow of the sky over the mountains and the river's ethereal reflection to the west of campus gently and magically slipped into twilight shadows each night. They remind us of the sting of winter's dawn air and of the mist rising from the Connecticut in the Upper Valley each morning, while Baker Library's clear and stirring bells summoned us to classes and the dining hall. They contrast the light, sounds, and visions we encountered every morning with those of the campus at noon and at dusk. His words—like no other Dartmouth song or memory—imprint in our minds the "splendor and the fullness" of the days and hours at Dartmouth that "passed like dreams."[61]

As a student, I listened with delight to McDuffee's sixteen simple lines sung by the Glee Club on the radio every night to end our daily dreamlike hours as WDCR (Dartmouth College Radio) signed off its broadcast. As an alumnus, fifty years after graduation, the evocation of the "gleaming, dreaming walls of Dartmouth" in this song fills me with nostalgia and thankfulness for the vision-like memories that still illuminate and enhance my life.[62]

---

[60] Widmayer, *Hopkins of Dartmouth,* 173.

[61] McDuffee, "Dartmouth Undying," in *Dartmouth Song Book,* 8–9.

[62] Ibid.

The Hopkins Center for the Arts (reflection of Baker Library),
September 1966

Graduation on the lawn of Baker Library, June 1967

Doug Webber, '69, with date at Tri-Kap party, February 1967

Xavier Mendoza, '67, hitchhiking in Europe, October 1965

EPILOGUE

Following graduation, I spent a last glorious summer working at the University of Uppsala. New friends and relationships made the summer of 1967 one of the best summers of my life! Classmate Brad Langley visited me in Sweden for a week.

After receiving my MA in English at the University of Wisconsin (1968), I served in the Peace Corps (1968–71), trained new Peace Corps volunteers at the School for International Training in Putney, Vermont (1971), and joined the Peace Corps' headquarters staff (1972–78). During my Foreign Service term appointment, I received my JD from the National Law Center, George Washington University (1976).

I practiced labor law for more than three decades (1979–2011) as a union attorney for the American Federation of Government Employees, AFL-CIO (AFGE), seeking justice for government employees and growing to love the labor movement and its members. In probably the final chapter of my legal career, I am again working to promote the Peace Corps' statutory mission—world peace—at the Peace Corps' headquarters.

With my wife and family, I returned to Hanover often in the two and a half decades after graduation to visit Dartmouth professors Allen, Eberhart, and Zeller and other local friends. Chauncey Allen and his wife were like grandparents to our children, Jason and Amy, as were our dear friends John and Jean Sibley in nearby Etna.[63] Other good friends included Bob and Jean Keene in Hanover.[64]

Returning to Hanover and to Dartmouth was always like coming home to my birthplace, Buffalo, New York. I knew the nooks and crannies of the Hanover streets and Dartmouth buildings, the curves and trees of the Grafton County roads, the nearby mountain trails, the Connecticut River's banks, and the outlines on the horizon of the sentinel, purple granite mountains—all of which called to me and pulled me into hugs of remembrance.

On one of those return trips, I stopped to visit Dartmouth's fine Hood Museum, which I always found to be a spiritual place. It displayed so much of the course of humanity in its treasures. I

---

[63]   Our deep friendship with the Sibleys, which began in Korea, is described in my memoir *The Time of the Monkey, Rooster, and Dog.*

[64]   Dr. Sibley taught at the Dartmouth Medical School, Bob Keene was the local Hanover dentist, and Jean Millane Keene (sister of classmate David Millane) was the Hanover High School librarian. Through the Allens and the Sibleys, we met the Keenes, who have been good friends since the early 1970s.

wondered about the history of Dartmouth and its future. Would someday the artifacts of Dartmouth hang on a museum's wall, engendering wonder and surmise but little else? What did it all mean?

On the wall of one of the galleries hung a large and very old tapestry of many colors. It had been woven long ago, but a mazelike design of faded green and white could still be distinguished.

On impulse, I examined the back of the tapestry, recalling the words of Thornton Wilder about a homemade rug:

> No figure could be traced on the reverse. It presented a mass of knots and frayed and dangling threads … These are the threads and knots of human life. You cannot see the design … History is *one* tapestry. No eye can venture to compass more than a hand's-breadth … There is much talk of design in the arias. Some are certain they see it. Some see what they have been told to see. Some remember that they saw it once but have lost it. Some are strengthened by seeing a pattern wherein the oppressed and exploited of the earth are gradually emerging from their bondage.

> Some find strength in their conviction that there is nothing to see. Some … [65]

Some of the 1967s tied huge knots and others small ones in the tapestry of Dartmouth. Whatever we did or did not do at Dartmouth, we all created our own threads and became thereby a part of the fabric of the College on the Hill forever. At our twenty-fifth reunion at Dartmouth in 1992, my wife and I met classmates whom I had not seen since graduation and others whom I never knew at Dartmouth. We all picked up our threads in the tapestry, and there was much talk of the design in the arias. I enjoyed reconnecting so much that since that year I have often attended Dartmouth events in Hanover and in Washington, DC. Meetings of the Dartmouth Club of Washington and the Dartmouth Lawyers Association, as well as annual autumn dinners of the DC area 1967s, have been especially memorable in promoting new friendships with members of the class of 1967 and other Dartmouth alumni. The pleasure of these new relationships with my previously unknown classmates and other Dartmouth graduates is immeasurable.

One last postgraduation event remains fixed in my mind as the best statement of all that is intangibly sublime about Dartmouth. Shortly after my new Korean wife had arrived in the United States from West Germany, Young and I attended a Dartmouth Glee Club concert at the Kennedy Center for the Performing Arts in Washington, DC, in April 1975. After the superb concert, there was a reception in an adjoining hall. It took us a while to find the reception room, so we arrived a little late—me in my usual rumpled suit and Young in her finest, most gorgeous, traditional native Korean dress. When we entered the large room, I noticed a knot of people crowding around a man in the center—evidently someone important.

---

[65] Thornton Wilder, *The Eighth Day* (New York: Harper and Row, 1967), 428–435.

Suddenly, the knot of people broke up as the man pushed through and strode toward us with a welcoming, friendly smile. He took Young's hands and boomed, "Great to meet you! How splendid you look in your gorgeous dress! I visited your homeland last week on my way home from the funeral of Chiang Kai-shek and was tremendously impressed by the beauty of Korea and friendliness of Koreans." Young was just beginning to master English but managed a conversation for several minutes with the vice president of the United States—Nelson Rockefeller, '30.

Although Young had no idea who he was, I was struck by how this important man—in a quintessential gesture of a member of the Dartmouth family—had singled out one of the few foreign faces in the room to make her feel welcome and accepted. Because of moments like this one, unexpectedly but joyfully, the Dartmouth community that I sensed in my first weeks on campus, as I looked over the campus and town from the top of Bartlett Tower, has increasingly flourished in my heart and mind as the years have passed since graduation half a century ago.

On that fine day in June 1967, we quietly thanked President Dickey, one by one, as he handed us our diplomas. The weathervane on top of Baker Library witnessed the grand and poetic symmetry manifest in the Dartmouth president's personal welcome to us in September 1963, in the Tower Room overlooking the elms on the college Green and in his personal farewell four years later at graduation under the same elms! As valued Dartmouth family members, we crossed the stage in the bright sunshine and exited down the stairs toward the rest of our lives. Six steps to the Green, and then we had to choose, one trail or another.

All passages that morning equally lay across grass no feet had yet trodden or with uncharted rivers. So we each chose, keeping the others for another day, but all knowing how way leads to way and doubting surely that we could ever come back. Whatever we were to miss or forget in our separate tracks or river traces from the Hanover plain, we all knew that we had briefly possessed together the precious—the caress of granite under foot, the songs of the leaves rustled by the hill winds, and the inexpressible joy of learning in the still north.

Moosilauke Ravine Lodge, Dartmouth College, April 1967

Wim deHaas, '69, sister Cecilia, me, Mom, Aunt Kate, and Dad, June 1967

The last American elms on the college green, January 1965

Baker Library at dusk, June 1967